Pirates Through the Ages

Primary Sources

Pirates Through the Ages

Primary Sources

Laurie Edwards
Sonia G. Benson, Contributing Writer
Jennifer Stock, Project Editor

GALE
CENGAGE Learning

Detroit • New York • San Francisco • New Haven, Conn • Waterville, Maine • London

GALE
CENGAGE Learning™

Pirates Through the Ages:
Primary Sources
Laurie Edwards

Project Editor: Jennifer Stock

Rights Acquisition and Management:
   Robyn Young

Text Acquisitions and Permissions:
   Sari B. Gordon

Composition: Evi Abou-El-Seoud

Manufacturing: Wendy Blurton

Imaging: John Watkins

Product Design: Kristine Julien

For product information and technology assistance, contact us at
Gale Customer Support, 1-800-877-4253.
For permission to use material from this text or product,
submit all requests online at **www.cengage.com/permissions.**
Further permissions questions can be emailed to
permissionrequest@cengage.com

Cover photographs reproduced by permission of The Art Archive/Granger Collection/The Picture Desk, Inc. (two pirates fighting, illustration from "Howard Pyle's Book of Pirates," 1921) and Mohamed Dahir/AFP/Getty Images (armed Somali pirate keeping watch along the coastline).

While every effort has been made to ensure the reliability of the information presented in this publication, Gale, a part of Cengage Learning, does not guarantee the accuracy of the data contained herein. Gale accepts no payment for listing; and inclusion in the publication of any organization, agency, institution, publication, service, or individual does not imply endorsement of the editors or publisher. Errors brought to the attention of the publisher and verified to the satisfaction of the publisher will be corrected in future editions.

Library of Congress Cataloging-in-Publication Data

Benson, Sonia.
   Pirates through the ages reference library / Sonia G. Benson, Elizabeth Shostak, Laurie Edwards.
      3 v. cm.
   Includes bibliographical references and index.
      ISBN 978-1-4144-8662-8 (set) -- ISBN 978-1-4144-8663-5 (almanac) -- ISBN 978-1-4144-8664-2 (biographies) -- ISBN 978-1-4144-8665-9 (primary sources)
      1. Pirates--History--Handbooks, manuals, etc. I. Shostak, Elizabeth, 1951- II. Edwards, Laurie, 1954- III. Title.
   G535.B38 2011
   910.4'5--dc22   2010051978

Gale
27500 Drake Rd.
Farmington Hills, MI, 48331-3535

ISBN-13: 978-1-4144-8662-8 (set)
ISBN-13: 978-1-4144-8663-5 (Almanac)
ISBN-13: 978-1-4144-8664-2 (Biographies)
ISBN-13: 978-1-4144-8665-9 (Primary Sources)
ISBN-13: 978-1-4144-8666-6 (Cumulative Index)

ISBN-10: 1-4144-8662-6 (set)
ISBN-10: 1-4144-8663-4 (Almanac)
ISBN-10: 1-4144-8664-2 (Biographies)
ISBN-10: 1-4144-8665-0 (Primary Sources)
ISBN-10: 1-4144-8666-9 (Cumulative Index)

This title is also available as an e-book.
ISBN-13: 978-1-4144-8667-3 ISBN-10: 1-4144-8667-7
Contact your Gale, a part of Cengage Learning sales representative for ordering information.

Printed in Singapore
1 2 3 4 5 6 7 15 14 13 12 11

Table of Contents

On April 8, 2009, in waters about 350 miles (563 kilometers) off the coast of Somalia, four pirates boarded the *Maersk Alabama* in a botched attempt to seize the cargo ship. After a stand-off with the ship's crew, the Somali pirates took the captain, Richard Phillips (1963–), hostage and sped off in a life boat. They were soon surrounded by military warships and helicopters from several nations, and for five days the pirates held the captain at gunpoint on the small boat. Footage of the hostage situation was broadcast to millions of television viewers throughout the world. In the end, U.S. Navy snipers killed the pirates and rescued Phillips. But piracy experts noted that the rescue of Phillips was the exception; at the time of his rescue, pirates held hundreds of other hostages in Somalia. The *Maersk Alabama* incident, only one among hundreds of pirate attacks in the waters off Somalia over the period of a few years, brought international attention to the rise in piracy in the twenty-first century, after many twentieth-century history books had pronounced piracy a thing of the past.

For most of us, it is difficult to connect the Somali pirates—young men and boys in t-shirts and jeans using modern technology and carrying automatic weapons—with the familiar image of pirates we have known since childhood: the swarthy seafarers with peg-legs or eye patches wearing tri-cornered hats and bearing parrots on their shoulders, who are known for phrases like "avast, me hearties," "shiver me timbers," and "aarr." The familiar image, a product of both fact and fantasy, is based on the historical era known as the golden age of piracy, a brief period during the late eighteenth and early nineteenth century when famous pirates like Blackbeard (Edward Teach; c. 1680–1718), William Kidd (c. 1645–1701), and Bartholomew Roberts (1682–1722) ruled large areas of the

Caribbean Sea. But Somali piracy and golden age piracy both take their place in a long, global history of similar pirate eras, periods when seas in certain regions became infested with pirates who managed to resist law enforcement agents for extended periods of time.

Who were these pirates? Pirates through the ages have been as diverse as the rest of the human population. Pirate leaders have ranged from poor English sailors to highly successful Chinese businessmen and ferocious Scandinavian warriors. Like most criminal paths, piracy has drawn courageous adventurers, sadistic psychopaths, and many who fall somewhere in between. Most were drawn to piracy as a rare means to lift themselves out of poverty, but not all pirates chose their trade. Many sailors were forced into it by pirates who raided their ships. Others, on the other hand, traveled long distances and some even converted to new religions for the opportunity to get rich by raiding ships at sea. Pirates have come from all nationalities and races. The Chinese pirates included women among their ranks, and there were also several notorious European women pirates, but overall, the overwhelming majority of pirates have been men.

On land and at sea, pirates have always sought places where they could carry out their plundering (robbing of goods by force) while living outside the law. They spent much of their lives on the high seas, the open waters of the ocean that are outside the limits of any country's territorial authority. At sea, most pirates have established their own codes of conduct and social structures. Pirates also need land to carry out large-scale operations. In pirate havens, usually remote sea ports or islands without any strong governmental presence, pirates have been able to establish rough societies of their own where they live and carry out their business under their own rules. In pirate havens, as at sea, pirates defied law enforcement authorities—but only for a time. After every major pirate era, law and order has been restored, pirate havens have been destroyed, and many notorious pirates have faced prison or the hangman's noose.

Pirates have fascinated people from ancient times to the present day. Studying them provides insight into history and human nature in all its complexity. Historians study pirates in a surprisingly wide variety of contexts, such as the wars they fought in, their contribution to the settlement of new lands, the social institutions they have established at sea, and the social classes from which they arose. Lawmakers and international diplomats ponder the unique challenges of trying to stop piracy by establishing law and order on the high seas. Fiction writers, poets, playwrights, and filmmakers have all been drawn to the romantic aspects of piracy, such as the courage and ingenuity of the raiders, their thrilling adventures, the freedom of the seas, and the brotherhood of pirates.

The abundance of legends and writings about pirates has led to a strangely comfortable image of piracy in modern times. Children dress as pirates for Halloween, watch pirate cartoons on TV, and play pirate video games. In studying real piracy, though, it quickly becomes apparent that pirates are dangerous, and often violent, criminals. Pirates have murdered, raped, tortured, and enslaved their victims. They have disrupted trade and made sea travel a terrifying experience. Though they may fascinate us with their adventures at sea, they are predators who do a great deal of harm in the world.

Pirates v. privateers

Many of history's major pirate eras began with governmental policies that encouraged the licensing of privateers, private ships or ship owners commissioned by their government to raid enemy ships during wartime. The actual work that pirates and privateers do is the same. They attack ships, usually merchant vessels, or coastal communities, and they use violence or the threat of violence to rob their victims of valuables, sometimes taking the ship itself as a prize. The main difference between pirates and privateers is that pirates work solely for their own profit, while privateers, at least in theory, work for their country. While piracy is illegal, privateering is considered legal, at least by the nation that licenses the privateers.

The history of pirates cannot be separated from the history of privateers. Since ancient times, warring nations have frequently enlisted privateers to destroy their enemies' trade and harass military shipping. Ancient Greece, the Ottoman Empire, late eighteenth-century Vietnam, and the European nations of Spain, England, the Netherlands, and France, to name a few, all relied heavily on privateers in war-time. Privateers often greatly aided their countries. Some privateers, such as Englishman Francis Drake (1540–1596), were considered heroes and went on to prestigious careers in their countries. Other privateers, however, took a very different path. When wars ended, they found themselves armed, equipped with sea vessels, and highly skilled at raiding enemy ships, but suddenly unemployed. Many simply continued to raid ships as pirates. The nations that had originally enlisted the privateers' services soon found they had no control over their activities, and often had to muster new naval forces to pursue them.

The many names for sea raiders—corsairs, buccaneers, filibusters, freebooters, picaroons, sea rovers, sea dogs—all signify people who raid at or from the sea, but whether they mean "pirate," "privateer," or a little of both may differ in context.

Coverage and features

Pirates Through the Ages: Primary Sources presents eighteen full or excerpted written works, poems, interviews, or other documents that were influential throughout the history of piracy. Included are the tale of the kidnapping of Julius Caesar by pirates, a letter from a captive of the Barbary corsairs, a pirate trial transcript, and an example of ship's articles. Also featured are literary works such as *Treasure Island* and *The Corsair*, and interviews with Somali and Strait of Malacca pirates. More than fifty photographs and illustrations, a timeline, sources for further reading, and an index supplement the volume

U·X·L Pirates Through the Ages
Reference Library

Pirates Through the Ages: Almanac presents a comprehensive history of the major pirate eras throughout history and around the globe. The volume's twelve chapters cover ancient and medieval pirates, the Barbary corsairs, the privateers of Spanish Main and the United States, the buccaneers of the Caribbean, the golden age of piracy, piracy in Asia, modern piracy, and pirates in popular culture. Each chapter features informative sidebar boxes highlighting glossary terms and issues discussed in the text. Also included are nearly sixty photographs and illustrations, a timeline, a glossary, a list of research and activity ideas, sources for further reading, and an index providing easy access to subjects discussed throughout the volume.

Pirates Through the Ages: Biographies profiles twenty-six pirates and privateers. Included are some of the most famous pirates of the golden age, such as Blackbeard, William Kidd, and Bartholomew Roberts; fierce corsairs of the Barbary Coast, including Barbarossa and Dragut Reis; and English and American privateers such as Francis Drake, John Paul Jones, and Jean Lafitte. Also featured are buccaneers such as Henry Morgan and William Dampier; female pirates Cheng I Sao, Anne Bonny and Mary Read, and Grace O'Malley; and pirate hunter Woodes Rogers. The volume includes more than fifty photographs and illustrations, a time-line, sources for further reading, and an index.

A cumulative index of all three volumes in the U•X•L Pirates Through the Ages Reference Library is also available.

Comments and suggestions

We welcome your comments on *Pirates Through the Ages: Primary Sources* and suggestions for other topics to consider. Please write: Editors, *Pirates Through the Ages: Primary Sources*, Gale Cengage Learning, 27500 Drake Road, Farmington Hills, Michigan 48331-3535; call toll free: 1-800-877-4253; fax to 248-699-8097; or send e-mail via http://www.gale.cengage.com.

Timeline of Events

2000 BCE: The Phoenicians begin maritime trading in regions of the Mediterranean; as trade expands, piracy emerges.

1220–1186 BCE: The Sea People, a band of sea raiders, dominate the Mediterranean Sea, attacking merchant ships and coastal towns.

c. 750 BCE: Greek poet Homer writes the ***Odyssey***; the epic poem is the first known written description of piracy.

421–339 BCE: Greek city-states engage pirates to attack their enemies in the Peloponnesian Wars in a system similar to what will later become known as privateering.

74 or 75 BCE: Roman statesman Julius Caesar is captured by Cilician pirates and held for ransom. The event is later recounted in ***Lives of Noble Grecians and Romans*** by Plutarch.

June 8, 793: Vikings attack the religious center at Lindisfarne, England.

1100s: A group of Germanic towns form the Hanseatic League to secure trade routes in the Baltic Sea and fight piracy.

1200s: The Wokou, a group of pirates that originated in Japan, attack the coasts of Korea and China.

1243: England's Cinque Ports, a league of sea towns, begins to license private merchant ships to raid enemy ships and ports. This is considered the origin of the privateer system that Europe would use for centuries to come.

1392: A powerful band of pirates known as the Victual Brothers attacks Norway's major city, Bergen, and sets up headquarters in Visby, Sweden.

1492: Spain captures Granada from the Moors and begins to expel the Moors from Spain. Tens of thousands of Spanish Muslims migrate to the Barbary Coast in northern Africa.

1492: Explorer Christopher Columbus, serving Spain, arrives on a Caribbean island, beginning an era of Spanish exploration and colonization in the Americas.

1494: The Catholic pope issues the Treaty of Tordesillas. Under the treaty, Portugal receives authority to control the non-Christian lands in the designated eastern half of the world, and Spain is awarded the lands in the west.

1516: Barbary corsair Aruj leads a large force of corsairs in an attack on the city-state of Algiers. The corsairs gain control of the city and the surrounding region.

1523: French privateer Jean Fleury captures two Spanish ships returning to Spain from Mexico. They are loaded with Aztec treasure that conquistador Hernán Cortéz was sending to the Spanish king.

1530: The Spanish king leases the island of Malta to the Knights of Malta under the condition that they fight "enemies of the Holy Faith." The Knights begin raiding Muslim ships and enslaving Muslim captives.

1550s: Wealthy Chinese businessman Wang Zhi commands a large force of Wokou pirate fleets, comprised of hundreds of junks and, by some estimates, about twenty thousand pirates.

1562: To protect its ships from piracy, Spain requires all ships carrying goods from the Spanish Main to Spain to join one of the two treasure fleets formed annually.

1567: In the Battle of San Juan de Ulúa, John Hawkins and his fleet of illegal traders are badly defeated by Spanish naval forces in Mexico. The battle is recounted in ***The Third Troublesome Voyage Made with the* Jesus of Lübeck, *the* Minion *and Four Other Ships to the Parts of Guinea and the West Indies, in the Years 1567 and 1568***

1577–60: English privateer Francis Drake circumnavigates (sails around) the globe, raiding Spanish ships in the Pacific and bringing home an enormous booty.

1628: Dutch privateer Pieter Pieterszoon Heyn, commanding an enormous fleet, captures a Spanish treasure fleet.

1600–40: A group of French hunters, called buccaneers, establish a rough lifestyle in the Caribbean, living part-time on the island of Tortuga and hunting feral animals on the northwest coast of Hispaniola.

1606–8: English pirate Jack Ward and Dutch pirate Simon de Danser join the Barbary corsairs. They are among the first in a long line of "renegades," or Europeans who converted from Christianity to Islam and raided Christian ships and ports with the Barbary corsairs.

Late 1620s: Hoping to expel the buccaneers, Spanish colonial officials exterminate feral animals in the northwestern region of Hispaniola. The buccaneers, no longer able to hunt, become full-time sea raiders.

1642: Robert Adams writes a **Letter from a Captive of the Corsairs**, pleading for his family to pay his ransom so he will be released from captivity among the Barbary corsairs.

1655: English ruler Oliver Cromwell sends naval forces to attack Santo Domingo, Hispaniola. The English forces fail to take over Santo Domingo, but take control of Jamaica. Under the English, Port Royal, Jamaica, becomes a pirate haven.

1661: Chinese pirate commander Kho Hsing Yeh attacks the Dutch colony at Formosa (present-day Taiwan) with a fleet of nine hundred junks and twenty-five thousand troops, pushing the Dutch military off the island. Under Kho Hsing Yeh and his sons, Formosa will remain a pirate kingdom for twenty years.

1668: Privateer Henry Morgan, chief of the buccaneers in Port Royal, leads a raid on the well-defended port city of Portobelo, Panama, where treasure from Peru is held for shipping to Spain on the annual treasure fleets.

1678: Alexander O. Exquemelin's **_The Buccaneers of America_** is first published in Dutch.

1690: The golden age of piracy begins.

1690s: The African island of Madagascar in the Indian Ocean becomes a pirate base in the Pirate Round, a course in which pirates raid African slave traders and merchant ships transporting valuable Asian goods from the shores of India and the Middle East back to Europe.

June 7, 1692: A major earthquake strikes Port Royal, Jamaica, killing thousands, toppling part of the city into the sea, and forcing pirates to look for another base of operations.

August 1695: Pirate captain Henry Every raids the well-armed *Ganj-i-sawii*, the Indian emperor's richly laden treasure ship, making every man in his crew wealthy. The raid inspires many heroic legends in England.

1701: After a lengthy trial in England, William Kidd is hung for piracy, though he claims to have been fulfilling his obligations as a privateer. His body is hung over the Thames River as a warning to all pirates.

1710: In India, Maratha navy commander Kanhoji Angria captures the British East India Company's island headquarters off Bombay and sets up a well-fortified pirate base there.

1714: Pirates of the Caribbean, led by Benjamin Hornigold, Blackbeard, and Charles Vane, establish a base in Nassau, a port in the Bahamas; other pirates soon join them there.

February 1717: Samuel Bellamy and his crew seize an English slave ship, the *Whydah*, near Cuba, and refit it for piracy.

May 1718: With a fleet of heavily armed pirate vessels, Blackbeard blockades the harbor of Charleston, North Carolina.

September 5, 1718: By this date, Bahamas governor Woodes Rogers has granted pardons to more than six hundred pirates on the condition that they stop raiding.

November 1718: English troops commanded by Lieutenant Robert Maynard battle with Blackbeard's fleet; Blackbeard is killed in hand-to-hand combat.

1720: The Trial of Anne Bonny and Mary Read is held in Jamaica. The story of these two female pirates causes a sensation in Europe and the Americas.

1721: England passes the Piracy Act, which punishes people who trade with or aid pirates.

March 1722: In the largest pirate trial of the golden age, 268 pirates who had sailed under the command of Bartholomew Roberts are tried at Cape Coast Castle, a slave-trading center in West Africa.

1724: *A General History of the Robberies and Murders of the Most Notorious Pirates* is published by Captain Charles Johnson. The book describes the adventures of several pirates, including **"The Life of Captain Roberts"** and **"The Life of Captain Evans"**

1730: The golden age of piracy ends.

April 19, 1775: The Battles of Concord and Lexington begin the American Revolution.

March 1776: The Continental Congress passes legislation allowing American privateers to raid British warships and merchant ships.

September 23, 1779: Continental Navy commander John Paul Jones defeats a Royal Navy warship and utters his famous line, "I have not yet begun to fight."

1788: With the aid of Chinese pirates, the Vietnamese Tay Son rebels defeat Vietnam's military and take control of the country.

1796: The English government issues a **Letter of Marque against the French** to John Maciver, captain of *The Swallow*.

1804: The United States sends its recently established naval forces to Tripoli in an attempt to force the Barbary corsairs to stop demanding tribute payments from U.S. merchant ships in the Mediterranean.

1807: Chinese pirate chief Cheng I dies, having organized and led the largest pirate confederation ever known to history, comprised of an estimated 40,000 to 70,000 pirates. His wife Cheng I Sao takes command of the pirate empire.

1810: Cheng I Sao surrenders to officials in **"The Pirate Surrender Document of 1810"**, accepting a general pardon for the pirates in her confederation, ending the huge and powerful Chinese pirate empire.

1812: As the United States prepares for war with Britain in the War of 1812, it once again enlists the aid of American privateers.

1814: Lord Byron publishes ***The Corsair***, a long poem in which the pirate captain Conrad is portrayed as a brooding, romantic hero. The poem is an instant success.

January 1815: In the Battle of New Orleans, the last battle of the War of 1812, privateer Jean Lafitte aids U.S. forces in defeating the British invasion of the city.

1830s: A combined force of British Royal Navy and English East India Company ships set up an antipiracy base in Singapore. After a long series of fierce battles with the pirates of the Strait of Malacca and surrounding areas over the next thirty years, the antipiracy forces destroy the pirates.

1856: The leading powers of Europe sign the Declaration of Paris, which prohibits privateering. The United States does not sign.

1861: In the first year of the American Civil War, Southern privateers raid scores of Union ships.

1883: Robert Louis Stevenson publishes his children's adventure story *Treasure Island*. His pirate character, Long John Silver, becomes the best-known pirate in popular culture.

1904: J.M. Barrie's play *Peter Pan, or The Boy Who Would Not Grow Up* is first produced. The play features a group of children, led by Peter Pan, who defeat a group of pirates.

1982: The **United Nations Convention on the Law of the Sea**, which authorizes official ships of all states to seize known pirate ships on the high seas, is signed by 158 nations.

1984: Underwater explorer Barry Clifford discovers the pirate ship *Whydah* off Cape Cod. Relics recovered from the sunken ship and can be viewed today at the Whydah Museum in Provincetown, Massachusetts.

1992: The International Maritime Bureau (IMB), a division of the International Chamber of Commerce (ICC), establishes the IMB Piracy Reporting Centre, based in Kuala Lumpur, Malaysia, to track pirate attacks around the world.

1998: Political unrest in Indonesia leads to a surge in pirate activity in the Strait of Malacca.

1998: Chinese pirates posing as customs officials hijack a Hong Kong cargo ship, the *Cheung Son*, killing the entire twenty-three-member crew. China captures and prosecutes the pirates, executing thirteen of them.

2000: Piracy peaks worldwide, with a reported 469 attacks during the year; 65 percent of the attacks occur in Southeast Asia.

2003: *Pirates of the Caribbean: The Curse of the Black Pearl*, the first in a series of Disney pirate movies featuring Captain Jack Sparrow, is a huge box-office success.

2004: Under the Regional Cooperation Agreement on Combating Piracy and Armed Robbery against Ships in Asia (ReCAAP), Malaysian, Indonesian, and Singapore naval forces begin to work together to combat piracy.

2005: Indonesian pirate John Ariffin participates in the hijacking of the tanker *Nepline Delima* in the Strait of Malacca. Ariffin recounts this event in **"Dark Passage"**, an interview with *National Geographic* reporter Peter Gwin.

June 2, 2008: The UN Security Council passes Resolution 1816, which authorizes foreign warships to enter Somali waters to stop piracy by any means necessary.

April 8, 2009: The world watches the aftermath of the botched hijacking of the U.S. cargo ship *Maersk Alabama*, after four Somali pirates take the ship's captain, Richard Phillips, hostage. Philips recounts this event in an interview for *Yankee* titled **"Captain Richard Phillips and the Pirates: What's Ahead for the Vermont Captain"**.

April 16, 2009: Reporter Jay Bahadur publishes **"I'm Not a Pirate, I'm the Saviour of the Sea"**, his interview with a Somali pirate.

2009: Two hundred seventy-one pirate attacks were attributed to Somali pirates—more than half of the worldwide total.

May 2010: The Anti-Piracy Caucus releases its ***2010 International Piracy Watch List***, citing problems with intellectual property piracy in five nations.

July 2010: A new court near Mombasa, Kenya, built with international donations through the United Nations, is established as a place to try pirates from the region for their crimes.

act of reprisal: A document granting permission to individuals to raid the vessels of an enemy in response to some harm that enemy had done.

admiralty court: A court that administers laws and regulations pertaining to the sea.

antihero: A leading character or notable figure who does not have the typical hero traits.

artillery: Large weapons, such as cannons, that discharge missiles.

asylum: Refuge or protection in a foreign country, granted to someone who might be in danger if returned to his or her own country.

barbarians: People who are not considered civilized.

barge: A large, flat-bottomed boat used to transport cargo, usually over inland waterways.

barnacle: A shell-like marine animal that attaches itself to the underwater portion of a ship's hull.

barque: A simple vessel with one mast and triangular sails.

bey: The word for a local ruler in Tripoli and Tunis.

bireme: A swift galley ship with two banks of oars, and sometimes a square sail.

blunderbuss: A short musket with a flared muzzle.

bond: A type of insurance in which one party gives money to another party as a guarantee that certain requirements will be followed. If these requirements are not followed, the party that issued the bond keeps the money permanently.

booty: Goods stolen from ships or coastal villages during pirate raids or attacks on enemies in time of war.

buccaneer: A seventeenth-century sea raider based in the Caribbean Sea.

caravel: A small, highly maneuverable sailing ship.

careening: A regular process of cleaning the bottom of a ship.

cat-o'-nine-tails: A whip with nine knotted cords.

cleric: A member of the clergy, or church order.

clinker-built: Construction for boats using overlapping wooden planks.

city-state: An independent, self-governing city and its surrounding territory.

coast guard: A government agency responsible for enforcing laws on the seas and navigable waters.

commerce raiding: Also *guerre de course*; a naval strategy in which a weaker naval power attacks its stronger opponent's commercial shipping.

convoy: A collection of merchant ships traveling together for protection, often escorted by warships.

copyright laws: Laws that grant the creator the exclusive right to distribute, copy, use, or sell his or her product.

corsair: A pirate of the Barbary Coast.

cutlass: A short, heavy, single-edged sword.

dey: The word for a local ruler in Algiers.

digital technology: A data technology system that converts sound or signals into numbers, in the form of a binary format of ones and zeros.

duel: A prearranged fight with deadly weapons to settle a quarrel under specific rules.

dynasty: A succession of rulers from the same family line.

Execution Dock: The place in London where pirates were hanged; their bodies were often displayed to discourage others from turning to piracy.

extortion: The use of authority to unlawfully take money.

failed state: A state without a functioning government above the local level.

flintlock pistol: A small and comparatively lightweight gun that loads through the front of the barrel.

flota: A Spanish treasure fleet that transported goods and riches from the New World to Spain every year.

frigate: A three-masted, medium-sized warship.

galiot: A small, fast galley using both sails and oars.

galleon: A large, square-rigged sailing ship with three or more masts that was used for commerce and war.

galley: A long, low ship used for war and trading that was mainly powered by oarsmen, but might also use a sail.

grapeshot: A cluster of small iron balls usually shot from a cannon.

grenado: An early form of hand grenade comprised of hollow balls made of iron, glass, or wood and filled with gunpowder.

guild: An association for people or towns with a similar trade or interest.

harem: The area of a Muslim household historically reserved for wives, concubines, and female relatives.

high seas: The open waters of the ocean that are outside the limits of any country's territorial authority.

hijack: To take over by force.

hypocrisy: Pretending to have qualities or beliefs one does not really have.

impalement: A process of torture and execution by inserting a long stake through the length of the body and then leaving the person to die a slow and painful death.

impressment: The practice of forcibly recruiting sailors to serve in the navy.

indentured servant: A person working under a contract that commits him or her to an employer for a fixed period of time, typically three to seven years.

intellectual property: A product of someone's intellect and creativity that has commercial value.

junk: A Chinese form of sailboat.

jurisdiction: The sole right and power to interpret and apply the law in a certain area.

keel: A strong beam that extends along the entire length of the bottom of a ship and supports its frame.

knight: A man granted a rank of honor by the monarch for his personal merit or service to the country.

letter of marque: A document licensing a private ship owner to the seize ships or goods of an enemy nation.

mangrove: A tropical tree or shrub characterized by an extensive, impenetrable system of roots.

maritime: Relating to the sea.

maritime law: The set of regulations that govern navigation and trade on the seas.

maroon: To strand an individual on a deserted island or shore with few provisions.

matchlock: A musket in which gun powder is ignited by lighting it with a match.

melodrama: A drama, such as a play, film, or television program, characterized by exaggerated emotions, stereotypical characters, and an extravagant plot.

mercenary: A seaman or soldier hired by a government to fight its battles.

militia: A volunteer military force made up of ordinary citizens.

monopoly: Exclusive control or possession of something.

musket: A muzzle-loading shoulder gun with a long barrel.

mutiny: An open rebellion by seamen against their ship's officers.

myth: A traditional story that is partly based on a historical event and serves to explain something about a culture.

nautical mile: A unit of distance used for sea navigation. One nautical mile equals 6,080 feet (1.9 kilometers). One mile across land equals 5,280 feet (1.6 kilometers).

navigator: A person who charts the routes of ships at sea.

nostalgia: A bittersweet longing for something from the past.

organized crime syndicate: A group of enterprises run by criminals to carry out illegal activities.

pagan: A person who does not accept the Christian religion.

parody: A spoof, or a work that mocks something else.

patent: A government grant that gives the creator of an invention the sole right to make, use, and sell that invention for a set period of time.

piragua: A dugout canoe.

pirate base: A place where pirates lived under their own rule and maintained their own defense system.

pirate haven: A safe place for pirates to harbor and repair their ships, resupply, and organize raiding parties.

plunder: To rob of goods by force, in a raid or in wartime.

prahu: A swift, light, seagoing vessel propelled by oars and used by the pirates of Southeast Asia.

privateer: A private ship or ship owner commissioned by a state or government to attack the merchant ships of an enemy nation.

prize: The goods, human captives, and ships captured in pirate raids.

rack: A piece of equipment used for torture; a person tied on a rack is slowly stretched by the wrists and ankles, causing extreme pain.

ransom: A sum of money demanded for the release of someone being held captive.

reprisal: An act of revenge against an enemy in wartime.

rigging: The system of ropes, chains, and other gear used to support and control the masts and sails of a sailing vessel.

rudder: A vertical, flat piece of wood or metal attached with hinges to a ship's stern (rear) that is used to steer the ship.

sack: To plunder a captured city.

scurvy: A disease caused by a lack of vitamin C, characterized by spongy and bleeding gums, bruising, and extreme weakness.

sea shanty: A sailor's work song.

ship's articles: The written sets of rules and conditions under which pirates operated on any given expedition.

ship of the line: A large, heavy warship designed for line of battle combat.

siege: A military blockade that isolates a city while an attack is underway.

sloop: **A fast vessel with a single fore-and-aft rigged mast, meaning that the mast was positioned for sails set lengthwise along the ship.**

smuggling: Illegally importing and exporting goods.

swashbuckler: A daring adventurer; also a drama about a swashbuckler.

tanker: A ship constructed to carry a large load of liquids, such as oil.

territorial waters: Waters surrounding a nation over which that nation exercises sole authority.

terrorism: The systematic use of violence against civilians in order to attain goals that are political, religious, or ideological.

timbers: The frames or ribs of a ship that are connected to the keel and give the hull its shape and strength.

trawler: A fishing boat that uses open-mouthed fishing nets drawn along the sea bottom.

tribute: Payment from one ruler of a state to another, usually for protection or to acknowledge submission.

Tower of London: A fortress in London, England, that was famously used as a prison.

vigilante: Someone who takes the law into his or her own hands without the authority to do so.

walk the plank: A form of punishment in which a person is forced to walk off the end of a wooden board extended over the side of a ship and into the sea.

war of attrition: A conflict in which a nation tries to wear down its opponent in small ways, hoping to gradually weaken the enemy's forces.

The following is a list of the copyright holders who have granted us permission to reproduce excerpts from primary sources documents in *Pirates Through the Ages: Primary Sources*. Every effort has been made to trace copyright; if omissions have been made, please contact us.

Copyrighted excerpts reproduced from the following books:

- Adams, Robert. From "Letter from Robert Adams to Captain Robert Adams," in *Piracy, Slavery, and Redemption: Barbary Captivity Narratives from Early Modern England*. Edited by Daniel J. Vitkus. Columbia University Press, 2001. Republished with permission of the Columbia University Press, 61 W. 62nd St., New York, NY 10023.

- Byron, Lord George Gordon. *The Works of Lord Byron: Poetry Vol III*, Charles Scribner's Sons, 1900.

- Exquemelin, Alexander O. *The Buccaneers of America,* Mineola, NY: Dover Publications, Inc., 1969. Copyright © 1969 by Dover Publications, Inc. Reproduced by permission.

- Homer. From *The Odyssey of Homer*. Translated by Richard Lattimore. Harper & Row Publishers, 1965, 1967. Reproduced by permission.

- Johnson, Captain Charles. From *A General History of the Robberies and Murders of the Most Notorious Pirates*. The Lyon's Press, 1998, 2002. Reproduced by permission.

- Murray, Dian H. From *Pirates of the South China Coast 1790–1810.* Stanford University Press, 1987. Copyright © 1987 by the Board of Trustees of the Leland Stanford Junior University. All rights reserved. Used with the permission of the author.

Copyrighted excerpts reproduced from the following periodicals:

- Allen, Mel. "Captain Richard Phillips and the Pirates: What's Ahead for the Vermont Captain," *Yankee*, 2010. Reproduced by permission.
- Bahadur, Jay. "I'm Not a Pirate, I'm the Saviour of the Sea," *Times Online*, 2009. Reproduced by permission of the author.
- Gwin, Peter. "Dark Passage," *National Geographic Magazine*, 2007. Reproduced by permission.

Copyrighted excerpts reproduced from the following other souces:

- United Nations. "Part VII: High Seas," *UN Convention on the Law of the Sea of 10 December 1982*, 1982. Reprinted with the permission of the United Nations.

Odysseus's Raid on the Kikonians

Excerpt from Book IX of *The Odyssey of Homer*
Published by Harper & Row Publishers, 1967

"I sacked their city and killed their people / and out of their city taking their wives and many possessions / we shared them out, so none might go cheated of his proper / portion."

Piracy, or the robbing of goods at sea, dates back to ancient times. From 1200 to 700 BCE, the area around the Mediterranean Sea was home to many pirates. The Mediterranean Sea is surrounded by Africa, Europe, and Asia. The coastline is rocky and farming was difficult in this area due to the poor soil. Since they could not make their living by farming, Mediterranean peoples began to trade with each other. Mountains in the region made land travel long and difficult, so traders traveled by sea, where they were attractive targets for pirates.

The ancient Mediterranean was a place of great turmoil, and war was common. During this time, many groups lost their lands and were forced to wander abroad in search of new homes. As cities fell, their warriors sometimes formed bands of roving pirates and plundered (robbed of goods by force) villages along the seacoast. Some early sea raiders also worked together.

The Sea People

One of the earliest organized pirate groups in history were the Sea People. Around 1220 BCE the Sea People roamed the area and destroyed major cities around the Mediterranean Sea. Historians have found evidence that the Sea People attacked Anatolia (present-day Turkey), Syria, Palestine, and Egypt. Most coastal areas fortified walls around their palaces and cities to protect themselves from this threat from the seas, because the Sea People

The Trojan War

According to Greek mythology, the Trojan War began when Eris, the Greek goddess of discord, was not invited to the wedding of the sea goddess Thetis. Angered, Eris attended the wedding anyway, ready to cause chaos. She brought a golden apple that said, "For the Fairest," which she threw into the middle of the room. Three beautiful goddesses, Hera, Athena, and Aphrodite, each assumed the apple was meant for her. They asked Zeus, the king of the gods, to determine which of them was the fairest. Zeus refused to get involved and declared that Paris, the prince of Troy, would settle the argument. Each goddess promised Paris a gift if he would choose her. Hera offered him power; Athena said she would give him wealth or victory in battle, but Aphrodite won by promising him the most beautiful woman in the world, and she gave him Helen.

But Helen was married to Menelaus, the king of Sparta. Paris waited until Menelaus left town, then he took Helen and sailed home. The Greeks assembled troops and sailed for Troy, but when Menelaus asked for his wife, Priam, the king of Troy, refused to return her. The Greeks attacked.

For ten years the Greeks tried to get into the city, but they could not get through the thick walls. Then Odysseus came up with a plan. The Greeks made a large, hollow horse and left it as a gift for the Trojans. When the Trojans took it inside the city, they did not realize that Greek warriors had hidden inside. The Greeks slipped out at night, opened the gates for their army, and sacked (captured and robbed) Troy.

razed and burned important trading ports across the eastern Mediterranean, particularly palaces, government buildings, and temples.

Yet, no one knows for sure who the Sea People were or where they came from. In spite of many descriptions of these sea raiders in ancient writings and in Egyptian carvings that show their clothing, weapons, and ships, scholars have been unable to pinpoint their origin. Some records indicate they may have come from the north, possibly central Europe. An interesting theory posed by geoarcheologist Eberhard Zangger (1958–) is that the ancient Sea People may have been from Troy. Whatever their origin, there is no doubt that the Sea People were a powerful and feared group who lived by plundering cities and settlements along the Mediterranean coast.

The ancient Greek civilization developed from 800 to 450 BCE, and records from this time show that piracy was a continuing problem. The pirates themselves left no traces that archaeologists could use to identify them. Most of the evidence comes from written accounts that ancient civilizations left behind along with the legends they told. *The Odyssey* is considered one of the first written sources on ancient pirates.

The Odyssey

The Odyssey is an epic (a long poem that tells the story of a hero) about Odysseus, a warrior venturing home after the Trojan War, a ten-year war fought between Greece and Troy. During their journey, Odysseus and his men often gather food and supplies by raiding coastal villages. At that time people saw piracy as an honorable way to make a living, and soldiers often supported themselves in this way as they traveled. In fact, as he travels home, Odysseus is a guest at the palace in Scheria. While there, he tells about the Trojan

War and gains status in the minds of his listeners by describing the booty he obtained during his voyages. (Booty is the goods stolen from ships or coastal villages during pirate raids or attacks on enemies in time of war.)

About the author

Little is known about Homer, the author of *The Odyssey*. One ancient Greek historian, Herodotus (c. 484–c. 425 BCE), claimed that Homer had been born to Critheis, an unwed orphan girl. To avoid disgrace she moved to another town, and her son was born near the river Meles, so he was named Melesigenes, which means "Born of the Meles." Critheis worked as a maid for a teacher named Phemius. He offered to marry her and adopt her son, and he also promised that he would train the boy to be a great scholar.

Phemius did teach the boy as he had agreed. After his adoptive father died, Melesigenes continued to run the school until a patron, impressed with his knowledge, asked Melesigenes to travel with him. During their trip, Melesigenes developed eye trouble and went blind. So he stopped traveling and instead studied poetry.

Though he was soon known for his skillful writing of poems, he needed money to live. He asked if the town of Cumae would support him, and in return he would compose poetry for them. Although most people agreed, one man remarked that if they fed this "Homer," they would soon have many more. ("Homer" was the name they gave blind people, and it became the name he was known by.)

A man in Phocaea named Thestorides offered to let Homer live in his home and paid him a small amount of money to create poetry. Later, Homer found out that Thestorides had been making money by reciting Homer's poems in another town. Homer went to the town to expose Thestorides' deception, and the people there persuaded him to become a schoolteacher for their children. And in that town of Chian, he married, had two daughters, and became wealthy.

Dating *The Odyssey*

Most scholars now discount Herodotus's tale as fanciful. Although they do not know when or where Homer lived, they are convinced he did not live during the twelfth century BCE, which is when *The Odyssey* is set. Instead, they estimate that he lived between 750 and 700 BCE. If they are correct, that means Homer would have been writing about events that happened five hundred years before he was born.

Greek poet Homer, the author of The Odyssey. © CLASSIC IMAGE/ALAMY.

One of the reasons for dating Homer's life so much later than the events he wrote about is the complexity of his works. Experts say that it would be impossible to memorize such long poems and pass them on from generation to generation, so they believe *The Iliad* and *The Odyssey* were originally written down, not recited from memory like most ancient poetry. Because the ancient Greeks did not have a writing system until about 750 BCE, that is when scholars assume these works were composed. In addition, some of the battle techniques mentioned in *The Odyssey* did not come into use until that time.

Where Homer lived is also a mystery. Seven different cities have been named as Homer's birthplace. The two most likely are the island of Chios and the city of Smyrna (present-day Izmir, Turkey). The majority of scholars believe Homer probably lived and worked in Ionia, along the west coast of Turkey, because his poems show an Ionic dialect.

Some people have even questioned whether Homer actually existed. They suggest that the two poems may have been written by several different authors or compiled from older folklore. Most scholars, though, believe Homer, whoever he was and wherever he lived, played a part in composing both epic poems, which would make his works the earliest surviving works by a Greek author.

About the poem

Many scholars think Homer may have been able to read and write, and so used writing to compose at least some of the poem. Divided into twenty-four books, *The Odyssey* would have been an extremely lengthy poem to memorize. Even though *The Odyssey*, or parts of it, may have been written down, some of the elements in the poem indicate that it was spoken aloud. Certain words and scenes repeat, which allowed performers to give different variations, or riffs, as they delivered these familiar phrases.

In Greece, oral poetry was chanted to the accompaniment of a *phorminx*, a four-stringed instrument similar to a lyre. *Rhapsodes*, professionals who recited epic Greek poetry, would have used four tones to express the rhythm and meter of Homer's poetry. They also added acting to their recitations. To become proficient in this art, rhapsodes probably went through a long apprenticeship with a master bard to learn these traditions, which were handed down through the generations the same way the poems were.

The Odyssey reveals many details about Greek culture as far back as the twelfth century BCE, which is when this epic poem is set. Homer is believed to have lived during the Iron Age (the period in history marked by the introduction of iron tools and weapons), but the weapons and armor he mentions are bronze, and the Bronze Age (characterized by the use of bronze implements) preceded the Iron Age. Yet some of the warfare tactics described in the poem were not used until Homer's time, so it appears that he has combined elements of various civilizations into this stirring poem of adventure, with its tales of battles, ocean voyages, and piracy.

Background of the story

The Odyssey is the sequel to *The Iliad*, which told the story of the Trojan War. *The Odyssey* begins ten years after the Trojan War is over, and the Greeks have headed home. Some have returned to find things are the same;

A statue of Odysseus.
© WORLD PICTURES/ALAMY.

others have faced many changes. But Odysseus, the hero of the story, is still far from home. At this point it has been twenty years since he left his wife to go off to war. The poem details all the troubles he has faced and the places he has been in the years following the end of the war.

The story opens with Odysseus's son, Telemachus, searching for his missing father with the assistance of the goddess Athena. Meanwhile, Odysseus, who has been stuck on the island of Calypso, sails off on a raft, but is shipwrecked. A Phaeacian princess finds him and invites him to the palace. When the tale of the Trojan War is told during the feast, Odysseus weeps. This leads him to tell of his own wanderings since the war ended.

Things to remember while reading the excerpt from Book IX of *The Odyssey*:

- *The Odyssey* has been translated from the Greek, so some of the original beauty of the poetic language, rhyme, and rhythm have been lost.
- The Greek name of this epic poem was *Odysseia*, which means "the story of Odysseus." The English word *odyssey*, meaning a significant and difficult journey, came from this Greek title.
- *The Odyssey* has twenty-four books; this excerpt is from Book IX. In Books IX through XII, Odysseus tells the Phaeacians the story of his wanderings, so it is a series of flashbacks remembering earlier events.
- Homer used epithets, or descriptive phrases, to round out his rhythm patterns and make the poem easier to sing. The epithets he used (e.g., strong-greaved) give added meaning to each character's name.
- The Greeks had many gods and goddesses, but their deities were much like people. The gods and goddesses fought, made mistakes, and had many failings, but they also had special powers. Each god or goddess was in charge of a specific area or activity. All of these gods and goddesses play an important role in *The Odyssey*. Their decisions, anger, or assistance help or hinder Odysseus's journey throughout the tale.
- Zeus was the greatest of the Greeks gods. The Greeks believed he caused their luck or fate.
- The Kikonians are also sometimes called the Cicones, and the Achaians (Greeks) are also referred to as Achaeans.
- Many people think *Cyclops* means "one-eyed," but it really means "circular eye." Often the Cyclops is pictured with one eye; however, sometimes it has three or even two large eyes. The reason most people think it had one eye is because of the way Odysseus blinds it.

• • •

The Odyssey of Homer

Book IX

... But come, I will tell you of my voyage home with its many
troubles, which Zeus inflicted on me as I came from Troy land.
  'From Ilion the wind took me and drove me ashore at Ismaros
by the Kikonians. I sacked their city and killed their people,
and out of their city taking their wives and many possessions
we shared them out, so none might go cheated of his proper
portion. There I was for the light foot and escaping,
and urged it, but they were greatly foolish and would not listen,
and then and there much wine was being drunk, and they slaughtered
many sheep on the beach, and lumbering horn-curved cattle.
But meanwhile the Kikonians went and summoned the other
Kikonians, who were their neighbors living in the inland country,
more numerous and better men, well skilled in fighting
men with horses, but knowing too at need the battle
on foot. They came at early morning, like flowers in season
or leaves, and the luck that came our way from Zeus was evil,
to make us unfortunate, so we must have hard pains to suffer.
Both sides stood and fought their battle there by the running
ships, and with bronze-headed spears they cast at each other,
and as long as it was early and the sacred daylight increasing,
so long we stood fast and fought them off, though there were more
    of them;
but when the sun had gone to the time for unyoking of cattle,
then at last the Kikonians turned the Achaians back and beat them,
and out of each ship six of my **strong-greaved** companions
were killed, but the rest of us fled away from death and destruction.
  'From there we sailed on further along, glad to have escaped death,
but grieving still at heart for the loss of our dear companions.
Even then I would not suffer the flight of my oarswept vessels
until a cry had been made three times for each of my wretched
companions, who died there in the plain, killed by the Kikonians.

• • •

What happened next ...

Odysseus and his crew finally escape, but they have lost six men per ship.
Zeus sends a violent storm that blows them to the land of the Lotus-Eaters,

Strong-greaved: Wearing
greaves, or leg armor made
of bronze.

where Odysseus's men end up drugged by the intoxicating fruit of the lotus and never want to leave. Odysseus has to drag them to the ship and tie them up, so he can sail away from the island.

Next Odysseus's crew find a lovely island with water, wild goats to hunt, and a beach. His men want to stay there, but Odysseus takes one ship to check out the people who live inland. He discovers a large cave as well as a pen made of stones and pine trees, filled with goats and sheep.

Odysseus and his men make themselves at home in the cave and help themselves to some cheese and cook some meat. Then the giant who lives there, a Cyclops, returns and rolls a huge stone across the doorway, blocking their escape. When he sees the crew, he asks if they are pirates, but Odysseus replies that they are sailors who were blown off course. That night the Cyclops eats two of the crew members for his dinner.

In the morning when the Cyclops leaves, he rolls the stone back across the cave entrance to trap them inside. The men make plans to escape, and Odysseus sharpens a large stick, then hides it. After the Cyclops returns, he eats two more men. Odysseus offers him some wine, which he drinks greedily, then falls asleep. Odysseus heats the stick, then drives it into the Cyclops's eye. The blinded Cyclops feels around for the men, but they evade him by clinging to the undersides of the goats the giant lets out into the pasture. After they escape, they take some of the Cyclops's flocks.

What Odysseus and his crew do not realize is that the Cyclops is Poseidon's son. Poseidon, the god of sea, is angry with Odysseus for blinding his son, so he prevents the sailors from returning home and keeps Odysseus at sea for ten more years.

Piracy continued to grow in the ancient Mediterranean as warring Greek city-states authorized pirates to attack their enemies. (A city-state is an independent, self-governing city and its surrounding territory.) Pirate havens, or safe places for pirates to harbor and repair their ships, resupply, and organize raiding parties, developed along trade routes, making sea travel extremely dangerous. Greek governments began antipiracy campaigns the fourth century BCE, but had little success. It was not until the rise of the Roman Empire in the late–first century BCE that piracy finally declined and ships could sail the Mediterranean without fear of pirate attacks.

Did you know . . .

- In Odysseus's world, pirates were not punished for raids or violence, but because they had angered the gods. So Odysseus was free to rob, maim, or kill someone, but if he harmed a god or

Cyclops returns to his cave with a flock of sheep while Odysseus and his terrified men hide at the back of the cave. MARY EVANS PICTURE LIBRARY/ EDWIN WALLACE/EVERETT COLLECTION.

a god's relative, as he did with the Cyclops, he was punished for it.

- For centuries scholars have wondered if Homer made up the island of Ithaca, because the geography of the Greek island by that name does not match Homer's descriptions, but in 2003 amateur archeologist Robert Bittlestone theorized that the forces of nature had changed the island. He began research that showed earthquakes and landslides had closed the sea channel between Ithaca and another island, turning two islands into one and changing its shape. The use of high-tech imaging systems in the area has revealed that many of the places Homer mentioned had once been laid out the way he said.

- The Greeks made sacrifices to their gods. They usually killed a sheep or cow in the god's name. Odysseus's sacrifices eventually won him Zeus's favor, and the great god helped the roving warrior finally return home to Ithaca.

Consider the following ...

- Many people see Odysseus as a hero; others claim he was a pirate. Judging by what you have read here, how would you classify him and why?

- After returning home from a battle, warriors (who have spent years defending their comrades, killing enemies, fighting for their lives, and living by their wits) often have trouble adjusting to a quiet domestic life. How might boredom combined with this set of skills lead naturally to pirating?

- The events in the excerpt could be based on actual happenings, but some of the other parts of *The Odyssey*, such as the tale about the Cyclops, seem fantastical. Why do you think this is so?

- How did the Greeks' perceptions of their gods differ from many religions that have only one God who is the embodiment of all that is good and perfect? In what ways might these ideas have affected the Greeks' religious practices and daily lives?

For More Information

BOOKS

Cooney, Caroline B. *Goddess of Yesterday*. New York: Delacorte, 2002.

Day, Malcolm. *100 Characters from Classical Mythology: Discover the Fascinating Stories of the Greek and Roman Deities*. Hauppauge, NY: Barron's, 2007.

Ormerod, Henry A. *Piracy in the Ancient World.* Baltimore: Johns Hopkins University Press, 1996.

Quintus Smyrnaeus. *The Fall of Troy,* translated by A.S. Way. Loeb Classical Library Volume 19. London: William Heinemann, 1913. Available online at www.theoi.com/Text/QuintusSmyrnaeus1.html (accessed on January 3, 2011).

PERIODICALS

Bordewich, Fergus M. "Odyssey's End? The Search for Ancient Ithaca," *Smithsonian* (April 2006). Available online at www.smithsonianmag.com/ people-places/10021506.html#ixzz0uqDYzZMx (accessed on January 3, 2011).

2

Julius Caesar and the Cilician Pirates

Excerpt from "Caesar"

Published in Lives of Noble Grecians and Romans *by Plutarch*

Translated by John Dryden, 1683

"[Caesar] was left among a set of the most bloodthirsty people in the world. . . . Yet he made so little of them, that when he had a mind to sleep, he would send to them, and order them to make no noise."

Although the ancient Greeks often considered piracy an acceptable, or even honorable, profession, as time went on pirates became classified as outlaws. Until about 68 BCE the area around the Mediterranean Sea served as a haven for pirates, and, for much of that time, piracy was seen as a means for gaining status and wealth.

Piracy may have initially begun in the Mediterranean because much of the barren, rocky shoreline did not support farming. Most people depended on fishing for their livelihoods, but some turned to piracy. Because most ships of the time moved slowly and sailed close to the coastline, robbery at sea was fairly easy. With many hidden inlets, pirates could conceal themselves until their prey had no means of escape.

Pirates not only attacked ships, but also raided on land, so most large cities were constructed several miles from the coast. In some cases these large towns also had sister ports on the sea for trading, but they had walled areas between them. Rome's main port was Ostia; Athens had the port of Piraeus. Sea robbers usually did not venture too far inland, but they troubled the shores all around the Mediterranean.

Rulers often did little to stop sea robbery, because for many provinces, piracy was a lucrative source of slaves. Rome, in particular, needed slaves to work the *latifundia*, or large plantations, owned by wealthy

Romans. Many slaves were transported to Italy to meet this demand. The waters around Crete, an island off the east coast of Greece, became known as the Golden Sea, because slave trading and piracy were so profitable there. Pirates' nests also sprang up in other nearby areas. Some of the most notorious places for slave trade were Cilicia and Delos. Kidnapping people and selling them into slavery remained commonplace until about 230 BCE.

The feared Cilician pirates

Located in present-day Turkey, Cilicia was home to bands of pirates who roamed the seacoast, ready to attack ships, especially slow-moving vessels filled with grain headed for Rome. These Cilician pirates plagued the eastern Mediterranean during the late second and early first centuries BCE.

During the three Mithridatic Wars (c. 89–84 BCE; 83–c. 82 BCE; and c. 73–63 BCE), Cilician pirates grew bolder. Mithridates, the king of Pontus, hired them to help in his fight against Rome. He even armed the pirates with faster ships so they could more easily attack the Roman navy. By 67 BCE Cilician pirates had become a major force in the Mediterranean. Many governments allowed the pirates to operate unhindered, because the government leaders benefited from the slave trade and from rising prices when grain ships were hijacked.

Rome had once protected many of the nations bordering the Mediterranean Sea, but the Cilicians took advantage of Rome's preoccupation with its civil wars to prey on the unguarded seas. The pirates had many harbors and watchtowers, which gave them an advantage in stealth, and with their swift, light sailing vessels, they easily overtook other ships.

Julius Caesar is captured by pirates

Sometimes pirates captured rich or well-connected citizens. In those cases they made more money by demanding a ransom for their illustrious prisoners. (A ransom is a sum of money demanded for the release of someone being held captive.) Such was the case when the Cilician pirates captured Julius Caesar (100–44 BCE).

Gaius Julius Caesar had been born into a wealthy and prestigious family in Rome. During Caesar's youth, his kinsman, Gaius Marius (c. 157–86 BCE), took over command of the Roman army, displacing the previously appointed leader, Sulla (also known as Lucius Cornelius Sulla Felix; c. 138–78 BCE), and beginning a rivalry that pitted the two men against each other for the control of Rome.

After Sulla took over as dictator in 82 BCE, Caesar lost his inheritance and was ordered to divorce his wife, Cornelia, who was related to Sulla's former rival. Caesar refused and spent the next years of his life on the run. Caesar joined the army, which was fighting in the east. It was during this time that he was captured by Cilician pirates.

Record of Caesar's capture

This account of Caesar's capture by pirates comes from a book of biographies written by the Greek author Plutarch of Chaeronea (also known as Mestrios Ploutarchos; 46–c. 120 CE). Plutarch grew up in central Greece in the first and second century CE. He traveled widely and became a Roman citizen.

Because Plutarch wrote his biography long after Caesar had died, some of the facts he recorded may not be accurate. Roman author Suetonius (c. 71–c. 135) later narrated the events of Caesar's life, and at times the reports contradict each other. Suetonius, who had access to the emperor Hadrian's (76–138) libraries, searched for anecdotes and scandals connected with Caesar's life, whereas Plutarch tried to convey a more factual review of events.

Historians differ as to the date of Caesar's capture by pirates. Some place it as early as 81 BCE; others indicate it occurred several years after that. Some even suggest it may have been as late as 74 BCE. Caesar's purpose for the trip is also subject to debate. One account says he was headed to Rhodes to study rhetoric. Plutarch says Caesar had sailed to Bithynia, the kingdom of Nicomedes, where Caesar was seized near the island of Pharmacusa.

One thing both authors agree on, though, is Caesar's fearlessness, even cockiness, onboard ship. Even at such a young age, he was sure of himself and not afraid to take charge in a situation that would have frightened most people. Perhaps his youth was what saved him from the pirates' wrath; they allowed him to get away with ordering them

Caesar: Conqueror of the Ancient World

When pirates abducted him, Julius Caesar was a young man. Later he became prominent in Roman politics, becoming first a *quaestor* (financial administrator; 69 BCE), next an *aedile* (official in charge of public works, police, grain supply, and games; 65 BCE), and then a *praetor* (judge; 62 BCE). After serving as a governor in Spain, which was a Roman province at the time, he returned to Rome and was elected consul (chief magistrate) in 59 BCE with the help of Roman generals Pompey (106–47 BCE) and Crassus (c. 115–53 BCE). Next, as governor of Roman Gaul, he expanded the empire to include present-day Belgium and France.

By this time he and Pompey were engaged in a rivalry for control of the Roman Empire. Pompey had the power, because Caesar was out of the country, and Pompey tried to use Roman laws to eliminate his competitor. But Caesar defied his orders, crossed the Rubicon River with an army, and defeated Pompey, who fled to Egypt, where he was assassinated. Caesar took over Rome in 48 BCE as consul and dictator, a position that traditionally lasted for six months at a time, but he retained it until 44 BCE, when a group of senators assassinated him.

Greek author Plutarch chronicled the life of Julius Caesar, including the tale of his capture by Cilician pirates.
EDWARD GOOCH/HULTON ARCHIVE/GETTY IMAGES.

around. Though Caesar was in his twenties, most likely the pirates viewed him as a spoiled boy who did not realize the danger of his situation.

Things to remember while reading the excerpt from "Caesar":

- Plutarch's account begins with Julius Caesar as a young man, but many scholars believe his biography may have originally begun with Caesar's childhood. If it did, that material has been lost.
- Caesar entertains the pirates by making speeches. He was known for his natural speaking ability; he even traveled to Rhodes to learn from

a famous teacher, Apollonius Molon. Talented at keeping an audience's attention, Caesar used this skill later as a Roman politician.

- Junius, the governor of Asia who judged these pirates, thought they would be better off free. He did not want them killed or imprisoned, because he was profiting from their endeavors.
- Crucifixion (hanging or nailing criminals on a cross until they died) was a common punishment for criminals and rebels in the Roman Empire until it was outlawed by emperor Constantine I (d. 337) in 337 CE.

● ● ●

Caesar

. . . He was taken near the island of Pharmacusa by some of the pirates, who, at that time, with large fleets of ships and innumerable smaller vessels, infested the seas everywhere.

When these men at first demanded of him twenty **talents** for his ransom, he laughed at them for not understanding the value of their prisoner, and voluntarily **engaged** to give them fifty. He presently despatched [dispatched] those about him to several places to raise the money, till at last he was left among a set of the most bloodthirsty people in the world, the Cilicians, only with one friend and two attendants. Yet he made so little of them, that when he had a mind to sleep, he would send to them, and order them to make no noise. For thirty-eight days, with all the freedom in the world, he amused himself with joining in their exercises and games, as if they had not been his keepers, but his guards. He wrote verses and speeches, and made them his **auditors**, and those who did not admire them, he called to their faces illiterate and barbarous, and would often, in **raillery**, threaten to hang them. They were greatly taken with this, and attributed his free talking to a kind of simplicity and boyish playfulness. As soon as his ransom was come from **Miletus**, he paid it, and was discharged, and proceeded at once to man [hire] some ships at the port of Miletus, and went in pursuit of the pirates, whom he surprised with their ships still stationed at the island, and took most of them. Their money he made his prize, and the men he secured in prison at **Pergamus**, and he made application to Junius, who was then governor of Asia, to whose office it belonged, as **praetor**, to determine their punishment. Junius, having his eye upon the money, for the sum was considerable, said he would think at his leisure what to do with the prisoners, upon which Caesar took his leave of him, and went off to Pergamus, where he ordered the pirates to be brought

Talent: A unit of weight or measure for gold and silver; estimated at 71–75 pounds (32.3–34.3 kilograms).

Engaged: Committed.

Auditors: Audience.

Raillery: Jest; joking.

Miletus: A city along the coast of present-day Turkey.

Pergamus: Also called Pergamon or Pérgamo; an ancient Greek city off the coast of present-day Turkey.

Praetor: Judicial officer.

Julius Caesar sets out to capture the pirates who had kidnapped him. PETER NEWARK HISTORICAL PICTURES/THE BRIDGEMAN ART LIBRARY.

forth and crucified; the punishment he had often threatened them with whilst he was in their hands, and they little dreamt he was in earnest. . . .

• • •

What happened next . . .

Although the pirates assumed Caesar was joking when he threatened them, he quickly gathered his forces after Junius refused to assist him and caught the pirates while they were still in port. He captured more than 350 pirates and crucified the 30 who had held him captive.

But Caesar's actions did not stop other pirates from preying upon the Italian coast. Although rulers outwardly condemned piracy, many, like Junius, secretly supported it for the wealth or prestige it brought them. For the next decade, Cilician pirates continued to plague Rome, while also supplying Roman citizens with slaves and driving up the price of grain.

After the Cilicians kidnapped two Roman praetors, destroyed government ships, set fire to Rome's own port of Ostia in 67 BCE, and then pillaged inland villages, Rome took action to stop these sea robbers. The tribune (official who looked after citizens' rights) Aulus Gabinius suggested that they appoint a military leader to pursue the pirates and that this person should be granted authority extending not only to the seas but also inland to all the Roman provinces surrounding the sea.

Although the common people wanted Pompey to get this position, Roman senators feared that giving one person so much power could lead to his becoming a dictator and seizing control of the government the way Sulla had done fifteen years before. Even though Pompey had maneuvered this appointment, he acted unwilling to accept it in order to ease their doubts. The conflict over this issue developed into a riot. But with the support of the tribunes and Julius Caesar, the law, called the *lex Gabinia*, passed in spite of the Senate's opposition.

To accomplish his mission, Pompey was supplied with five hundred ships, five thousand horses, 120,000 troops, and unlimited access to the Roman treasury. He divided his fleet into thirteen *legates* (assistants or squadrons) and gave each one control of a section of the Mediterranean. They targeted not only Cilicia but also Delos, Illyria, and Crete, which were the main pirate strongholds at that time. His forces kept the pirates from uniting, while the men under his command patrolled the middle of the sea in sixty of the best warships and drove the pirates toward his squadrons, who captured them.

One of Pompey's first moves was to open the way for Rome's food supplies to get through. In about forty days, he cleared the seas by destroying more than one thousand pirate ships and capturing more than four hundred vessels. During that time, he attacked and killed about ten thousand pirates, and restored communications between Spain, Africa, and Italy.

Within three months he overtook the remaining pirates near their capital, Coracesium, and captured their fortress. The battle was soon over. According to the Roman historian Florus in *The Epitome*, the pirates

Roman military leader Pompey the Great was given the task of eradicating piracy in the Mediterranean.
© INTERFOTO/ALAMY.

"did no more than meet the first onslaught; for as soon as they saw the beaks of our ships all round them, they immediately threw down their weapons and oars, and with a general clapping of hands, which was their sign of entreaty, begged for quarter [mercy]."

Pompey was a skilled strategist as well as a strong military leader. He offered amnesty (freedom from punishment) and even rewards to those pirates who surrendered. About twenty thousand pirates took advantage of his proposition, and he granted them plots of land in Cilicia and resettled them as farmers. In this way he regained control of the seas.

This conquest was not as difficult as it might have been because several years before, Publius Servilius Vatia had defeated western Cilicia. Some scholars also question whether Pompey did a thorough job, because some pirates were resettled in areas that were unsuitable for farming, and a few years later the governor of Asia was accused of extorting money to protect Greek cities from pirates. Some say it was not until decades later that the Mediterranean became relatively pirate free. Nevertheless, Pompey was credited with vanquishing piracy, and the relative peace he established lasted until after the fall of the Roman Empire in the fifth century.

Did you know ...

- English writer William Shakespeare (1564–1616) wrote a play called *Julius Caesar* that shows the dictator's assassination and the events that followed it. The main character in the play is Marcus Brutus, Caesar's friend and, later, assassin.
- Julius Caesar had three Roman wives during his lifetime: Cornelia, who died in 68 BCE, was the daughter of Lucius Cornelius Cinna (d. 84 BCE), a distinguished leader; Pompeia, whom he divorced after a scandal involving her possible love affair, was the granddaughter of Sulla; and, finally, Calpurnia, the daughter of an aristocrat, whom some say had a premonition of his assassination. Most of these marriages were for political gain. He may also have had a son with Cleopatra VII (69–30 BCE), ruler of Egypt.

Consider the following ...

- Most people were terrified in the presence of pirates, fearing what the ruffians might do to them, yet Caesar showed no fear. Why do you think this was?
- The pirates thought Caesar was joking when he threatened to hang them all. Why did none of them take him seriously?
- The Roman Empire greatly depended on slave labor to maintain its plantations. What changes might have occurred in the Roman economy and lifestyle if piracy had been outlawed sooner?
- From this account it seems that Caesar's time as the pirates's prisoner was not a hardship. Why do you think he chose to execute his captors?
- A pirate once questioned Alexander the Great (356–323 BCE) as to why pirates, who act in the same manner as conquerors, were

punished while conquerors were honored. Caesar, too, used naval forces to gain power, yet he punished the pirates. Compare and contrast a conqueror's conduct with that of a pirate.

- Following the terrorist bombing of the World Trade Center on September 11, 2001, the American government passed the USA PATRIOT Act (2001), which allowed law enforcement agencies to search private citizens' records. Those documents had previously been protected by privacy laws. Many defended the new law as a way to protect the United States from further attacks. Some writers likened that to the way Romans reacted to the pirates by passing the *lex Gabinia*. What similarities and differences exist between the reactions to these events?

For More Information

BOOKS

Appian of Alexandria. "The Mithridatic Wars." In *History of Rome*. Translated by Horace White. Cambridge, MA: Harvard University Press, 1912. Available online at www.livius.org/ap-ark/appian/appian_mithridatic_00.html (accessed on January 3, 2011).

Davis, William Stearns, ed. *Readings in Ancient History: Illustrative Extracts from the Sources*. Vol. 2: *Rome and the West*. Boston: Allyn and Bacon, 1912–1913.

De Souza, Philip. *Piracy in the Graeco-Roman World*. Cambridge: Cambridge University Press, 1999.

Florus, Lucius Annaeus. "The War Against the Pirates." In *The Epitome of Roman History*. Translated by J. Davies and J.S. Watson. Cambridge, MA: Harvard University Press, 1929, p. 195. Available online at http://penelope.uchicago.edu/Thayer/E/Roman/Texts/Florus/Epitome/1L*.html (accessed on January 3, 2011).

Smith, William, and Eugene Lawrence. *A Smaller History of Rome*. New York: Harper & Brothers, 1881.

PERIODICALS

De Souza, Philip. "Ancient Rome and the Pirates." *History Today* 51, no. 7 (2001).

Doyle, Noreen. "Mediterranean in Peril: From Their Island Home, These Pirates Frightened Even Mighty Rome." *Dig* (July–August 2008).

Goerke-Shrode, Sabine. "The Die Is Cast." *Calliope* (December 2006).

Harris, Robert. "Pirates of the Mediterranean." *New York Times* (September 30, 2006). Available online at www.nytimes.com/2006/09/30/opinion/30harris.html?pagewanted=all (accessed on January 3, 2011).

Hollingsworth, Anthony. "According to the Biographers: Julius Caesar according to Plutarch and Suetonius." *Calliope* (December 2006).

Wolverton, Joe, II. "Fear and Fatal Power: When Cilician Pirates Attacked a Major Port of Rome, Gnaeus Pompeius Magnus—Pompey the Great— Manipulated the Fear of the People to Acquire Immense Power." *New American* (May 24, 2010).

WEB SITES

Hooker, Richard. "Rome: Julius Caesar," *Washington State University.* http:// wsu.edu/~dee/ROME/JULIUS.HTM (accessed on January 3, 2011).

Lendering, Jona. "Cilician Pirates," *Livius: Articles on Ancient History.* www.livius.org/cg-cm/cilicia/cilician_pirates.html (accessed on January 3, 2011).

3

English Privateers Battle the Spanish at San Juan de Ulúa

Excerpt from *The Third Troublesome Voyage Made with the* Jesus of Lübeck, *the* Minion *and Four Other Ships to the Parts of Guinea and the West Indies, in the Years 1567 and 1568*
By John Hawkins

Reprinted in Voyages of the Elizabethan Seamen to America: Select Narratives from the 'Principal Navigations' of Hakluyt, *edited by* Edward John Payne, M.A.

Published by The Clarendon Press, 1893

"The Viceroy, now seeing that the treason must be discovered, forthwith stayed our master, blew the trumpet, and of all sides set upon us. Our men which warded [stood guard] ashore, being stricken with sudden fear, gave place, fled, and sought to recover succor [help or safety] of the ships."

Although piracy, the act of robbing ships at sea, has always been illegal, until the nineteenth century the governments of many countries employed privateers, or private ship owners commissioned by a state or government to attack the merchant ships of an enemy nation. In times of war, privateers were granted licenses, called letters of marque, which allowed them to legally seize shiploads of gold, silver, and other goods from enemy ships. The privateers were required to turn over a portion of their spoils to the government, keeping the rest for themselves. There were several benefits to this arrangement. Privateer attacks weakened the enemy, brought money into the government treasury, and made privateers wealthy. But there were also risks. Privateers who were captured by the enemy nation were treated as pirates and could be executed.

In the sixteenth century, tensions between England and Spain escalated, leading to war in 1588. In part, this conflict stemmed from the fact that Spain held a strict monopoly, or exclusive control, on colonization and trade in the Americas. England wanted to gain access to the wealth of the Americas. Another major factor was religion. The king of Spain was Catholic, and opposed Protestantism, the religion of England. Throughout these hostilities, the English used privateers to strike out at Spain. Among the most successful English privateers were John Hawkins (1532–1595) and his cousin, Francis Drake (1540–1596).

John Hawkins enters the slave trade

John Hawkins was the son of a wealthy merchant. He became a skilled seaman and trader, and inherited his father's business around 1553. Several years later, Hawkins began planning a slaving expedition. One of the greatest commodities at this time was slaves. Slave labor was in high demand in the Americas, and millions of slaves were transported from Africa to work on plantations. Spain had a monopoly on African slave trade in the Americas, but Hawkins was certain he could break into this profitable business. He gained the support of various investors and, beginning in 1562, Hawkins made three trips to Africa to collect slaves. On his first two expeditions, Hawkins made large profits. Then he planned a third expedition.

On October 2, 1567, Hawkins left Plymouth, England, with a fleet of six ships. Hawkins's cousin, Francis Drake, joined the expedition. Hawkins commanded the *Jesus of Lübeck*, a ship belonging to Queen Elizabeth I (1533–1603). When they arrived on the coast of West Africa, the English set about capturing Africans for the slave trade. The English took their prisoners and sailed to the Americas to sell them.

The weather in the Caribbean Sea at that time of year was dangerous. A storm hit as the ships passed Cuba. Hawkins's battered ship sprang leaks large enough for fish to swim through. The crew hoped to stop in Florida, but the water was too shallow along the coast. They headed for the nearby Mexican port of San Juan de Ulúa (also spelled Ullua).

John Hawkins. © DEREK BAYES ASPECT/LEBRECHT MUSIC & ARTS/CORBIS.

When Hawkins sailed into the port, the Spaniards thought his fleet belonged to Don Martín Enriquez (d. 1583), their newly appointed Mexican viceroy, so they did not fire on the approaching ships. Hawkins tried to convince the Spanish that his intentions were peaceful—he only wanted to repair his vessels and gather supplies—but once Enriquez arrived a few days later, the Spanish attacked.

The Third Troublesome Voyage describes Hawkins's final expedition for slaves and the attack by the Spanish at San Juan de Ulúa. This account was written by Hawkins himself.

John Hawkins battles the Spanish at San Juan de Ulúa. LOOK AND LEARN/THE BRIDGEMAN ART LIBRARY INTERNATIONAL.

Things to remember while reading the excerpt from *The Third Troublesome Voyage Made with the* Jesus *of Lübeck,* the Minion *and Four Other Ships to the Parts of Guinea and the West Indies, in the Years 1567 and 1568*:

- Two of the ships on this voyage, the *Jesus of Lübeck* and the *Minion*, were Queen Elizabeth's naval vessels. Captains got one-third of the bounty; the rest went to the investors—merchants, courtiers, councilors, and the queen—so the expedition had to make a profit.
- The English and Spanish were rivals in the slave trade. When the English arrived at Spanish ports, the Spanish colonists usually refused to trade, but sometimes under cover of night made secret

exchanges. In a few ports, however, the Spanish refused to allow the English to even land.

- The Spanish Inquisition was going on at the time of this voyage. During the Inquisition, anyone not of the Catholic faith was tortured until they agreed to convert (change their religion). Those who refused were usually put to death. The Spanish at San Juan de Ulúa considered the English pirates to be not only criminals but also infidels, or unbelievers who opposed the Catholic Church and needed to be punished.

- Hawkins's fleet of six English ships set sail on October 2, 1567, but only two returned. The first ship did not dock in England until January 20, 1569; the second ship returned to port on January 25, 1569.

• • •

The Third Troublesome Voyage Made with the *Jesus of Lubeck*, the *Minion* and Four Other Ships to the Parts of Guinea and the West Indies, in the Years 1567 and 1568 by Master John Hawkins

Now we had obtained between 400 and 500 negroes, wherewith we thought it somewhat reasonable to seek the coast of the West Indies, and there, for our negroes and other our merchandise, we hoped to obtain whereof to **countervail** our **charges** with some gains. Whereunto we proceeded with all diligence, furnished our watering, took fuel, and departed the coast of Guinea the third of February, continuing at the sea with a passage more hard than before hath been accustomed till the 27 day of March, which day we had sight of an island called Dominica, upon the coast of the West Indies, in 14 degrees. From **thence** we coasted from place to place, making our traffic with the Spaniards as we might, somewhat hardly, because the king had **straitly** commanded all his governors in those parts by no means to **suffer** any trade to be made with us. Notwithstanding, we had reasonable trade, and courteous entertainment, from the isle of Margarita unto Cartagena. . . .

Shortly after this, the 16 of September, we entered the port of St. John de Ullua, and in our entry, the Spaniards thinking us to be the fleet of Spain, the chief officers of the country came aboard us; which, being deceived of their expectation, were greatly dismayed: but immediately, when they saw our demand was nothing but **victuals**, were **recomforted**. I found also in the same port 12 ships which had in them by the report £200,000 in gold and silver; all which, being in my possession, with the king's island, as also the passengers

Countervail: Match.

Charges: Expenses.

Thence: There, or that place.

Straitly: Strictly.

Suffer: Allow.

Victuals: Food.

Recomforted: Relieved.

before in my way **thitherward** stayed, I set at liberty, without the taking from them the weight of a **groat**. Only, because I would not be delayed of my **dispatch**, I **stayed two men of estimation** and sent post [a letter] immediately to Mexico, which was 200 miles from us, to the Presidents and Council there, shewing [showing] them of our arrival there by the force of weather, and the necessity of the repair of our ships and victuals, which wants we required as friends to King Philip to be furnished of for our money; and that the Presidents and Council there should with all convenient speed take order that at the arrival of the Spanish fleet, which was daily looked for, there might no cause of quarrel rise between us and them, but for the better maintenance of **amity** their commandment might be had in that behalf. This message being sent away the 16 day of September at night, being the very day of our arrival, in the next morning, which was the 17 day of the same month, we saw open of the **haven** 13 great ships. . . .

Also the place of the haven was so little [narrow], that of necessity the ships must ride one aboard the other, so that we could not give place to them, nor they to us. And here I began to **bewail** that which after followed, for now, said I, I am in two dangers, and forced to receive the one of them. That was, either I must have kept out the fleet from entering the port, the which with God's help I was very well able to do; or else suffer them to enter in with their accustomed **treason**, which they never fail to execute, where they may have opportunity to **compass** it by any means. If I had kept them out, then had there been present shipwreck of all the fleet, which amounted in value to six millions, which was in value of our money £1,800,000, which I considered I was not able to answer, fearing the Queen's Majesty's indignation in so weighty a matter. Thus with myself revolving the doubts, I thought rather better to abide the jut of the uncertainty than the certainty. . . .

Now was our first messenger come and returned from the fleet with report of the arrival of a Viceroy, so that he had authority, both in all this province of Mexico, otherwise called Nueva España, and in the sea; who sent us word that we should send our conditions. . . . Thus, following our demand, we required victuals for our money, and licence [license] to sell as much **ware** as might furnish our wants, and that there might be of either part twelve gentlemen as hostages for the maintenance of peace; and that the island, for our better safety, might be in our own possession during our abode there, and such **ordnance** as was planted in the same island, which were eleven pieces of brass [cannons]: and that no Spaniard might land in the island with any kind of weapon. These conditions at the first he somewhat misliked. . . . But in the end he concluded to our request with a writing from the Viceroy, signed with his hand and sealed with his seal, of all the conditions concluded. . . . Thus at the end of three days all was concluded and the fleet entered the port, saluting one another as the manner of the sea doth require. . . . Then we laboured 2 days, placing the English ships by themselves and the Spanish by themselves, the captains of

Thitherward: Going in that direction.

Groat: A coin worth about four pennies.

Dispatch: Message.

Stayed two men of estimation: Left two trustworthy men.

Amity: Friendship.

Haven: Harbor.

Bewail: Express deep sorrow.

Treason: Betraying a trust.

Compass: Devise.

Ware: Goods or merchandise.

Ordnance: Weapons and ammunition.

each part and inferior men of their parts promising great amity of all sides; which even as with all **fidelity** it was meant on our part, so the Spaniards meant nothing less on their parts; but from the mainland had furnished themselves with a supply of men to the number of 1,000, and meant the next Thursday, being the 23 of September, at dinner-time, to set upon us on all sides.

The same Thursday, in the morning, the treason being at hand, some appearance shewed [showed], as shifting of weapon from ship to ship, planting and bending of ordnance from the ships to the island where our men **warded**, passing to and fro of companies of men more than required for their necessary business, and many other ill likelihoods, which caused us to have a **vehement** suspicion. And **therewithal** [we] sent to the Viceroy to enquire what was meant by it, which sent immediately strait commandment to **unplant** all things suspicious, and also sent word that he in the faith of a Viceroy would be our defence [defense] from all **villainies**. Yet we being not satisfied with this answer, because we suspected a great number of men to be hid in a great ship of 900 tons which was moored near unto the *Minion*, sent again to the Viceroy the master of the *Jesus*, which **had the Spanish tongue**, and required to be satisfied if any such thing were or not. The Viceroy, now seeing that the treason must be discovered, forthwith stayed our master, blew the trumpet, and of all sides set upon us. Our men which warded ashore, being stricken with sudden fear, gave place, fled, and sought to recover **succor** of the ships. The Spaniards, being before provided for the purpose, landed in all places in multitudes from their ships, which they might easily do without boats, and **slew** all our men on shore without mercy. A few of them escaped aboard the *Jesus*. The great ship, which had by the estimation 300 men placed in her secretly, immediately fell aboard the *Minion*, but by God's appointment, in the time of the suspicion we had, which was only one half-hour, the *Minion* was made ready to avoid, and so leesing [releasing] her **headfasts**, and haling [dragging] away by the **sternfasts**, she was gotten out. Thus with God's help she defended the violence of the first brunt of these 300 men. The *Minion* being passed out, they came aboard the *Jesus*, which also with very much **ado** and the loss of many of our men, were defended and kept out. Then were there also two other ships that assaulted the *Jesus* at the same instant, so that she had hard getting loose, but yet with some time we had cut our headfasts and gotten out by the sternfasts. Now when the *Jesus* and the *Minion* were gotten about two ships' length from the Spanish fleet, the fight began so hot on all sides that within one hour the admiral of the Spaniards was supposed to be sunk, their vice-admiral burned, and one other of their principal ships supposed to be sunk, so that the ships were little able to annoy us.

Then it is to be understood that all the ordnance upon the island was in the Spaniards' hands, which did us so great annoyance that it cut all the masts and yards of the *Jesus*, in such sort that there was no hope to carry her away.

Fidelity: Trustworthiness.

Warded: Stood guard.

Vehement: Strong.

Therewithal: With that.

Unplant: Remove.

Villainies: Evil deeds.

Had the Spanish tongue: Spoke Spanish.

Succor: Help or safety.

Slew: Killed.

Headfast: A rope that secures the bow of a ship to the dock.

Sternfast: A rope that secures the stern of a ship.

Ado: Difficulty.

Also it sunk our small ships, whereupon we determined to place the *Jesus* on that side of the *Minion*, that she might abide all the **battery** from the land, and so be a defence for the *Minion* till night, and then to take such relief of victuals and other necessaries from the *Jesus* as the time would suffer us, and to leave her. As we were thus determining, and had placed the *Minion* from the shot of the land, suddenly the Spaniards had fired two great ships, which were coming directly with us, and having no means to avoid the fire, it bred among our men a marvellous fear, so that some said, Let us depart with the *Minion*. Others said, let us see whither the wind will carry the fire from us. But to be short, the *Minion*'s men, which had always their sails in a readiness, thought to make sure work, and so, without either consent of the captain or master, cut their sail, so that very hardly I was received into the *Minion*.

The most part of the men that were left alive in the *Jesus* made shift and followed the *Minion* in a small boat. The rest, which the little boat was not able to receive, were enforced to abide the mercy of the Spaniards, which I doubt was very little. So with the *Minion* only and the *Judith*, a small bark [boat] of 50 tons, we escaped; which bark the same night **forsook** us in our great misery. We were now removed with the *Minion* from the Spanish ships two bow-shoots, and there rode all that night. The next morning we recovered an island a mile from the Spaniards, where there took us a north wind, and being left only with two anchors and two cables (for in this conflict we lost three cables and two anchors) we thought always upon death, which ever was present, but God preserved us to a longer time.

The weather **waxed** reasonable, and the Saturday we set sail, and having a great number of men and little victuals, our hope of life waxed less and less. Some desired to yield to the Spaniards; some rather desired to obtain a place where they might give themselves to the **infidels**; and some had rather abide with a little **pittance** the mercy of God at sea. So thus, with many sorrowful hearts, we wandered in an unknown sea.

• • •

What happened next . . .

The two English ships barely escaped from the Spanish and began the journey home. They snatched whatever food they could along the coast. They ate rats, mice, dogs, cats, parrots, and monkeys. When they reached the lower end of the Bay of Mexico, half the crew wanted to stop, but the rest preferred to set out to sea. The boats were overloaded, so those who wanted to search for food and water were sent ashore. The rest of the crew sailed off without them.

Battery: Attack.

Forsook: Left.

Waxed: Grew.

Infidels: Natives.

Pittance: Tiny amount.

English sailors battle the Spanish at San Juan de Ulúa.
PRIVATE COLLECTION/THE
BRIDGEMAN ART LIBRARY
INTERNATIONAL.

Many men fell ill and died along the way, but the weakened crew continued on to Vigo, Spain, hoping to find English ships for protection and fresh crew members at the port there. When they arrived, they obtained much-needed supplies and repaired their vessels before setting sail for England. The *Judith* reached Plymouth on January 20, 1569, and everyone assumed that the other vessels had been lost at sea.

The Fate of the English Privateers in Captivity

Job Hortop was a teenage powder-maker until he was pressed (forced) into service as a gunner on the *Jesus of Lübeck* . He was in the group that went ashore along the Bay of Mexico. Soon after they arrived, Chichimichi Indians attacked them, but after seeing the English were unarmed, the natives fed them but also stripped them of their clothing. Later, the Spanish imprisoned the English who survived and took them to the viceroy in Mexico.

The prisoners served as deckhands on the voyage to Spain, but they conspired to escape, so the captain put them in stocks. In Spain two of the conspirators were burned to death, but the other men, including Hortop, were forced to be galley slaves.

As slaves, they received daily rations of a pound and a half of black biscuits and water. They slept on wooden boards and had their heads and beards shaved once a month. Galley slaves rowed the ship and suffered from hunger, thirst, cold, and frequent whippings.

Hortop worked as a galley slave for twelve years before he was sent to a prison in Seville, Spain, for four years. A Spaniard paid Hortop's ransom, and Hortop served him for seven years. In October 1590 Hortop gained his freedom, sailed to England, and later wrote of his captivity.

Another captured privateer who wrote about his adventures was Miles Philips, who was captured by the Inquisition. Philips endured a forced march through the jungle to the viceroy's home, where he worked in the garden with about one hundred men, who all shared two sheep and some small loaves of bread as rations for four months.

Some prisoners were taken as slaves by other Spaniards. The Inquisitors tortured the others and burned some alive. Philips was sent to a monastery for five years. After that he endured many ordeals, including being locked in leg and neck irons, which he escaped, and spent years trying to return to his homeland, finally succeeding in 1582.

But five days later, the *Minion* docked at Cornwall, England. Only fifteen of the original one hundred crewmen survived. All told, a total of about seventy or eighty of the four hundred seamen made it back to England. The *Minion* was beyond repair, but the *Judith* made later voyages. After the English government totaled the losses from the expedition, they declared that the four horses loaded with gold and silver that Hawkins had brought back from the voyage were not enough to cover expenses.

As for the English sailors who had been left behind, they suffered at the hands of the Spanish. Many died of starvation or from cruelty. Hawkins spent many years negotiating for the release of these prisoners, but with little success. Some crew members captured by the Spanish were brought before the Inquisition and whipped or tortured. Many were sentenced as galley slaves to force them to recant, or publicly turn against, their faith.

Those who refused to convert were burned alive in the marketplace of Seville, Spain.

Both Hawkins and Drake were furious at the Spanish for breaking their promise and spent the rest of their lives getting revenge on them. Hawkins became a member of Parliament, the English legislature, in 1591. Later he took over as rear admiral of the Royal Navy. Using his knowledge of shipbuilding, Hawkins designed better ships, which helped the English defeat the Spanish Armada (navy) in 1588. He set up blockades to intercept Spanish treasure ships and prevent Spain from rearming. Hawkins was knighted in 1588; he died at sea in 1595.

Francis Drake became one of England's most successful privateers. After serving with Hawkins, Drake became the first Englishman to circumnavigate (sail around) the globe. He set sail on December 13, 1577, sailing around South America and along the west coast of North America and attacking Spanish possessions. His reputation earned him the Spanish name *El Draque*, meaning "The Dragon." After Drake returned to England with enough treasure to pay off the national debt, the queen gave him a fortune and knighted him in 1581. Drake also helped defeat the Spanish Armada in 1588.

Did you know ...

- After the Battle of San Juan de Ulúa, the viceroy told King Philip II of Spain (1527–1598) that he had only pretended to make peace so he could capture the English.
- Hawkins and Drake were separated after the attack, and, back in England, Hawkins accused Drake of desertion and cowardice. Hawkins claimed that Drake had sailed away on the *Judith*, leaving Hawkins and his crew to make their own way home. But Drake said that he had only followed Hawkins's orders. The episode left a permanent stain on Drake's reputation.

Consider the following ...

- Because the Spanish considered the English crew to be pirates, they felt it was their duty to capture them. What do you think about the way the Spaniards handled this?
- Should the English have left when the *Jesus* was first in trouble? Did the *Minion* do the right thing by leaving men behind? Why or why not?

- After all the trials and tribulations the fleet's crew had been through, how do you think the survivors felt when they heard the court's decision that the voyage was not worth the cost?
- What must it have been like for men who had spent a long time living and working together to deal with the deaths, abandonment, or capture of so many of their crew?

For More Information

BOOKS

Cabrera de Cordova, Luis. *Filipe Segundo Rey de España*. Madrid: Luis Sanchez, 1619.

Hakluyt, Richard. "Job Hortop." In *The Tudor Venturers*. London: Folio Society, 1970.

Kelsey, Harry. *Sir John Hawkins: Queen Elizabeth's Slave Trader*. New Haven, CT: Yale University Press, 2002.

Kraus, Hans P. "The Unfortunate Voyage of the San Juan de Ulúa, 1567–1569." In *Sir Francis Drake: A Pictorial Biography* by Hans P. Kraus. Amsterdam: N. Israel, 1970. Available online at www.loc.gov/rr/rarebook/catalog/drake/drake-2-unfortunatevoy.html (accessed on January 3, 2011).

Rediker, Marcus. *The Slave Ship: A Human History*. New York: Penguin, 2008.

Walling, Robert Alfred John. *A Sea-Dog of Devon: A Life of Sir John Hawkins*. Denver: BiblioLife, 2009.

PERIODICALS

Helgerson, Richard. "*I, Miles Philips*: An Elizabethan Seaman Conscripted by History." *PMLA* (May 2003).

WEB SITES

Long-Price, Simon. "Sir John Hawkins." *BBC*. www.bbc.co.uk/kent/content/articles/2007/03/23/abolition_john_hawkins_feature.shtml (accessed on January 3, 2011).

4

Letter from a Captive of the Corsairs

"Letter from Robert Adams to Captain Robert Adams"

Originally written in 1642

Reprinted in Piracy, Slavery, and Redemption: Barbary Captivity
Narratives from Early Modern England

Published by Columbia University Press, 2001

"And, dear father, I humbly beseech you, for Christ Jesus'
sake, to take some course [action] for my deliverance, for if neither the
king take no course, nor my ransom come, I am out of all hope ever to
behold my country again."

Many stories about pirates praise the excitement and romance of the
high seas, but captives who lived to tell of their experiences spoke of
harsh conditions, cruelty, and despair. Knowing they might never see their
loved ones again, fearing whippings and punishments, forced to labor
under the hot sun, most longed for freedom and sent letters to relatives
begging to be ransomed. (A ransom is a sum of money demanded for the
release of someone being held captive.)

From 1492 to 1820, fierce pirates called corsairs roamed the Barbary
Coast, an area in the Mediterranean Sea roughly encompassing the present-
day countries of Morocco, Algeria, Tunisia, and northwest Libya. The
North African nations that were home to the corsairs were called the
Barbary States and included the kingdom of Morocco, Algiers, Tripoli,
and Tunis. For several centuries, the latter three states were part of the
Ottoman Empire, ruled by the Muslim Ottoman Turks. After a revolt in
Algiers in 1659, Ottoman rulers maintained little control. The Barbary
Coast republics chose their own rulers and survived by raiding. Europeans
captured in corsair raids were held for ransom or sold into slavery. It is

European prisoners captured by Barbary corsairs. © BETTMANN/CORBIS.

estimated that the corsairs may have taken as many as 1.25 million Europeans as slaves. Many countries paid a tribute to these pirates to prevent them from attacking their ships. (A tribute is payment from one ruler of a state to another, usually for protection or to acknowledge submission.)

Rise of the Barbary corsairs

In the eighth century, the Moors, a Muslim people from regions of the Sahara Desert and the Mediterranean coast of Africa, invaded the Iberian Peninsula (part of present-day Spain and Portugal). Christians in Iberia lived under Muslim rule for nearly two centuries. Then the Roman Catholic Church launched the Crusades, a series of military campaigns to take control of the Holy Land (roughly the present-day territory of Israel, the Palestine territories, and parts of Jordan and Lebanon) from the Muslims. Inspired by the religious fervor of the Crusades, Catholics in Spain rose up against the Moors.

In 1492 the Spanish conquered Granada in southern Spain and drove out the last of the Moors, who settled across the Mediterranean Sea in Morocco and Algiers, then spread throughout the Maghreb, an area of North Africa that Europeans called the Barbary Coast. There were few ways to earn a living on the Barbary Coast, where farming was poor, so many of the expelled Moors turned to sea raiding. Piracy also allowed them to gain revenge for their exile and the brutality of the Crusades by plundering (robbing of goods by force) European ships and capturing slaves.

The 1600s saw the rise of corsairs who attacked ports in Portugal, Spain, Italy, France, England, the Netherlands, and islands off the coasts of these nations. Sometimes these pirates traveled as far north as Ireland and even Iceland. In 1627 Algerian corsairs seized more than four hundred men, women, and children from Icelandic coastal towns. According to one captive who escaped, the pirates selected young people who would make the best slaves. They herded the elderly into a church that they then set ablaze. Anyone who resisted was killed. A few years later, in 1631, the corsairs raided the village of Baltimore, Ireland, and kidnapped more than one hundred people. As the raids grew more daring, many coastal cities and even some entire islands were abandoned.

Not all the corsairs were from Africa or the Ottoman Empire, however. Some European sea raiders, seeing the profits that could be made by pirating, abandoned their national loyalties, converted to Islam, and became corsairs of the Barbary Coast. These converts were called renegades. They aided the North African corsairs by introducing them to European shipbuilding techniques.

As they grew bolder, Barbary pirates not only attacked ships, but plundered villages. They even sailed into England's Thames River, coming very close to London. After they raided a town, they often returned to get ransoms for many of their prisoners. If relatives were unable to pay, sometimes moneylenders provided cash in exchange for the families' houses or land.

Treatment of Barbary captives

Robert Adams was taken by Barbary pirates in 1625, during the peak of the slave trade. In the years between 1605 and 1634, piracy off the coast of North Africa reached its zenith; at that time, estimates indicate that the Barbary States had about thirty-five thousand captives. To keep this number constant, the corsairs needed a steady supply of replacement slaves, because many prisoners died from starvation, disease, and cruelty. The pirates also supplied slaves for the Ottoman Empire and the Middle East.

As Robert Adams reported, prisoners were often treated cruelly both aboard ship and on land. First they were stripped of their clothing and often beaten. If no one ransomed them, they remained in chains in the hold of the ship and were fed only black barley bread and water. Some unlucky captives never got off the vessel; instead, they served as galley slaves, where they were chained to their places at the ship's oars and forced to row without stopping for ten to twenty hours a day. If they weakened or tried to rest, they were whipped. Falling asleep could mean being thrown into the sea after a merciless flogging. Most remained chained in place for as long as six months at a time, so they slept, ate, and went to the bathroom in that spot. Rowers might serve for up to two decades.

Other slaves were taken in neck chains to be auctioned off. The ruler of the Ottoman Empire received a percentage of all captured slaves. He could also buy as many as he wanted at a low price. One Englishman captured in the 1600s, Francis Brooks, wrote *Barbarian Cruelty* (1693), which described his ordeal. He tells of the prisoners being taken to the palace where the guards cursed at them and whipped them with cords or sticks to force them to work all day long. Many slaves constructed buildings or walls for the capital, often carrying heavy buckets of dirt on their heads. Their captors also tried to get them to become Muslims. Some prisoners changed their religion to gain easier jobs, and mothers often converted so they could stay with their children. Women usually became maids or were added to the ruler's harem, the area of a Muslim household historically reserved for wives, concubines, and female relatives.

At night the slaves were herded into an underground vault, where they slept on the cold ground, so many became ill. When Mully Ishmael (also spelled Moulay Ismail; 1645–1727), the sultan of Morocco, discovered that some of his slaves were too weak to work, he had them killed. The captives and guards alike feared his temper, because he beat or slaughtered those who angered him. Some of the punishments included being run through with a lance (sometimes multiple times), being shot, being pelted with stones, or being dragged to pieces behind a mule. As many as 15 to 30 percent of the captives died from disease or starvation.

An American prisoner about a century later said he and his fellow captives were chained together, and each also had to drag a heavy ball and chain around his ankle. Guards beat them with sticks, often hitting innocent men beside them at the same time. One punishment mentioned

A corsair captain offers a female captive for sale at a slave market in Algiers. MARY EVANS PICTURE LIBRARY/EVERETT COLLECTION.

by many captives was having their bare feet beaten, making walking painful. These prisoners worked from before dawn until sundown cutting stone, then spent the night in jail. Like Robert Adams, these prisoners were encouraged to write letters to friends and relatives telling of their hard lives and begging to be ransomed.

Things to remember while reading the "Letter from Robert Adams to Captain Robert Adams":

- Adams writes his letter from Salley (also spelled Sallee). This was Salé, Morocco, a sister city to the present-day capital of Rabat. Salé was a thriving pirate haven, or a safe place for pirates to harbor and repair their ships, resupply, and organize raiding parties.

- The term *corsair* is mainly used for Barbary pirates during the sixteenth century and later. At that time, the Ottoman Empire ruled Algiers, Tunis, and Tripoli, but not Morocco. The Barbary pirates increased their attacks during this time, and the slave trade was at its peak.

- Little is known about Robert Adams. The only information available is the letter he wrote to his father, a sea captain.

- In England at this time, first sons were usually named after their grandfathers, and they inherited the family property when their parents died. Second sons were usually named after their fathers, so Robert Adams may have been a second son.

- Records of a Captain Robert Adams show that he served with the East India Company in the early 1600s and made voyages to the East Indies (Southeastern Asia) as well as to the American colonies. Adams was well respected and never lost a ship, so he was entrusted with important documents that were sent to England and to the king of Spain. But whether this Captain Adams was the father of the young man who wrote this letter is not known.

• • •

Letter from Robert Adams to Captain Robert Adams

To his most loving father, Captain Robert Adams, at his house, in Ratcliff, give this—I pray you pay the **post**—from a poor captive in Salley.
[written on the back of the letter in a different hand:]
4 November 1625.
—From Robert Adams, a poor captive at Salley, to his father.
—For the King.
[in the margin:] I pray let me hear an answer from you, soon as possible you can.
From Salley, this 4th of November, **anno** 1625.
Loving and kind Father and Mother, my humble duty remembered unto you, both praying to God continually for your health as my own.

You may please to understand that I am here in Salley, in most miserable captivity, under the hands of most cruel **tyrants**. For after I was sold, my **patroon** made me work at a mill like a horse, from morning until night, with chains upon my legs, of 36 pounds weights apiece, my meat [food] nothing but a little coarse bread and water, my lodging in a dungeon underground,

Post: Postage.

Anno: In the year.

Tyrants: Harsh rulers.

Patroon: Slave master.

where some 150 or 200 of us lay altogether, having no comfort of the light but a little hole, and being so full of **vermin** for want of **shift** and not being allowed time for to pick [the lice off] myself that I am almost eaten up with them, and every day beaten to make me either **turn Turk** or come to my ransom. For our master's boy had told my patroons that I was the owner's son of the ship and you were able to ransom home forty such as I was, which was not sooner known but they forced me to come to my ransom and agree to them, though I always pleaded poverty. For then they made me **grind** more then I did formerly, and continually beat me, and almost starved me. So, though unwilling, I agreed at 730 **ducats** of Barbary, for I was forced to it, being brought so low for want of sustenance that I could not go [walk] without a staff.

So I have six months' time for my ransom to come, whereof three months are gone, and if it come not, then I must arm myself to endure the most misery of any creature in the world. Therefore I humbly desire you on my bended knees, and with sighs from the bottom of my hart [heart], to **commiserate** my poor distressed estate [state] and seek some means for my delivery out of this miserable slavery. For here are some 1500 Englishmen here in as bad case as myself, though something better **used**, for they misuse none but such as are able to pay their ransom. And, dear father, I humbly beseech you, for Christ Jesus' sake, to take some **course** for my deliverance, for if neither the king take no course, nor my ransom come, I am out of all hope ever to behold my country again.

Thus ceasing to trouble you, I rest
Your most dutiful and obedient son till death,
Robert Adams.

Mr. Legg is here at ransom for 730 Barbary ducats likewise. I have sent three or four letters before this by several men and never heard from you.

• • •

What happened next . . .

No one knows the fate of Robert Adams. Perhaps, as happened with some of the wealthier captives of the Barbary corsairs, his parents paid the ransom, and he was set free. Other captives were not as lucky. Adams's letter indicates that he had written several previous letters that had gone unanswered. With the precarious nature of sea travel and the many pirates roaming the seas, the ships carrying these letters may have been lost at sea or the couriers of Adams's letters may have been kidnapped themselves. If that was the case, then Adams may have remained a prisoner the rest of his life.

Vermin: Pests such as lice, fleas, rats, or mice.

Shift: A change of clothes.

Turn Turk: Convert to Islam.

Grind: Work hard.

Ducats: Gold coins.

Commiserate: Feel sympathy for.

Used: Treated.

Course: Action.

The Barbary corsairs ruled the Mediterranean until the late 1700s. They demanded tribute from any nation whose ships sailed near their coastline. Most European countries gave in and paid money to stop the raids. England, under King Charles II (1630–1685), won some naval victories and negotiated agreements with the Barbary States. The English signed treaties in 1671 with Algiers, in 1675 with Tunis, and in 1676 with Tripoli. Other countries tried to take advantage of England's relationship with the North African states by posing as English ships to gain safe passage. This angered the corsairs, and they broke the pacts. After England won a decisive victory in 1682, they forced Algiers to sign another treaty ensuring that no person aboard an English ship would be bought, sold, or enslaved.

Other nations also either attacked the Barbary States or tried to negotiate with them, but the corsairs often did not honor the treaties, so European ships and sailors continued to be lost. Most countries did not want to use military means to control the piracy because war was costly, but, even more importantly, they wanted the corsairs to plunder other nations' ships. The more countries that lost goods and personnel to the marauders, the better it was for their own commerce. If the European nations had united, they could have overtaken the pirates. Instead, they let the corsairs roam unchecked and continued paying tribute for safe passage and ransom for captured citizens.

Until the American Revolution (1775–83; the American colonists' fight for independence from England) began, the American colonies had operated under the protection of the English treaties with the Barbary States, and they had the backing of the English navy to enforce any violations. During the war, France offered to protect the Americans against piracy. After the colonies won their independence, they tried to negotiate treaties with England for protection, because the Royal Navy was a strong force against Barbary pirates. Concerned that lower-cost American goods would hurt their economy, England refused to sign an agreement. Consequently, Morocco corsairs captured an American ship a year later. Then corsairs from Algiers seized two American vessels in July 1785 within a few days of each other. Historians sometimes consider these acts as the start of the Barbary Wars, but it was not until thirty-three years later that tension escalated into two wars.

For many years John Adams (1735–1826), president of the United States from 1797 to 1801, argued with Thomas Jefferson (1743–1826), who was then ambassador to France but would become the next American

U.S. Navy forces bombard Tripoli in 1804, during the First Barbary War. MPI/ARCHIVE PHOTOS/GETTY IMAGES.

president. The two wrote letters back and forth discussing the issue of paying tribute to the Barbary pirates versus forming a navy and defeating the bandits at sea. Early in Adams's presidency, the U.S. government signed the Treaty of Tripoli with the beys (local rulers) of Tripoli and Algiers, agreeing to pay them for safe shipping. When Jefferson became president (served 1801–1809), he refused to give in to Tripoli's demands for more money, so the bey declared war on the United States, which sparked the First Barbary War, called the Tripolitan (1801–5). Not until the Second Barbary War, the Algerine, in 1815, was the matter officially settled. From then on America no longer had to pay tribute, but most European countries continued making payments until 1820, when France conquered Algiers and the threat of the Barbary corsairs came to an end.

Did you know ...

- It is estimated that Barbary pirates captured and sold into slavery as many as 1.25 million Europeans. By comparison, about ten million to fifteen million Africans were enslaved by the Europeans.

Pirates Through the Ages: Primary Sources

- Many Barbary prisoners penned tales of their hardships after they had been ransomed from captivity. These sold well to European audiences who loved to read of adventure and danger. Fiction authors, too, played on this interest to attract wider readership. In Daniel Defoe's (1660–1731) novel *Robinson Crusoe* the title character is captured by a Sallee Rover, a Barbary corsair from Salé, Morocco. And in *Don Quixote*, author Miguel de Cervantes (1547–1616) includes the story of Spaniard who escaped from Algiers, where the author himself had been held prisoner for more than five years.
- Another Robert Adams, a sailor who lived almost two centuries later, was also captured by Barbary pirates and later escaped. In 1816 he wrote the story of his three years as a slave in the Arabian Desert.
- The United States Navy was established in March 1794 to fight the Barbary Wars.
- The U.S. Marine Corps battle song memorializes the Barbary Wars with the phrase "To the shores of Tripoli."

Consider the following ...

- Robert Adams says that the pirates were crueler to captives they planned to ransom. Why might this have been so?
- Compare and contrast the African slave experience in America with that of European slaves in the Barbary States.
- John Adams and Thomas Jefferson had different solutions to the pirate problem. One president paid tribute to the corsairs; the other fought them. If you could discuss the situation with them, what policy would you recommend?

For More Information

BOOKS

Bak, Greg. *Barbary Pirate: The Life and Crimes of John Ward, the Most Infamous Privateer of His Time.* Gloucestershire, England: The History Press, 2010.

Brooks, Francis. *Barbarian Cruelty.* London: J. Salusbury and H. Markman, 1693. Available online at http://penelope.uchicago.edu/morocco/index.xhtml (accessed on January 3, 2011).

Davis, Robert. *Christian Slaves, Muslim Masters: White Slavery in the Mediterranean, the Barbary Coast, and Italy, 1500–1800.* Edited by Rab Houston and Edward Muir. New York: Palgrave Macmillan, 2003.

A buccaneer. MARY EVANS
PICTURE LIBRARY/EVERETT
COLLECTION.

5

The Buccaneers of America

Excerpt from *The Buccaneers of America*
  By Alexander O. Exquemelin
  Originally published in 1684
  Reprinted by Dover Publications, Inc., 1969

"If anyone has a quarrel and kills his opponent treacherously, he is set against a tree and shot dead by the one whom he chooses. But if he has killed his opponent like an honourable man—that is, giving him time to load his musket, and not shooting him in the back—his comrades let him go free."

Buccaneers were a group of seventeenth-century sea raiders who operated in the Caribbean Sea. Warm weather, numerous waterways and islands, and feuding conquerors allowed piracy, or the act of robbing at sea, to flourish. Many islands in the Caribbean had jagged coastlines, which gave pirates places to hide and led to notorious pirate lairs developing in the area. In some cases the pirates even took over islands. Tortuga, an island north of Hispaniola (present-day Haiti and the Dominican Republic), became the center of buccaneer activity in the 1600s. Encouraged by the governors of the area, who often shared in the profits, buccaneers attacked richly laden ships transporting the wealth of the Americas to Europe.

How buccaneers became pirates

The buccaneers were a group of hunters who had left the Caribbean settlements to live on their own as hunters. Many had been prisoners, runaway servants, or escaped slaves. Cattle and hogs ran wild on many of the Caribbean islands, so meat was plentiful. The native Caribs taught the

Ekin, Des. *The Stolen Village: Baltimore and the Barbary Pirates.* Dublin: O'Brien Press, 2006.

Forester, C.S. *The Barbary Pirates.* New York: Sterling Point, 2008.

January, Brendan. *The Aftermath of the Wars Against the Barbary Pirates.* Brookfield, CT: Twenty-First Century Books, 2009.

Lunsford, Virginia West. *Piracy and Privateering in the Golden Age Netherlands.* New York: Palgrave Macmillan, 2005.

Tinniswood, Adrian. *Pirates of Barbary: Corsairs, Conquests, and Captivity in the Seventeenth-Century Mediterranean.* New York: Riverhead, 2010.

PERIODICALS

Caplan, Dennis. "John Adams, Thomas Jefferson, and the Barbary Pirates: An Illustration of Relevant Costs for Decision-Making." *Issues in Accounting Education* 18, no. 3 (August 2003): 265–73. Available online at www.docstoc.com/docs/27026398/The-Barbary-Pirates (accessed on January 3, 2011).

Davis, Robert C. "Counting European Slaves on the Barbary Coast." *Past & Present* 172 (2001): 87–124.

Hotson, Leslie. "Pirates in Parchment." *The Atlantic Monthly* 140, no. 2 (August 1927): 208–15. Available online at www.theatlantic.com/past/docs/issues/27aug/hotson.htm (accessed on January 3, 2011).

WEB SITES

Davis, Robert. "British Slaves on the Barbary Coast," *British History in-depth.* www.bbc.co.uk/history/british/empire_seapower/white_slaves_01.shtml (accessed on January 3, 2011).

Gawalt, Gerard W. "America and the Barbary Pirates: An International Battle Against an Unconventional Foe," *The Library of Congress American Memory.* http://memory.loc.gov/ammem/collections/jefferson_papers/mtjprece.html (accessed on January 3, 2011).

Sumner, Charles. "White Slavery in the Barbary States: a Lecture Before the Boston Mercantile Library Association, February 17, 1847." *Internet Archive.* www.archive.org/stream/whiteslaveryinba00sumn/whiteslaveryinba00sumn_djvu.txt (accessed on January 3, 2011).

hunters to cure meat over a fire to preserve it. The Caribs called the frame they used for this a *boucan*. The French adopted the word and created the verb *boucaner*, which meant to smoke meat using a *boucan*. They called those who made the dried meat strips *boucaniers*, which when translated into English became *buccaneers*.

The buccaneers lived in small groups of two to five men. Many of the buccaneers lived in homosexual unions called *matelotage*. Matelots, as the members of the union were called, took care of each other in sickness and battle. They shared all their property in common and did not marry or raise families.

The buccaneers traded the hides and jerky from the animals they hunted. To survive, they also engaged in occasional sea raids. Their main targets were Spanish ships. The Spanish colonial government on Hispanola did not like having these attackers living among them, so in the 1620s they began to take steps to drive the buccaneers out. First, the Spanish killed off the wild livestock that the buccaneers hunted, hoping that, with the source of their livelihood gone, the buccaneers would leave. Instead, the buccaneers turned more and more to piracy.

They built small, fast barques (vessels with one mast and triangular sails) of cedar that could easily sail into the wake (waves behind a boat) of the clumsy, larger merchant ships. Then they used grappling hooks to board the vessels, and with cutlasses and pistols took over the ships, overpowering the crews in hand-to-hand combat.

Tortuga: the buccaneer's base

The buccaneers established a base on Tortuga. This island was an ideal location, because there was only one accessible port, which could be easily guarded against attack. The buccaneers began calling themselves the Brethren of the Coast in 1640. They lived under their own rules, and every buccaneer had a say in how the group was governed.

Around this time, European countries were fighting for control of the various Caribbean islands. The French West India Trading Company opened warehouses on Tortuga to do business with the buccaneers, and the island virtually became a French colony. But in 1654 the Spanish drove the French and English from the island and established a fort. The following year the English took over Jamaica. England sent colonist Elias Watts and a few families to Tortuga to start plantations. The Spanish governor gave up the island without a fight. Watts allowed buccaneers to live there in exchange for a portion of their loot.

In 1660 a Frenchman, Jérémie Deschamps (1615–1675), took over the island from Watts. The West India Company named Bertrand d'Ogeron governor of Tortuga in 1665. He encouraged the buccaneers to engage in bolder acts. To settle them in town, d'Ogeron had a shipful of women sent from Europe and auctioned them off. The buccaneers did not have to marry the women but had to live with them as partners rather than slaves. Under d'Ogeron's leadership, the buccaneers were at their most numerous and most deadly.

The mysterious Exquemelin

Much of what is known about the buccaneers comes from a book by Alexander O. Exquemelin titled *The Buccaneers of America*, originally published in Dutch in 1678. However, very little is known for certain about the author himself. No one knows for sure who Exquemelin was or where he came from. The only facts about his life that have been recorded are from his early twenties on, when he departed from Havre-de-Grace, France, for the Caribbean. According to some sources, the author is A.O. Exquemelin, whose initials stand for Alexandre Olivier. But an English edition of the book lists the author as John Esquemeling, perhaps an English spelling of the last name. Even more curiously, the French version published in 1686 indicated that the author's last name was Oexmelin and that he was French. That raises the questions of why he wrote the book in Dutch and how he learned Dutch so well while he was a buccaneer. The claim that he was French led historians to wonder if he might have been a Huguenot, a French Protestant group that was driven from France during the religious persecutions of the sixteenth and seventeenth centuries. With the exception of the French translation, most prefaces to early editions of the book suggest that the author was either Flemish (from Flanders in the Netherlands) or Dutch.

Exquemelin was most likely born around 1645 and died after 1707. He sailed to Tortuga in 1666, and *The Buccaneers of America* details his adventures in the New World. After serving the French West India Company for three years, he became a buccaneer, most likely as a barber-surgeon. Exquemelin tells of life on the high seas under several pirates, including Henry Morgan (c. 1635–1688). In 1674 Exquemelin ended his career as a buccaneer and returned to Europe, where he settled in Amsterdam. There he qualified to be a surgeon in 1679. His name is on the register of the Dutch Surgeons' Guild that year. Yet, he seems to have later returned to buccaneering, because his name appears on a ship's muster-roll (crew list) as a surgeon during an attack on Cartagena, Venezuela, in 1697.

Exquemelin's tale

The Buccaneers of America begins with Exquemelin sailing from France on May 2, 1666, on the *St. John* in the service of the French West India Company. A group of ships departed together with a man-of-war for protection against pirates. (A man-of-war is a heavily armed warship.) Near Barbados an English privateer chased them, but the *St. John* was faster and managed to elude it. (A privateer is a private ship or ship owner commissioned by a state or government to attack the merchant ships of an enemy nation.) Exquemelin's ship survived a number of storms and arrived safely in Tortuga on July 7 with all the goods and passengers intact, which was not often the case. Exquemelin then described the beauty of the island.

Exquemelin had gained his passage on the ship by agreeing to become an indentured servant, working on a plantation for the West India Company. (An indentured servant is a person working under a contract that commits him or her to an employer for a fixed period of time, typically three to seven years.) Because the plantation lost money, the West India Company sold it along with the contracts of all the indentured servants. Exquemelin's contract was bought by another master, who mistreated him. When Exquemelin became sick and seemed about to die, his owner sold him to a surgeon. Exquemelin recovered his health and stayed with the doctor for a year. The surgeon then offered Exquemelin his freedom on the condition that Exquemelin repay him when he had earned enough money. Exquemelin decided that the fastest way to earn the money would be to join the buccaneers.

Things to remember while reading the excerpt from *The Buccaneers of America*:

- This book was originally written in Dutch in 1678. A few years after it was published, translations came out in several different languages, but, following a lawsuit, the English publishers changed some of the material in the book. The selection used here is from the first English translation to be based on the original Dutch version.
- *The Buccaneers of America* is divided into three parts. The first part describes the French arrival in Hispaniola and describes the island

The title page of the original Dutch version of The Buccaneers of America, *published in 1678.* © INTER-FOTO/ALAMY.

of Tortuga. This passage comes from that first part of the book. The second part of the book describes the buccaneers, their way of life, and their attacks on the Spanish, especially under Henry Morgan. The third part details the burning of Panama City, which is why the book's full title is *The Pirates of Panama; Or, The Buccaneers of America: A True Account of the Famous Adventures and Daring Deeds of Sir Henry Morgan and Other Notorious Freebooters of the Spanish Main.*

- Freebooters are sailors who plunder (rob of goods by force), similar to pirates but usually not as well organized or as violent.
- Spain controlled most of the territories in the area, including Mexico, Florida, Cuba, Hispaniola, and the coast of Venezuela, all of which was known as the Spanish Main. Buccaneers gained much of their wealth from looting Spanish galleons.

• • •

The Buccaneers of America

… The French on Hispaniola have three sorts of employment—hunting, planting and privateering. When a man has finished his service, he seeks out a partner and they pool all they possess. They draw up a document, in some cases saying that the partner who lives longer shall have everything, in others that the survivor is bound to give part to the dead man's friends or to his wife, if he was married. Having made this arrangement, some go off marauding, others to hunt, and others to plant tobacco, as they think best.

There are two sorts of hunters: those who hunt bulls for the hides, and those who go after wild boar, to sell the meat to the planters. The hunters of bulls became known as *boucaniers*. Formerly there used to be a good five or six hundred of them on the island, but now they are less than three hundred strong; the cattle have become so scarce the hunters have to be very quick and skilful to catch any.

The men stay a whole year, sometimes even two years, without leaving the woods, and then cross over to Tortuga to fetch necessaries—powder and shot, muskets, linen and so forth. When they arrive, they **squander** in a month all the money which has taken them a year or eighteen months to earn. They drink brandy like water, and will buy a whole cask of wine, **broach** it, and drink until there's not a drop left. Day and night they roam the town, keeping the feast of **Bacchus** so long as they can get drink for money. The service of **Venus** is not forgotten, either. In fact, the tavern-keepers and whores make ready for the coming of the hunters and the privateers in the same way as their fellows in Amsterdam prepare for the arrival of the East India ships and **men-of-war**. Once their money is all spent and they've had all they can on credit, back they go to the woods again, where they remain for another year or eighteen months.

Now we shall describe the sort of life they lead there. Having met at the **rendezvous**, they separate into troops of five or six hunters, with their indentured servants if they have any. Each band seeks a well situated place near the open fields, where they set up their tents and make a hut in which to store the hides when dry.

Squander: Spend wastefully.

Broach: Pierce a cask to open it.

Bacchus: Greek god of wine and revelry.

Venus: Roman goddess of love and pleasure.

Men-of-war: Armed ships.

Rendezvous: Arranged meeting place.

In the morning, as soon as it begins to get light, the hunters call up their hounds and go into the forest, along the trails where they hope to meet most bulls. Immediately [when] they have shot a beast, they take what they call their brandy—that is, they suck all the marrow from the bones before it is cold [as a tonic, or strengthener]. After this, they **flay** the beast properly, and one of them takes the hide to their rendezvous. They carry on like this until every man has got a hide; this takes until about noon—sometimes later, sometimes sooner. When they are all met together at the rendezvous, if they have **bond-servants**, these have to stretch out the hides to dry, and prepare the food. This is always meat, for they eat nothing else.

Having eaten, every man takes his gun and they go off to shoot [wild] horses for sport, or to bring down birds with a single bullet. Or they may shoot at targets for a prize—usually at an orange tree, to see who can shoot off the most oranges without damaging them, but only nicking the stem with a single bullet—which I've often seen done.

Sundays they spend carrying the hides down to the beach and putting them in the boats. There was once a bondsman who badly wanted to have a rest, and told his master God had ordained seven days in a week—six for labour and the seventh for rest. His master did not interpret matters this way. He thrashed the lad unmercifully with a stick, saying 'Get on, you bugger; my commands are these—six days shalt thou collect hides, and the seventh shalt thou bring them to the beach.' . . .

When the provisions are on board and the ship is ready to sail, the buccaneers resolve by common vote where they shall cruise. They also draw up an agreement or *chasse partie*, in which is specified what the captain shall have for himself and for the use of his vessel. Usually they agree on the following terms. Providing they capture a prize, first of all these amounts would be deducted from the whole capital. The hunter's pay would generally be 200 **pieces of eight**. The carpenter, for his work in repairing and fitting out the ship, would be paid 100 or 150 pieces of eight. The surgeon would receive 200 or 250 for his medical supplies, according to the size of the ship.

Then came the agreed awards for the wounded, who might have lost a limb or suffered other injuries. They would be compensated as follows: for the loss of a right arm, 600 pieces of eight or six slaves; for a left arm, 500 pieces of eight or five slaves. The loss of a right leg also brought 500 pieces of eight or five slaves in compensation; a left leg, 400 or four slaves; an eye, 100 or one slave, and the same award was made for the loss of a finger. If a man lost the use of an arm, he would get as much as if it had been cut off, and a severe internal injury which meant the victim had to have a pipe inserted in his body would earn 500 pieces of eight or five slaves in **recompense**.

Flay: Strip off the hide.

Bond-Servants: Indentured servants.

Pieces of eight: Silver Spanish coins.

Recompense: Payment for something lost.

These amounts having first been withdrawn from the capital, the rest of the prize would be divided into as many portions as men on the ship. The captain draws four or five men's portions for the use of his ship, perhaps even more, and two portions for himself. The rest of the men share uniformly, and the boys get half a man's share.

When a ship has been captured, the men decide whether the captain should keep it or not: if the prize is better than their own vessel, they take it and set fire to the other. When a ship is robbed, nobody must plunder and keep his loot to himself. Everything taken—money, jewels, precious stones and goods—must be shared among them all, without any man enjoying a penny more than his fair share. To prevent deceit, before the booty is distributed, everyone has to swear an oath on the Bible that he has not kept for himself so much as the value of a **sixpence**, whether in silk, linen, wool, gold, silver, jewels, clothes or shot, from all the capture. And should any man be found to have made a false oath, he would be banished from the **rovers**, and never more be allowed in their company.

The buccaneers are extremely loyal and ready to help one another. If a man has nothing, the others let him have what he needs on credit until such time as he can pay them back. They also see justice done among themselves. If anyone has a quarrel and kills his opponent treacherously, he is set against a tree and shot dead by the one whom he chooses. But if he has killed his opponent like an honourable man—that is, giving him time to load his musket, and not shooting him in the back—his comrades let him go free. The duel is their way of settling disputes.

When they have captured a ship, the buccaneers set the prisoners on shore as soon as possible, apart from two or three whom they keep to do the cooking and other work they themselves do not care for, releasing these men after two or three years. . . .

• • •

What happened next ...

In his book Exquemelin discusses several well-known pirates of the time, including Pierre le Grand and Francis L'Olonnais (c. 1635–1668). And though the preface to his book indicates that Exquemelin was present at all the events he describes, many scholars have questioned whether this was true. Some believe that his descriptions of Pierre le Grand's exploits differ enough from the facts that Exquemelin may have written down tales he heard about the pirate rather than ones he participated in. Others see Exquemelin as a reliable witness to the history of the buccaneers. Although some of the

Sixpence: English coin worth six pennies.

Rovers: Pirates.

A portrait of Henry Morgan from the 1684 edition of The Buccaneers of America. *Morgan did not like how he was portrayed in the book and sued its English publishers.* THE ART ARCHIVE/THE PICTURE DESK, INC.

exploits in his book may be exaggerated, most of the details of Exquemelin's stories of serving under Captain Henry Morgan seem to ring true.

Four years after Exquemelin settled in Amsterdam, the publisher Jan ten Hoorn printed the Dutch version of Exquemelin's book, *De Americaensche Zee-Roovers*, in 1678. The book was translated into German the following year and into Spanish in 1681. Then two English publishers picked it up in 1648. W. Crook released the first English edition and changed the title to *Bucaniers of America*. The other version was printed by Thomas Malthus and had the title *The History of Bucaniers*. These English translations came out while some of the buccaneers mentioned in the book were still alive.

Henry Morgan was upset about how he had been portrayed so he sued both publishers for libel and won £200 plus damages from each. Morgan resented Exquemelin's portrayal of him as cruel to prisoners. Exquemelin had also written that, when Morgan was a boy, his parents sold him to a plantation owner in Barbados. But following the lawsuit in 1685, the English publisher W. Crook printed the following retraction, as quoted by Walter Adolphe Roberts in *Sir Henry Morgan, Buccaneer and Governor*: "John Esquemeling hath mistaken the Origin of Sir Henry Morgan, for he was a Gentleman's Son of good Quality, in the County of Monmouth, and was never a Servant unto anybody in his life, unless unto his Majesty, the late King of England." Since that time many different translations of the book have appeared, and the buccaneers of the Caribbean live on in the pages of Exquemelin's book.

Did you know ...

- In addition to their base on Tortuga, the buccaneers also had a base at Port Royal, Jamaica.
- During Colonial times, many European countries encouraged piracy in the Caribbean to weaken or destroy rival nations' trade, which bettered their own financial state and allowed them to obtain more money for their goods.
- Former pirates and privateers sometimes ended up as governors or officials on various Caribbean islands. For example, Henry Morgan was appointed lieutenant governor of Jamaica.
- Many Caribbean pirates attacked the Spanish Main, an area that included the Spanish colonies in the Americas, especially Central America and the northern part of South America. The Spanish Main had abundant gold, silver, and precious gems. Most of these treasures were located inland and had to be transported to the coast by mule. Pirates often attacked these mule trains or raided the port cities of Portobelo and Darien in Panama and Cartagena in Venezuela.

Consider the following ...

- Exquemelin describes Captain Henry Morgan in glowing terms. For example, Chapter 9 is titled "His [Morgan's] exploits, and the most remarkable actions of his life." The author devotes ten of his eighteen chapters to Morgan's deeds. Why would this be so when Morgan was such a notorious pirate?

- In what ways did colonial society contribute to the development of the buccaneers? How did putting former pirates and privateers in positions of authority affect the growth of piracy in the New World?
- What effects do you think buccaneers and pirates had on the original natives of the Caribbean and the American continents?

For More Information

BOOKS

Burgess, Douglas R., Jr. *The Pirates' Pact: The Secret Alliances Between History's Most Notorious Buccaneers and Colonial America.* New York: McGraw-Hill, 2009.

Burney, James. *History of the Buccaneers of America.* Cambridge, U.K.: Cambridge University Press, 2010.

Roberts, Walter Adolphe. *Sir Henry Morgan, Buccaneer and Governor.* New York: Covici Friede Publishers, 1933, p. 28.

PERIODICALS

Richard Frohock. "Exquemelin's Buccaneers: Violence, Authority, and the Word in Early Caribbean History," *Eighteenth-Century Life* 34, no. 1 (Winter 2010): 56–72.

Rogers, Nicholas. "Caribbean Borderland: Empire, Ethnicity, and the Exotic on the Mosquito Coast," *Eighteenth-Century Life* 26 (Fall 2002)117–38.

WEB SITES

Pirates of the Caribbean, in Fact and Fiction. http://blindkat.hegewisch.net/pirates/pirates.html (accessed on January 3, 2011).

6

The Trial of Anne Bonny and Mary Read

Excerpt from "Transcript of Bonny and Read's Trial"

Published in The Tryals of Captain John Rackham and other Pirates

Printed by Robert Baldwin, 1721

"Two Women, Prisoners at the Bar, were then on Board the said Sloop, and wore Mens Jackets, and long Trouzers, and Handkerchiefs tied about their Heads; and that each of them had a Machet and Pistol in their Hands, and cursed and swore at the Men."

During the period known as the golden age of piracy, which spanned the end of the seventeenth century through the first three decades of the eighteenth century, pirates roamed the Caribbean Sea and the east coast of North America, severely damaging European trade routes. In the early 1700s England cracked down on pirates. Within a few decades, the golden age had come to end. Many colorful pirates met their ends because the king had passed an act intended to rid the seas of raiders. The Act for the More Effectual Suppression of Piracy allowed local authorities to hold trials and convict pirates. In 1720 a jury convened in St. Jago de la Vega, Jamaica, for the trial of John "Calico Jack" Rackham (1682–1720) and his crew. Rackham and most of his shipmates were condemned for piracy on November 16–17, 1720. The most surprising members of Rackham's crew were two women, Anne Bonny (1700–c.1782) and Mary Read (c. 1690–1721), who were tried separately on November 28.

Antipiracy law

An Act for the More Effectual Suppression of Piracy gave captains, governors, lieutenant governors, or council members, whether they were in colonies, on plantations, or onboard ship, permission to try pirates. Criminals were to be tried before a jury of seven, but, if need be, any of those in authority could appoint people to serve as members of the court. The authorities who conducted the trial also could pronounce the sentence and carry out the punishment.

The act specified that the president of the court must first read the king's commission then take an oath to be an impartial judge and state that he had received no share of the pirated goods. The president then administered the same oath to each member of the court. Prisoners had the opportunity to plead guilty or not guilty, and the accused could ask the court to question any witnesses against them. Pirates could also bring their own witnesses for their defense.

Under this new law, raiding a ship or town was considered piracy, but violence toward a ship's captain as well as enticing another person to become a pirate was also a felony. Assisting a pirate in any way (e.g. by concealing goods, giving advice, or even entertaining one) meant being tried as an accessory to the crime. Accessories could suffer the same fate as the pirates and lose their property or their lives.

The king also offered rewards to commanders who bravely defended their ships and to those who took over or destroyed a pirate ship. The British Crown hoped these incentives, along with the fear of punishment, would encourage more people to turn against the pirates. At the same time, investing the local authorities in the colonies as well as ships' captains with the power to try pirates meant that these scourges of the seas could be dealt with speedily.

The antipiracy law made it imperative for governors to actively pursue pirates rather than to cooperate with them for a share of their goods. Knowing that they, too, could be hanged if they allowed pirates to come ashore, many colonial authorities who had previously assisted or ignored pirates, now began turning them in. Ships' captains also went after pirate crews, hoping for the promised reward. The American colonies took the lead in executing many pirates, but the pirate stronghold on the island of New Providence in the Bahamas continued to be a threat. To reduce piracy, Woodes Rogers (c. 1679–1732), governor of Jamaica, offered amnesty (freedom from prosecution) to all pirates who surrendered. Many took advantage of this policy and settled in New Providence.

The women pirates

New Providence is where the pirate "Calico Jack" Rackham first met Anne Bonny in 1719. Bonny was born in County Cork, Ireland, to a

Anne Bonny, "Calico Jack" Rackham, and Mary Read. © THE PRINT COLLECTOR/ HERITAGE/THE IMAGE WORKS. REPRODUCED BY PERMISSION.

housemaid named Peg Brennan. Various sources date her birth from 1697 to 1705, although March 8, 1700, is often given. Her father was William Cormac, a lawyer. Cormac tried to pass his illegitimate daughter off as the son of a relative. When that ruse did not work, Cormac took Anne and her mother to South Carolina to avoid the scandal. In 1716, teenaged Anne married the pirate James Bonny. The couple sailed to New Providence, where James took advantage of the governor's amnesty offer.

Rackham had also been lured to New Providence by the governor's offer and retired from piracy. He fell in love with Anne Bonny. The two lovers stole a ship and, with six other pirates, took off for the high seas in August 1720.

Like Bonny, Read had been illegitimate, and she, too, had masqueraded as a boy when she was young. Her mother passed her off as her brother, who in reality had died, in order to keep receiving money for his upkeep from their grandmother. Read's grandmother died when she was teenager, and her mother sent Read to work as a footman, a type of servant. Read joined the navy, then fought as a soldier, married another soldier who later died, and then returned to sea. She became a sea robber when pirates seized her ship.

According to some sources, it was Rackham who had captured a Dutch ship she was on. However, some historians say Read accompanied Rackham and Bonny from the start. Read had been among a group of pirates who had taken advantage of the amnesty, so she could have been in New Providence at that time. Once aboard Rackham's ship, Read

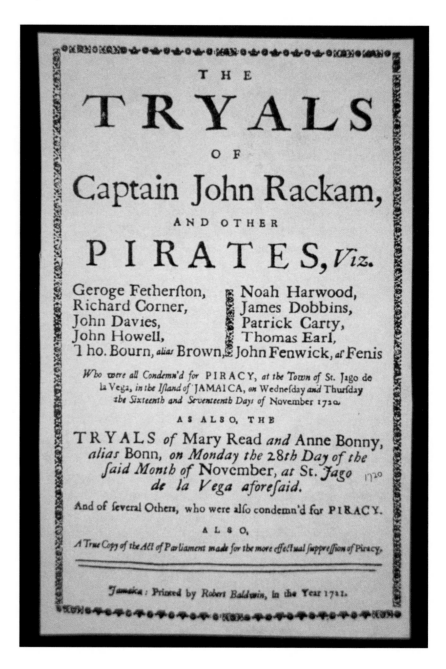

THE

TRYALS

OF

Captain John Rackam,

AND OTHER

PIRATES, *Viz.*

Geroge Fetherſton,   Noah Harwood,
Richard Corner,   James Dobbins,
John Davies,   Patrick Carty,
John Howell,   Thomas Earl,
Tho. Bourn, *alias* Brown, John Fenwick, *at* Fenis

Who were all Condemn'd for PIRACY, *at the Town of St. Jago de
la Vega, in the Iſland of* JAMAICA, *on Wednesday and Thurſday
the Sixteenth and Seventeenth Days of* November 1720.

AS ALSO, THE

TRYALS *of* Mary Read *and* Anne Bonny,
alias Bonn, *on Monday the* 28th *Day of the
ſaid Month of* November, *at St. Jago
de la Vega aforeſaid.*

And of ſeveral Others, who were alſo condemn'd for PIRACY.

ALSO,

A True Copy of the Act of Parliament made for the more effectual ſuppreſſion of Piracy,

Jamaica: Printed by Robert Baldwin, in the Year 1721.

The titlepage of The Tryals of Captain John Rackham and other Pirates. PRIVATE COLLECTION/PETER NEWARK HISTORICAL PICTURES/THE BRIDGEMAN ART LIBRARY INTERNATIONAL.

participated willingly in the pirate raids. Both she and Bonny fought as fiercely, and sometimes even more fiercely, than the men.

Only Bonny and Read resisted when a naval sloop commanded by Captain Jonathan Barnet tried to seize their ship in October 1720.

Witnesses said that the two women fought like wildcats and swore at the men who, too drunk to fight, remained below deck. Read yelled for them to join the fight and fired shots into the hold, injuring two men and killing one. Barnet captured their ship and towed it back to shore. The pirates were jailed to await trial.

Pirates on trial

When the jury convened in November 1720, the male pirates were tried and convicted first. Bonny expressed little sympathy for Rackham's plight, saying that "if he had fought like a Man, he need not have been hang'd like a Dog." On November 18, 1720, Rackham was hanged at Gallows-Point in Port Royal, Jamaica. His body was displayed in a cage on a gibbet (gallows) to discourage other would-be pirates. The other pirates tried with him were also executed.

Bonny and Read went to trial on November 28. The court, under the presidency of Nicholas Lawes, made the required proclamations and read the charges against them, after which they pled not guilty. The court then called witnesses who testified against them, sealing their fates.

Things to remember while reading the excerpt from the "Transcript of Bonny and Read's Trial":

- The transcript of the trial was published in *The Tryals of Captain John Rackham and other Pirates* in 1721. It has been reproduced the way it was originally written, and in places it contains punctuation errors or variant spellings used in the 1700s. For example, Bonny's name is spelled both *Ann* and *Anne*. The pirate John Rackham's name is recorded as *Rackam. Schooner* is written as *scooner, trousers* as *Trouzers, machete* as *Machet* and *murder* is spelled *murther*.
- Anne and Mary escaped the noose by "pleading their bellies," which meant they were both pregnant. No English court would kill an unborn child, so they were safe, at least until their babies were born.

● ● ●

Transcript of Bonny and Read's Trial

Then the Prisoners, *Mary Read, Ann Bonny*, alias *Bonn*, were brought to the Bar; and were told by the Register to **hearken** to their Charge.

Hearken: Listen.

Then the Register exhibited the Articles against them; which he read to them in the following Words, *viz.* . . . .

I. That they, the said *Mary Read*, and *Ann Bonny*, alias *Bonn*, and each of them, on the first Day of *September*, in the Seventh Year of Reign of Our said Lord the King, that now is, upon the high Sea, in a certain Sloop of an unknown Name, being; did **feloniously** and wickedly, consult, and agree together, and to and with, *John Rackam*, *George Fetherston*, *Richard Corner*, *John Davies*, *John Howell*, *Patrick Carty*, *Thomas Earl*, and *Noah Harwood*, to rob, plunder, and take, all such Persons, as well as Subjects of Our said Lord the King, that now is, as others, in Peace and **Amity** with His said Majesty, which they should meet with on the high Sea; and in Execution of their said Evil Designs, afterwards (to wit) on the Third Day of *September*, in the Year last mentioned, with Force and Arms, &c [etc.]. upon the high Sea, in a certain Place, distant about Two Leagues from Harbour-Island in *America*, and within the **Jurisdiction** of this Court, did piratically, feloniously, and in an hostile manner, attack, engage, and take, Seven certain Fishing-Boats, then being, Boats of certain Persons, Subjects of our said Lord the King, (to the Register aforesaid unknown) and then and there, Piratically, and Feloniously, did make an Assault, in and upon certain Fishermen, of our said Lord the King, (whose Names to the Register aforesaid unknown) in the same Fishing-Boats, in the peace of God, and of our said Lord the King, then and there being, and then and there, Piratically, and Feloniosly, did put the aforesaid Fishermen, in the said Fishing Boats then being, in **Corporal** Fear of their Lives; and then and there, piratically and feloniously did steal, take, and carry away the Fish, and Fishing-Tackle, the value of Ten pounds, of Current Money of Jamaica, the Goods and **Chattels** of the aforesaid Fisherman, then and there upon the high Sea aforesaid, in the aforesaid place, about two **Leagues** distant from Harbour-Island aforesaid, and within the Jurisdiction aforesaid, being found, in the said Fishing-Boat, in the Custody and Possession of the said Fishermen, from the said Fishermen, and from their Custody and Possession, then and there, upon the high Sea aforesaid, in the place aforesaid, distant about two Leagues from the Harbour Island aforesaid, and within the Jurisdiction aforesaid.

II. That afterwards, **to wit**, The first Day of October, in the Year last mentioned, they, the said *Mary Read*, and *Ann Bonny*, alias *Bonn*, and each of them, in the said Pirate Sloop being, by Force and Arms, &c [etc.]. Upon the high Sea, in a certain place, distant about three Leagues from the Island of Hispaniola in America; and within the Jurisdiction of this Court, did Piratically, and Feloniously, set upon, Shoot at, and take, two certain Merchant Sloops, then being, Sloops of certain Persons, Subjects of our said Lord the King (to the aforesaid Register unknown) and then and there, Piratically, and Feloniously, did make an Assault, in and upon, one James Dobbin, and certain other

Feloniously: Criminally or illegally.

Amity: Friendship.

Jurisdiction: Authority to apply the law.

Corporal: Physical or bodily.

Chattels: Property; the term could also refer to slaves.

Leagues: Distance of about 2.4 to 4.6 statute miles (3.9 to 7.4 kilometers). In England in the 18th century, it usually equaled 3 miles.

To wit: That is to say.

Mariners (whose Names to the Register aforesaid are unknown) in the same Merchant Sloops, in the peace of God, of our said now Sovereign Lord the King, then and there being, and then and there, Piratically, and Feloniously, did put, the aforesaid Mariners, of the same two Merchant Sloops, in the aforesaid two Merchant Sloops then being, in Corporal fear of their Lives, and then and there afterwards, to wit, The said first Day of October, in the Year last mentioned, upon the high Sea, the place aforesaid, distant about three Leagues from Hispaniola aforesaid, America aforesaid, and within the Jurisdiction aforesaid, did steal, take, and carry away the said two Merchant Sloops, and the Apparel and Tackle of the same Sloops, of the Value of One Thousand Pounds of Current Money of Jamaica.

III. That they, the said Mary Read, and Anne Bonny, *alias* Bonn, and each of them, in the said Pirate Sloop being, afterwards (to wit) the Nineteenth Day of October, in the Year last mentioned, with Force and Arms, &c [etc.]. Upon the high Sea, at a certain place, distant about Five Leagues from Porto-Maria-Bay, in the Island of Jamaica aforesaid, and within the Jurisdiction of this Court, did Piratically, Feloniously, and in an Hostile manner, Shoot at, set upon, and take, a certain Scooner, of an unknown Name, whereof one Thomas Spenlow was Master, then being, a Scooner of certain Persons, Subjects of our said Lord the King (to the Register aforesaid unknown) and then and there, Piratically, Feloniously, and in an Hostile manner, did make an Assault, in and upon the said Thomas Spenlow, and certain other Mariners (whose Names to the Register aforesaid are unknown) in the same Scooner, in the Peace of God, and of our said now Lord the King, then and there being, and then and there Piratically and Feloniously, did put the aforesaid Thomas Spenlow, other Mariners of the same Scooner, in the Scooner aforesaid, then being, in Corporal Fear of their Lives; and then and there Piratically and Feloniously, did steal, take, and carry away, the said Scooner, and the Apparel and Tackle of the same Scooner, of the value of Twenty Pounds of Current Money of *Jamaica*.

IV. That they, the said *Mary Read*, and *Ann Bonny*, alias *Bonn*, and each of them, in the said Pirate Sloop being, afterwards (to *wit*) the 20th Day of *Octob.* in the Year last mention'd, with Force and Arms, &c [etc.]. upon the high Sea, at a certain Place, distant about one League from Dry-Harbour-Bay, in the Island of *Jamaica*, aforesaid, and within the Jurisdiction of this Court, did Piratically, Feloniously, and in an Hostile manner, set upon, board, and enter, a certain Merchant Sloop, called the *Mary*, then being a Sloop of certain Persons (to the Register aforesaid unknown) whereof *Thomas Dillon* Mariner was Master; and then and there, did make an Assault, in and upon the said *Thomas Dillon*, and certain other Mariners (whose Names to the Register aforesaid are unknown) in the same Sloop, called the *Mary*, in the Peace of God, and of our said now Lord the King, then and there being, and then and there, Piratically, and Feloniously, did put the aforesaid *Thomas Dillon*, and other the Mariners of the same Merchant Sloop, called the *Mary*, in the said Sloop called the *Mary* then being, in Corporal Fear of their Lives; and then and there Piratically, and Feloniously, did steal, take, and carry away, the said Sloop *Mary*, and the Apparel and Tackle of the same Sloop, of the value of Three hundred pounds, of Current Money of *Jamaica*.

William Norris, Reg'.

After the Articles were read, the Prisoners were severally asked by the Register, What they had to say? Whether they were Guilty of the Piracies, Robberies and Felonies, or any of them, in the said Articles mention'd, which had been read to them? Or not Guilty?

Whereto they both of them pleaded, *Not Guilty*.

Then the Register did call and produce Witnesses, to prove the said Articles, and Charge against the Prisoners; Who, being duly sworn, were examined by His Excellency the President, and the Court, in the presence and hearing of the Prisoners; And they deposed as follows, *viz.*

Dorothy Thomas **deposed**, That she, being in a Canoa [canoe] at Sea, with some Stock and Provisions, at the North-side of *Jamaica*, was taken by a Sloop, commanded by one Captain Rackam (as she afterwards heard;) who took out of the Canoa, most of the Things that were in her: And further said, That Two Women, Prisoners at the Bar, were then on Board the said Sloop, and wore Mens Jackets, and long Trouzers, and Handkerchiefs tied about their Heads; and that each of them had a Machet and Pistol in their Hands, and cursed and swore at the Men, to murther the Deponent; and that they should kill her, to prevent her coming against them; and the Deponent further said, That the Reason of knowing and believing them to be Women then was, by the largeness of their Breasts.

Thomas Spenlow, being sworn, deposed, That when he was taken by *Rackham*, the two Women, Prisoners at the Bar, were then on board *Rackam*'s sloop.

John Besneck, and *Peter Cornelian*, two Frenchmen, were produced as Witnesses, against the Prisoners at the Bar, and were sworn.

Mr. *Simon Clarke* was sworn Interpreter;

Then the said Two Witnesses declared, That the Two Women, Prisoners at the Bar, were on Board Rackam's Sloop, at the Time that *Spenlow*'s Scooner, and *Dillon*'s Sloop, were taken by Rackam; That they were very active on Board, and willing to do any Thing; That *Ann Bonny*, one of the Prisoners at the Bar, handed Gun-powder to the Men, That when they saw any Vessel, gave Chase, or Attacked, they wore Men's Cloaths; and, at other Times, they wore Women's Cloaths; That they did not seem to be kept, or detain'd by Force, but of their own Free-Will and Consent.

Deposed: Testified under oath.

Thomas Dillon, being sworn, declared, That on or about the Twentieth Day of *October* last, he was lying at Anchor, with the Sloop *Mary* and *Sarah*, whereof he was Master, in Dry-Harbour, in *Jamaica*; and that a strange Sloop came into the said Harbour, which fired a Gun at the Deponent's Sloop; whereupon the Deponent and his Men went ashore, in order to defend themselves, and Sloop; And that after several Shot had been fired at them, by the said Sloop, the Deponent hailed them, and one *Fetherston* (as the Deponent believ'd) answer'd, That they were English Pirates, and that they need not be afraid; and desired the Deponent to come on Board; whereupon the Deponent went on Board, and found that the said Sloop was commanded by one John Rackam; afterwards the said Rackam, and his Crew, took the Deponent's Sloop, and her Lading [cargo], and carried her with them to Sea; and further said, That the two Women, Prisoners at the Bar, were then on Board Rackam's Sloop; and that Ann Bonny, one of the Prisoners at the Bar, had a Gun in her Hand, That they were both very profligate [indecent], cursing and swearing much, and very ready and willing to do any Thing on Board.

After the aforesaid Witnesses had severally been examined, His Excellency the President, asked both the Prisoners at the Bar, if they, or either of them, had any Defence to make, or any Witnesses to be sworn on their behalf; or if they would have any of the Witnesses, who had been already sworn, cross examined; that if they would, they should propose and declare to the Court what Questions they, or either of them, would have asked? and if they had any, the Court, or himself, would **interrogate** them? Whereto they both of them answer'd, That they had no Witnesses, nor any Questions to ask.

Then the Prisoners were taken away from the Bar, and put into safe Custody, and all of the Standers by withdrew from the Court, except the Register.

Afterwards His Excellency the President, and Commissioners, then sitting, took the Evidence which had been given against the Prisoners into Consideration; and having maturely, and deliberately, considered thereof, and of the Circumstances of the Prisoners Case, all the Commissioners then sitting, and his Excellency the President, unanimously agreed, That *Mary Read*, and *Ann Bonny*, alias *Bonn*, were both of them Guilty, of the Piracies, Robberies and Felonies charged against them in the Third and Fourth Articles, of the Articles aforesaid.

Then the Prisoners before-named were brought back to the Bar, and His Excellency the President, acquainted them, That the Court had unanimously found them both Guilty of the Piracies, Robberies, and Felonies, charged against them, in the Third and Fourth Articles, of the Articles which had been Exhibited against them.

And being severally [separately] asked, Whether they, or either of them, had any Thing to say, or offer, Why Sentence of Death

Interrogate: Formally question.

should not pass upon them, for their said Offenses? And they, nor either of them, offering any Thing material, His Excellency the President, pronounced Sentence of Death upon them in the Words following, *viz.*

> *You* Mary Read, *and* Ann Bonny, *alias* Bonn, *are to go from hence to the Place from whence you came, and from thence to the Place of Execution; where you, shall be severally hang'd by the Neck, 'till you are severally Dead.*
> And God of His infinite Mercy be merciful to both of your Souls.

After Judgment was pronounced, as aforesaid, both the Prisoners inform'd the Court, that they were both quick with Child, and prayed that Execution of the Sentence might be stayed.

Whereupon the Court ordered, that Execution of the said Sentence should be **respited**, and that an Inspection should be made.

Then the Court adjourn'd 'till Monday the Nineteenth Day of *December* next.

William Norris, Reg.

• • •

What happened next ...

Although they had been sentenced to hang, both women claimed they were pregnant. After a doctor examined them and discovered they were telling the truth, they each received a stay of execution until their babies were born.

Read died in prison of fever and was buried on April 28, 1721, at St. Catherine's Church in Jamaica. Bonny's end is a mystery. The colonial office records do not show that she was paroled, pardoned, or set free, but neither is there a record of her death in prison. At some point she must have been released, or perhaps she escaped.

Did you know ...

- Bonny and Read were not the only the only female pirates in history. Some of the other women took to the high seas are Alvilda of Sweden, Grace O'Malley from Ireland (c. 1530–1603), England's Charlotte de Berry (born 1636), and Chinese pirate Cheng I Sao (1775–1844). Tales of female pirates date back to the third century BCE.

Respited: Postponed.

Alvilda, Swedish female pirate.
© NATIONAL MARITIME MUSEUM,
LONDON/THE IMAGE WORKS.
REPRODUCED BY PERMISSION.

- Stories abound as to Anne Bonny's final end. Some say she had a child named John Cormac Bonny and that her father, who was influential in South Carolina, arranged for her release.
- Those who claim to be Anne Bonny's descendants have said that she married Joseph Burleigh in 1721, had many children (some sources say eight, five of whom survived), and lived into her eighties. When she died on April 25, 1782, she was buried in York County, Virginia.

Consider the following ...

- Researchers say that people generally became pirates because they were poor or because they longed for adventure. What do you think motivated Anne Bonny and Mary Read?
- Women of this time were considered the weaker sex and incapable of strenuous jobs. How do you think men reacted when they discovered they had been bested by a female pirate?
- Although Anne Bonny may have lived a conventional life after her jail term, legends are told of her escaping from jail to return to piracy. How do you think she spent her later years?

For More Information

BOOKS

Druett, Joan. "She Captains." Chapter 7 of *She Captains: Heroines and Hellions of the Sea*. Simon & Schuster, 2000. Available online at www.joan.druett.gen.nz/she_captains_15250.htm (accessed on January 3, 2011).

Evans, William David, Anthony Hammond, and Thomas Colpitts Granger. *A Collection of Statutes Connected with the General Administration of the Law*. Vol. 6. 3rd ed. London: Thomas Blenkarn, Edward Lumley, and W.H. Bond, 1836.

Rediker, Marcus. "The Women Pirates: Anne Bonny and Mary Read." In *Villains of All Nations: Atlantic Pirates in the Golden Age*. Boston: Beacon Press, 2004, pp. 103–26.

Woodard, Colin. *The Republic of Pirates: Being the True and Surprising Story of the Caribbean Pirates and the Man Who Brought Them Down*. New York: Harcourt, 2007, pp. 311–20.

Zepke, Terrance. *Pirates of the Carolinas*. Sarasota, FL: Pineapple Press, 2005.

PERIODICALS

Rediker, Marcus. "When Women Pirates Sailed the Seas." *The Wilson Quarterly* 17, no. 4 (Autumn 1993): 102–10.

7

Bartholomew Roberts's Ship's Articles

Excerpt from "The Life of Captain Roberts"

Published in A General History of the Robberies and Murders of the
Most Notorious Pirates *by Captain Charles Johnson*

Originally published in 1724

Reprinted by The Lyon's Press, 1998, 2002

"If the robbery was only between one another, they contented themselves with slitting the ears and nose of him that was guilty, and set him on shore; not in an uninhabited place, but somewhere, where he was sure to encounter hardships."

Much of what is known about pirates and their lifestyles comes from *A General History of the Robberies and Murders of the Most Notorious Pirates*, written by Captain Charles Johnson in 1724. Johnson compiled biographies of notorious pirates who lived during the golden age of piracy, which began at the end of the seventeenth century and spanned the first three decades of the eighteenth century. Among the pirates Johnson chronicled was Bartholomew Roberts (1682–1722). Roberts is remembered as not only one of the greatest, but also one of the last golden-age pirates.

The reluctant pirate

Born John Robert in May 17, 1682, in Pembrokeshire, Wales, to a farming family, Roberts took to the sea as a youth. Little is known of his early years at sea. He may have honed his skills in the British Royal Navy. He became a merchant seaman, and in November 1718 he set sail for West Africa aboard a slave ship, the *Princess of London*. The ship ran into trouble as it reached the Guinea Coast, where it was attacked by the pirate

Bartholomew Roberts.
© LEBRECHT MUSIC AND
ARTS PHOTO LIBRARY/
ALMAY.

ship *Royal Rover.* Pirate captain Howell Davis (c. 1690–1719) forced some
of the members of the *Princess* crew to join the pirates. Roberts had no
wish to become a pirate, but he felt he had no choice. Davis, who was also

Welsh, wanted Roberts to sail with him. Roberts was a skilled navigator, so he was a valuable asset among the men, many of whom could not read or write.

In 1719 John Robert changed his name to Bartholomew Roberts, perhaps to protect his family. But many of his shipmates called him "Black Bart" or "Black Barty," because of his dark hair. Within six weeks Davis was killed during a Portuguese ambush off the African island of Principe, and the pirates elected Roberts as captain. They chose him for his knowledge and boldness. Although he had been an unwilling pirate, Roberts agreed to take over, believing, according to Johnson, "that since he had dipped his hands in muddy water, and must be a pirate, it was better being a commander than a common man."

After leveling the Portuguese settlement at Principe to revenge Davis's death, the pirates under Roberts's command sailed to Brazil, where they spent weeks searching for merchant ships but found none. Then Roberts spotted a fleet of forty-two Portuguese ships that were waiting for two men-of-war, or armed ships, to escort them. Roberts managed to capture a merchant ship and get away before the men-of-war arrived to stop him. The booty the pirates took included gold coins and a diamond-studded cross intended for the king of Portugal. (Booty is the goods stolen from ships or coastal villages during pirate raids or attacks on enemies in time of war.) Roberts, who loved finery, kept the diamond cross for himself.

While they were in Africa, Roberts and forty of his men chased a supply ship, but did not catch it. When they returned, they discovered that one of the crew, Walter Kennedy, had taken off with the *Royal Rover* and the treasure. Roberts immediately wrote a set of strict ship's articles to better control his crew. (Ship's articles are the written sets of rules and conditions under which pirates operated on any given expedition.)

Pirate rules

Having a set of rules aboard pirate ships was not unusual. Most pirates decided on their ship's articles before they sailed, so they would have no arguments about their duties or about dividing the spoils. They also set punishments for mutiny (open rebellion against the ship's officers), desertion, or fighting. The rules aboard Roberts's ship were a bit different than most, because Roberts, unlike many captains, did not believe in drinking or gambling. So he tried to control those behaviors as best he could.

Bartholomew Roberts's crew drinking and reveling wildly. Roberts did not approve of drinking or gambling, so he tried to control such behavior among his crew. PRIVATE COLLECTION/PETER NEWARK PICTURES/THE BRIDGEMAN ART LIBRARY INTERNATIONAL.

Although pirates disobeyed the law, most of them respected the Bible. To join a pirate crew, a candidate swore an oath on the Bible. Roberts also respected the Sabbath Day (the one day out of every week that the Bible commanded people to rest; for Christians that was Sunday) as evidenced by the eleventh rule that gave musicians that day off.

In addition to rules like these, other rules were fairly standard on most pirate ships. To govern lesser offenses not covered by the ship's articles, such as disobeying orders, abusing prisoners, quarreling, or neglecting to care for their weapons, the crew elected a quartermaster. He decided on the punishment; offenders were usually drubbed (beaten with a stick) or whipped. The quartermaster was also the first to board a captured ship. He kept an account of the booty taken.

Johnson indicates that Roberts's original list of rules most likely was lengthier, but after all the pirates signed and swore to the articles, the crew threw the document overboard. That way, if a government ship captured them, no written evidence could be found against them. Johnson also notes that "there is a great deal of room to suspect, the remainder contained something too horrid to be disclosed to any, except such as were willing to be sharers in the iniquity (evil) of them."

Things to remember while reading the excerpt from "The Life of Captain Roberts":

- Captain Charles Johnson, the author of *A General History of the Robberies and Murders of the Most Notorious Pirates* claimed to be an eye witness to the events he chronicled, but not much is actually known about him. (For more information on Johnson, see **The Life of Captain Evans**.)

- Because pirates threw their ship's articles overboard, no written list of rules was ever found. Roberts's ship's articles were reconstructed from the oral testimony of his crew, when they were asked what rules they remembered.

- If the pirates took a female prisoner, they selected a guard to protect the lady's virtue and prevent fighting among the crew. In August 1721, Roberts captured the *Onslow*, a Royal African Company frigate. There was a woman onboard named Elizabeth Trengrove. David Symson was the crew member charged with guarding Trengrove, but he later admitted to having sex with her.

- Although Johnson interpreted Roberts's rules to mean that Roberts was religious and a strict disciplinarian, Patrick Pringle in *Jolly Roger* suggests that the rules were practical rather than moral. For example, the rules about no women and gambling were intended to prevent fights. And candles out at eight o'clock was to prevent fire hazards, especially among drunken sailors. As for not working on the Sabbath, that was common in Europe at that time. No one worked on that day.

- Johnson made observations about many of the articles, seen in brackets within the excerpt below.

Pirates abusing female captives. If Roberts's pirates took a female prisoner, they placed a guard at the door to prevent fighting and to protect the woman from harm. © BETTMANN/CORBIS.

• • •

The Life of Captain Roberts

I

Every Man has a Vote in Affairs of Moment; has equal Title to the fresh Provisions, or strong Liquors, at any Time seized, & use them at pleasure, unless a Scarcity [no uncommon thing among them] make it necessary, for the good of all, to Vote a **Retrenchment**.

II

Every Man to be called fairly in turn, by List, on Board of Prizes, because, (over and above their proper Share,) they there on these Occasions allow'd a **Shift of Cloaths**: But if they **defrauded** the Company to the Value of a Dollar, in Plate, Jewels, or Money. Marooning was their Punishment. [This was a barbarous custom of putting the offender on shore, on some desolate or uninhabited cape or island, with a gun, a few shot, a bottle of water, and a bottle of powder, to subsist with, or starve. If the robbery was only between one another, they contented themselves with slitting the ears and nose of him

Retrenchment: Cut back. If supplies got low, the crew had to ration food and drink so it would last until they reached land.

Shift of Cloaths: Change of clothes.

Defrauded: Cheated.

that was guilty, and set him on shore; not in an uninhabited place, but somewhere, where he was sure to encounter hardships.]

III

No Person to game at Cards or Dice for Money.

IV

The Lights & Candles to be put out at eight o'Clock at Night. If any of the Crew, after that Hour, still remained inclined for Drinking, they were to do it on the open Deck; [which Roberts believed would give a check to their **debauches**, for he was a sober man himself, but found at length that all his endeavours to put an end to this debauch proved ineffectual].

V

To Keep their Piece, Pistols, & **Cutlash**, clean, & fit for Service. [In this they were extravagantly **nice**, endeavouring to outdo one another in the beauty and richness of their arms, giving sometimes at an auction (at the mast) thirty or forty pounds a pair, for pistols. These were slung in time of service, with different coloured **ribbands** over their shoulders, in a way peculiar to these fellows, in which they took great delight.]

VI

No Boy or Woman to be allow'd amongst them. If any Man were found seducing any of the latter Sex, and carried her to Sea, disguised, he was to suffer Death. [So that when any fell into their hands, as it chanced in the *Onslow*, they put a **sentinel** immediately over her to prevent ill consequences from so dangerous an instrument of division and quarrel; but then here lies the **roguery**; they contend who shall be sentinel, which happens generally to one of the greatest bullies, who, to secure the lady's virtue, will let none lie with her but himself.]

VII

To Desert the Ship, or their **Quarters** in Battle, was punished with Death, or Marooning.

VIII

No striking one another on Board, but every Man's Quarrels to be ended on Shore, at Sword & Pistol Thus: The Quarter-Master of the Ship, when the Parties will not come to any Reconciliation, accompanies them on Shore with what

Debauches: Periods of drinking to excess.

Cutlash: Cutlass; a short, heavy, single-edged sword.

Nice: Exacting.

Ribbands: Ribbons.

Sentinel: Guard.

Roguery: Reckless or malicious behavior.

Quarters: Assigned posts.

Assistance he thinks proper, & turns the Disputants Back to Back, at so many Paces Distance. At the Word of Command, they turn and fire immediately, (or else the Piece is knocked out of their Hands). If both miss, they come to their Cutlasses, and then he is declared Victor who draws the first Blood.

IX

No Man to talk of breaking up their Way of Living, till each had shared a 1000 £ [pounds]. If in order to this, any Man should lose a Limb, or become a Cripple in their Service, he was to have 800 Dollars, out of the publick Stock, and for lesser Hurts, proportionably.

X

The Captain and Quarter-Master to receive two Shares of a Prize; the Master, Boatswain, & gunner, one Share and a half and other Officers, one and a Quarter.

XI

The Musicians to have Rest on the Sabbath Day, but the other six Days & Nights, none without special Favour. . . .

• • •

What happened next ...

With the rules set, Roberts set out to attack shipping in the Caribbean Sea. From there, Roberts headed to Newfoundland, an island off the east coast of present-day Canada, and entered the harbor on June 1720 with his black pirate flag flying, drums pounding, and trumpets blaring. The townspeople all fled, leaving their twenty-two ships behind. The pirates looted and burned the ships, but they also destroyed fishing and crops.

Roberts returned to the Caribbean and captured so many ships that he virtually destroyed shipping there. In April 1721 Roberts captured and hanged the governor of Martinique. He then sailed for West Africa. Roberts spent months plundering the area and even took over the port of Whydah (present-day Ouidah).

Colonial forces were ready to take action against Roberts. On February 5, 1722, Chaloner Ogle (1681–1750) of the HMS *Swallow* caught up with Roberts. Believing that the *Swallow* was a merchant vessel, Roberts sent one of his ships, the *Ranger*, after the *Swallow*. Ogle led the *Ranger* out of sight of the shore, then turned, opened fire, and seized the *Ranger*. Then Ogle headed back to look for Roberts.

When Ogle returned on February 10, many of Roberts's men were hungover from celebrating the capture of a ship the previous day, but Roberts had them sail out to meet the ship. After Roberts realized that his men no longer controlled the *Ranger*, he knew he would have to pass the *Swallow* to get into the open sea. But as his ship passed the *Swallow*, Ogle opened fire. Roberts was struck the neck by grapeshot (a cluster of small iron balls shot from a cannon) and died. With their great leader gone, the crew fell apart. After the death of two more crew members, the rest surrendered.

Roberts had once said that he would prefer a short but merry life to one of poverty. He got his wish. He died before he turned forty, and, honoring his request, the crew weighted his body and threw it overboard so it would not be taken by the British. (The bodies of pirates were put on display to remind sailors that if they became pirates they would come to a bad end.)

Roberts's surviving crew members ended up in jail at Cape Corso Castle, a West African fort. Various groups of pirates were tried separately, but all of the captured pirates pleaded not guilty. Many claimed that they had been forced into piracy and had no choice. The court believed and acquitted seventy-four of them. Ogle and the officers of the *Swallow* testified against the rest of the convicted prisoners and told of their resistance. The court condemned most of them. Fifty-four pirates were hanged, and thirty-seven were sentenced to hard labor. The African members of the crew were sold into slavery.

Did you know . . .

- According to Johnson, a pirate captain, other than commanding the ship and getting the best cabin, often received little respect. The men were free to walk into his cabin, use his dishes, take some of his food, and even swear at him. Captains issued orders during attacks or battles, but most decisions were made by voting, and the majority ruled.
- Some of Roberts's crew were *gremetoes*, African sailors from what are today the nations of Liberia and Sierra Leone who were known to be skilled navigators of long canoes at sea.
- On the coast of Africa, Roberts's crew set fire to a ship that had on board about eighty slaves shackled to each other. The slaves who managed to jump overboard were eaten by sharks; the rest burned to death. Johnson thought the pirates should have been severely punished for their cruelty.
- During the 1720s a record number of pirates were caught and executed. From that point on, piracy declined in the Caribbean.

Consider the following . . .

- Johnson's book preface suggests that poverty and low wages drove many to piracy. How attractive do you think piracy would be if you were working long hours aboard ship for poor wages and often went hungry?
- Johnson indicates that Roberts was reluctant to join the pirates, but he did take over as captain and later became quite cruel and vengeful. What do you think caused this change in his behavior?
- If you lived in a town where pirates' bodies dangled from gibbets, how would that make you feel? Do you think it discouraged others from becoming pirates?

For More Information

BOOKS

A Full and Exact Account, of the Tryal of All the Pyrates, Lately Taken by Captain Ogle, on Board the Swallow Man of War, on the Coast of Guinea. London: J. Roberts, 1723.

Breverton, Terry. *Black Bart Roberts: The Greatest Pirate of Them All.* Gretna, LA: Pelican Publishing Company, 2004.

Hamilton, Sue. *Bartholomew Roberts.* Edina, MN: ABDO, 2007.

Nash, Jay. "Bartholomew Roberts' Black Flag." In *The Great Pictorial History of World Crime.* Vol. 2. Lanham, MD: Scarecrow Press, 2004.

Pringle, Patrick. "The Great Pirate Roberts." In *Jolly Roger.* Mineola, NY: Dover Publications, 2001, pp. 238–9.

Rediker, Marcus. "The New Government of the Ship." In *Villains of All Nations: Atlantic Pirates in the Golden Age.* London: Beacon Press, 2004.

Woodard, Colin. *The Republic of Pirates: Being the True and Surprising Story of the Caribbean Pirates and the Man Who Brought Them Down.* New York: Harcourt, 2007.

PERIODICALS

Hudson, Christopher. "The Real Jack Sparrow." *Daily Mail* (London; May 26, 2007). Available online at www.dailymail.co.uk/femail/article-457724/The-Real-Jack-Sparrow-He-eaten-Johnny-Depp-breakfast.html (accessed on January 3, 2011).

WEB SITES

"Bartholomew Roberts: The Great Pirate Roberts." *BBC.* www.bbc.co.uk/dna/h2g2/A6988756 (accessed on January 3, 2011).

Krystek, Lee. "The Golden Age of Piracy." *The Unmuseum.* www.unmuseum.org/pirate.htm (accessed on January 3, 2011).

"Reefs, Wrecks, and Rascals," *Mel Fisher Maritime Heritage Society.* www.melfisher.org/reefswrecks/golden.htm (accessed on January 3, 2011).

8

The Life of Captain Evans

"The Life of Captain Evans"

Published in A General History of the Robberies and Murders of
the Most Notorious Pirates *by Captain Charles Johnson*

Originally published in 1724

Reprinted by The Lyon's Press, 1998, 2002

"[T]hey found a small sloop at an anchor, belonging to Bermuda. They made bold and went aboard, and Evans informed the folks that belonged to her, that he was captain of the vessel, which was a piece of news they knew not before."

Wales produced some of the greatest pirates in western history. Henry Morgan (1635–1688), one of the most successful pirates to roam the Spanish Main, and Bartholomew Roberts (1682–1722), who captured more than four hundred ships in two years, were only a few of the most infamous Welsh sea rovers. However, not all Welsh pirates achieved such fame. Some, like John Evans (d. 1723), were petty pirates whose names might never have been remembered if it were not for Captain Charles Johnson's book *A General History of the Robberies and Murders of the Most Notorious Pirates*. A mention in Johnson's book of pirate biographies ensured that Evans's story would be passed down to future generations.

Welsh pirates

For a small country—it is just a peninsula on the western coast of Great Britain—Wales had more than its share of pirates. In the fifteenth and sixteenth centuries, Wales was called "a nursery and store-house of pirates," according to Dafydd Meirion in *Welsh Pirates*. Meirion also observed,

Welsh pirate Howell Davis. Some of the greatest pirates in history came from Wales.
© NATIONAL MARITIME MUSEUM, LONDON/THE IMAGE WORKS. REPRODUCED BY PERMISSION.

"Some sources say that Wales has produced more pirates per mile of coastline than any other country in Europe. Others contend that about half of the 17th century pirates were of Welsh descent." Although these conjectures are likely exaggerated, it is true that several of the most famous pirates during the golden age of piracy, which began at the end of the seventeenth century and spanned the first three decades of the eighteenth century, hailed from Wales. Bartholomew Roberts, Howell Davis (c. 1690–1719), Palgrave Williams—these names struck terror in the hearts of many during the seventeenth and eighteenth centuries.

Many pirates learned their trade in their home country of Wales, where pirating was an accepted way of life. Wealthy landowners profited by getting a portion of the stolen cargo, and supported the pirates' efforts. Even government officials, who should have stopped the flow of pirated goods, received a cut of the booty, so they saw to it that the loot reached markets throughout the British Isles. (Booty is the goods stolen from ships or coastal villages during pirate raids or attacks on enemies in time of war.) Rather than unloading goods in secret during the dead of night, pirates operated openly and sailed into major Welsh ports.

A weak English navy did little to curb piracy in Wales. After England went to war with Spain in 1588, England commissioned many Welshmen as privateers, or private ship owners commissioned by a state or government to attack the merchant ships of an enemy nation. Privateers robbed vessels returning from the New World filled with gold, silver, and gems. With the government backing their efforts, the pirates grew even bolder, and many were hailed as heroes in their homeland.

After the war, the English navy had increased in numbers and strength and thus was better able combat piracy. To evade authorities, Welsh pirates headed to the Mediterranean Sea, then to West Africa, and finally to the Caribbean Sea. Some of the greatest Welsh pirates plied their trade in the seas around the Caribbean islands. This area became a hotbed of pirate activity during the golden age of piracy.

Economy drives piracy

By the 1720s the golden age of piracy was coming to an end, but many sailors still found it easier to live by plundering (robbing of goods by force) than by honest work. The huge scale of piracy in the Caribbean over the past decades had decimated trade, so finding jobs on the islands proved difficult. Many pirates, John Evans included, had been seamen who were now out of work as fewer merchant ships ventured into the pirate-infested seas. For these unemployed sailors, piracy seemed their only option.

Although some pirates honed their skills, thrived on danger, and lived by their wits, others were amateurs who launched careers as sea robbers in the spur of the moment. John Evans was one of the latter. Driven by need, he and a few friends began with petty theft, taking goods from several houses to equip themselves for the mission. They did not even have a proper ship, only a canoe. The first ship they stole was a small sloop that they fitted with guns. (A sloop is a fast vessel with a single fore-and-aft rigged mast, meaning that the mast was positioned for sails set lengthwise along the ship.) In spite

Two pirates fighting with swords while the rest of the crew watches. When quarrels erupted among pirates, they were often settled with duels.

of the size of their vessel, they managed to take their first prize, a Spanish ship that netted them a large amount of money. Thus, they began their careers as freebooters, looking for ships to plunder. (Freebooters operated similarly to pirates, but were not as organized or as ruthless.)

Evans's career as a pirate was brief, and he gained little attention during his lifetime. His was a story like that of many seamen who were inexperienced in the art of handling a crew; his crew mutinied and killed him. Mutiny, or open rebellion against a ship's officers, was a very real threat for sea captains. If the crew did not agree with their captain's decisions, they might just get rid of him. Although some took the captain prisoner or killed him, most crews put it to a vote. Pirates generally operated in a democratic manner, electing their captain, and the majority ruled. If most of them wanted a new captain, they elected one. When quarrels erupted on board, though, they were often settled with duels using pistols and knives. As long as neither one shot the other in the back, the killing was not considered murder.

The puzzle of Captain Charles Johnson

Not much is known about Evans, beyond this brief story in Johnson's book, *A General History of the Robberies and Murders of the Most Notorious Pirates*. The book, first published in 1724, contains biographies and stories about pirates that Johnson claimed he had either witnessed with his own eyes or had heard about directly from the pirates themselves.

Johnson's claims led many to suppose that he was a sailor, possibly even a pirate himself, as he seemed to have a good knowledge of nautical terms and speech. But no Charles Johnson was found in any ship's records. Perhaps Johnson's claim that he was an eyewitness only meant that he had attended pirate trials and took note of the proceedings.

Historians have also looked at another Charles Johnson (1678–1748) who might have been the author. He was a playwright who in 1712 produced *The Successful Pyrate*. This unsuccessful play glamorized the life of English pirate Henry Every (also spelled Avery; c. 1653–c. 1699). This Charles Johnson, a lawyer turned author, was accused of plagiarizing much of his material. His style did not match the dynamic, gripping prose of the pirate biographies in Johnson's book, however.

Another theory was proposed by John Robert Moore (1890–1973), a professor at Indiana University. He believed Daniel Defoe (1660–1731), the author of *Robinson Crusoe* (1719), had written the pirate books under a pseudonym, or pen name. An expert on Defoe's work, Moore argued in his book *Defoe in the Pillory* (1939) that *A General History of Pirates* was written in Defoe's style. Because Defoe often wrote anonymously or under pen names, many of his works could only be identified by comparing them to his known writing or finding references to them in his correspondence.

Moore also noted that Defoe had researched pirates for three novels of his that were published between 1719 and 1720, including *Robinson Crusoe*. Based on Moore's research, some editions of the book were published listing Defoe as the author, and many libraries still catalog *A General History of Pirates* under Defoe's name.

Several decades later another professor, from Trent University in Ontario, Canada, challenged this long-held assumption. Arne Bialu-schewski published articles suggesting that the book had been written by publisher Nathaniel Mist (d. 1730), who ran the newspaper called *The Weekly Journal; or Saturday's Post*, later called *Mist's Weekly Journal*, where Defoe worked. A former sailor, Mist would have been familiar with the seafaring life. In addition, Mist's name appears in connection with the book in the registers at Her Majesty's Stationery Office, in a note by an Under Secretary of State, and in a pamphlet. Some argue that Defoe, who at that time was spying on Mist for the government, would not have given his book to a publisher he was trying to put out of business.

Like Defoe, many journalists wrote under pseudonyms during this period, because England prosecuted anyone who published articles critical of the government. So it is also possible that one of the other journalists working for Mist may have been the author Charles Johnson. Mist, as well as Defoe and the other reporters, all had access to the newspaper accounts of piracy and could have used them to compose the book.

The authorship of the book is not the only question that has been raised about *A General History of Pirates*. Although many scholars consider Johnson's book a valid source of information on pirates during the early 1700s, others believe some of the tales are embellished or exaggerated. Much of what Johnson wrote agrees with historical records and ships' logs, but not all of the material can be checked for accuracy. In spite of this, his book is still considered one of the best sources of material on key figures during the golden age of piracy.

Things to remember while reading "The Life of Captain Evans":

- Many of the pirates Johnson wrote about were famous, but not much is known about Captain Evans. New to freebooting, Evans seems to be more of a bumbler than a dramatic figure or even a successful pirate, so perhaps Johnson included him to lighten the mood or to warn that a seaman tempted into piracy would come to a bad end.

- In places Johnson seems to be writing with a bit of tongue-in-cheek humor, where his meaning is the opposite of what he says. For example, he says the men planned to be pirates, but they did not have a boat, which prevented them from reaching their "laudable" (admirable) goal. Later when Evans announces to those on the newly hijacked boat that he is its captain, Johnson notes drily that it was news the boat owners had not known before. Even Evans's death and the crew's revenge seem to be foolish accidents.
- The island of Nevis is located in the Caribbean Sea south of Puerto Rico. It got its name from the Spanish, who called it *Nuestra Señora de las Nieves* (Our Lady of the Snows), after a feast celebrated by the Catholic Church on August 5. The island of Nevis had many wealthy British plantation owners during the 1700s, so pirates like Evans found it a profitable place to raid.

● ● ●

"The Life of Captain Evans"

John Evans was a Welsh man, had been formerly master of a sloop belonging to Nevis, but losing his employ there, he sailed for some time out of Jamaica as mate, till happening in company of three or four of his comrades, and wages not being so good as formerly, and berths scarce, because of the great number of seamen; they agreed to go abroad in search of adventures. They sailed, or rather rowed out of Port Royal in Jamaica, the latter end of September 1722, in a canoe; and coming on the north side of the island, went ashore in the night, broke open a house or two, and robbed them of some money, and every thing else they could find that was portable, and brought the booty on board the canoe.

This was very well for the first time, but this kind of robbery did not please so well, they wanted to get out to sea, but having no vessel but their canoe, they were prevented in their **laudable** design; however, they kept a good look out, and **traversed** the island, in expectation that **providence** would send some unfortunate vessel as a sacrifice, and in a few days their wishes were accomplished; for at Dunns Hole, they found a small sloop at an anchor, belonging to Bermuda. They made bold and went aboard, and Evans informed the folks that belonged to her, that he was captain of the vessel, which was a piece of news they knew not before. After they had put their affairs in a proper **disposition** aboard, they went ashore to a little village for refreshments, and lived jovially the remaining part of the day, at a tavern, spending three pistols, and then departed. The people of the house admired

Laudable: Admirable.

Traversed: Traveled across.

Providence: Divine guidance.

Disposition: Order.

at the merry guests they had got, were mightily pleased, and wished for their company at another time, which happened too soon for their profit; for, in the middle of the night, they came ashore all hands, rifled the house, and carried what they could aboard their sloop.

The next day they weighed in the sloop, aboard of which they mounted 4 guns, called her the *Scowerer*, and sailed to Hispaniola; on the north part of which island they took a Spanish sloop, which proved an extraordinary rich prize, as it fell among so few persons as this company consisted of; for they shared upwards of 150 pounds a man.

In pursuance of the game, and beating up for the Windward Islands, the *Scowerer* met with a ship from New England, bound to Jamaica, 120 tons, called the *Dove*, Captain Diamond master, off Puerto Rico. They plundered her, and strengthened their own company, by taking out the mate, and two or three other men; they discharged the prize, and run into one of the islands for fresh water and necessaries, and stayed there some time.

The next prize they made, was the *Lucretia and Catherine*, Captain Mills, of 200 ton burden; they came up with her near the island of Disseada, January 11th. Upon seizing of this ship, the pirates began to take upon themselves the distribution of justice, examining the men concerning their master's usage of them, according to the custom of other pirates; but the captain overhearing the matter, put an end to the judicial proceedings, and fell to rummaging the ship, saying to them, 'What have we to do to turn reformers, 'tis money we want.' And speaking to the prisoners, he asked them, 'Does your captain give you **victuals** enough?' And they answering in the affirmative: 'Why then,' said he, 'he ought to give you work enough.'

After the taking of this prize, they went to the little island of Avis, with a design to clean, and carried the *Lucretia* along with them, in order to heave down the *Scowerer* by her; but meeting there with a sloop, the pirate gave chase till the evening, when she was within gun-shot of her; but fearing to lose company with the *Lucretia*, who was a heavy sailer, they left off; and saw her no more. This chase brought them to **leeward** of their port, so that they were obliged to look out for another place of retreat, and the island of *Ruby* not being far distant, they steered for that, and anchored there accordingly; but the next day a Dutch sloop coming as it were, into their mouths, they could not **forbear** dealing, and so making her their prize, they plundered her of what came, when shared, to 50 pounds a man.

They found this sloop more for their purpose than the *Lucretia*, to clean their own sloop by, as being much lower in the **waist**, and therefore capable of heaving her bottom farther out of the water, so she was discharged, and the Dutchman kept in her room; but not thinking it convenient to lay up here, for fear a discovery should be made, they turned their thoughts another way,

Victuals: Food.

Leeward: The side away from the wind.

Forbear: Hold themselves back from.

Waist: The middle deck.

and steered to the coast of Jamaica, where they took a sugar **drover**, and then run to the Grand Caymans, about thirty **leagues** to leeward of Jamaica, with intention to clean there; but an unhappy accident put an end to their piracies, which hitherto had proved very successful to them.

The **boatswain** of the pirates being a noisy **surly** fellow, the captain had at several times words with him, relating to his behaviour, who thinking himself ill-treated, not only returned ill language, but also challenged the captain to fight him on the next shore they came to, with pistols and sword, as is the custom among these outlaws.

When the sloop arrived, as above mentioned, the captain proposed the duel; but the cowardly boatswain refused to fight, or go ashore, though it was his own challenge. When Captain Evans saw there was nothing to be done with him, he took his cane, and gave him a hearty **drubbing**; but the boatswain not being able to bear such an **indignity**, drew out a pistol and shot Evans through the head, so that he fell down dead; and the boatswain immediately jumped overboard, and swam towards the shore; but the boat was quickly manned and sent after him, which took him up and brought him aboard.

The death of the captain in that manner, provoked all the crew, and they resolved the criminal should die by the most exquisite tortures; but while they were considering of the punishment, the gunner, transported with passion, discharged a pistol, and shot him through the body; but not killing him outright, the **delinquent** in very moving words, desired a week for repentance only; but another stepping up to him, told him, that he should repent and be damned to him, and without more ado shot him dead.

I should have observed, that when the *Lucretia and Catherine* was **suffered** to go away, the pirates detained their mate, who was now the only man aboard who understood navigation, and him they desired to take upon him the command of the sloop, in the room of Captain Evans deceased; but he desired to be excused that honour, and at length positively refused it; so they agreed to break up the company, and leave the mate in possession of the vessel. Accordingly they went ashore at the Caymans, carrying with them about 9,000 pounds among thirty persons; and it being fair weather, the mate and a boy brought the vessel into Port Royal in Jamaica.

• • •

What happened next ...

Johnson's story ends with Evans's crew deciding to disband, dividing the booty between them. They had made quite a bit of money and, because the crew was small, there were fewer people to divide the spoils among.

Drover: Cargo ship.

League: A measure of distance equaling about three miles (4.8 kilometers).

Boatswain: The officer in charge of the sails and rigging, as well as supervision of the deck crew.

Surly: Bad-tempered.

Drubbing: Beating.

Indignity: Insult.

Delinquent: Offender.

Suffered: Allowed.

New and stronger antipiracy laws were introduced in 1722 that put an end to piracy. The law frightened many citizens into turning in pirates. By giving informers a large share of the goods stolen by the pirates they informed on, the government made it more profitable to report pirates than to aid them, and a record number of pirates were hanged during the early 1700s.

Did you know . . .

- According to the Smithsonian about two thousand pirates were operating along the North American coast and in the Caribbean Sea around 1720, at the peak of the golden age of piracy.
- In his book *Welsh Pirates*, Dafydd Meirion cites statistics that he says are more likely to be true than the usual claims that Wales produced most of the pirates on the high seas. The statistics he uses say that 35 percent of the pirates came from England, 20 percent from the West Indies, 10 percent from Scotland, 8 percent from Wales, and 2 percent each from Sweden, Holland, France, and Spain.

Consider the following . . .

- After reading the statistics from Meirion's book in the section above, why do you think so many writers have suggested that Wales was responsible for most of the piracy on the high seas?
- Most pirate ships drew up rules called ship's articles to prevent fights. Evans being so inexperienced at pirating, do you think he and his crew had taken care of this before they set off? What clues led you to your conclusion?
- Did Captain Evans make the right choice when he beat the boatswain, or was there another way he could have handled the man's disrespectful attitude? Why do you think the boatswain refused to engage in a duel?
- If you were an out-of-work seafarer during Johnson's time, would the story of Captain Evans have discouraged you from becoming a pirate or would it have enticed you to head to the high seas to try your luck?
- Why do you think Charles Johnson chose to write under a pseudonym?

For More Information

BOOKS

Baer, Joel H., ed. *British Piracy in the Golden Age: History and Interpretation, 1660–1730.* London: Pickering & Chatto, 2007.

Breverton, Terry. *The Book of Welsh Pirates and Buccaneers.* Porth Glyndwr, Wales: Glyndwr Publishing, 2003.

Meirion, Dafydd. *Welsh Pirates.* Talybont, Wales: Y Lolfa Cyf, 2006, pp. 9, 32.

Moore, J.H. *Defoe in the Pillory.* Bloomington: Indiana University Publications, 1939.

Pringle, Patrick. "The Great Pirate Roberts." In *Jolly Roger.* Mineola, NY: Dover Publications, 2001, p. 48.

PERIODICALS

Bialuschewski, Arne. "Daniel Defoe, Nathaniel Mist, and the *General History of the Pyrates,*" *The Papers of the Bibliographical Society of America* 98, no. 1 (March 2004): 21–38.

Mathew, David. "The Cornish and Welsh Pirates in the Reign of Elizabeth," *English Historical Review* 3, no. 155 (1924): 337–48.

Rogers, Pat. "Nathaniel Mist, Daniel Defoe, and the Perils of Publishing," *The Library: The Transactions of the Bibliographical Society* 10, no. 3 (September 2009): 298–313.

WEB SITES

Devine, Darren. "Wales Was the True Home of Pirates." *Wales News.* www.walesonline.co.uk/news/wales-news/tm_objectid=15408625&method=full&siteid=50082&headline=the-welsh-pirates-who-struck-terror-on-the-seas-name_page.html (accessed on January 3, 2011).

Krystek, Lee. "The Golden Age of Piracy." *The Unmuseum.* www.unmuseum.org/pirate.htm (accessed on January 3, 2011).

9

Letter of Marque against the French

The Swallow, Letter of Marque against the French, Dated 12th July 1796

Reprinted in History of the Liverpool Privateers and Letters of Marque with an Account of the Liverpool Slave Trade, 1744–1812

Published by Liverpool University Press, 2004

"Know ye therefore, that we do … grant Letters of Marque and reprisals to, and do license and authorize the said John Maciver to set forth in a warlike manner the said ship called the '*Swallow*,' under his own command, and therewith by force of arms to apprehend, seize, and take the Ships, Vessels, and Goods belonging to France."

During the Middle Ages (also called the medieval era, which began in the late fifth century and continued through the end of the fifteenth century), European countries gathered armies to fight their enemies on land, but few had navies to protect themselves at sea, so they depended on privateers, or private ship owners commissioned by a state or government to attack the merchant ships of an enemy nation. To increase the size of their fleets, the monarchs issued letters of marque, documents licensing a private ship owner to the seize ships or goods of an enemy nation. Governments issued both letters of reprisal and letters of marque during wartime. Letters of reprisal were similar to letters of marque, but they limited the amount of property that could be taken. If an enemy attacked a ship and stole cargo, the captain who lost the shipment could get a letter of reprisal, allowing him to seize only the same amount of goods as the enemy had taken. Letters of marque, however, gave privateers unlimited access to enemy ships.

The line between pirate and privateer often blurred during the frequent periods of war and commercial competition between 1690 and 1865. Although privateers had the authority to attack ships, those

Sailors signing up to receive their letters of marque, granting them permission to sail as privateers. ROGER VIOLLET/GETTY IMAGES.

whose vessels they seized viewed them as pirates. And often privateers not only preyed on enemy ships, but also raided vessels that belonged to neutral or friendly nations. Whenever they raided these ships, they crossed the line into piracy.

Advantages of privateering

Privateering was advantageous to the privateers, their investors, and the government of the country that issued the letters of marque. Privateers were allowed to keep a portion of all goods they seized, so many captains and crews became wealthy. The investors, who provided the ships and paid to outfit them with guns and supplies, not only got those costs back, they also shared in the prizes, so they, too, often ended up with large fortunes. The government also benefited, because privateers gave part of the value of each captured ship to the king, which enriched the country's treasury.

For countries with small navies, having ships outfitted by private investors and commanded by citizens added to their small fleets. Sometimes the ships the privateers seized were turned into additional privateering vessels; these new boats increased the size of the fleet without any costs for building or equipping them. Privateers also assisted the navy not only by eliminating enemy ships, but also by distracting warships, which could not engage in sea battles, because they had to accompany and protect trade ships from pirates and privateers.

Besides helping the war effort, privateers damaged the enemy's trade, which in turn hurt their foe's economy, another aid to their own country. They also prevented their enemies from getting food and supplies. Economic problems often forced countries to surrender, so privateers could contribute greatly to bringing this about.

With all these benefits, it is not surprising that some privateers kept operating even after the war ended, often with unofficial government approval.

The great age of privateering

By the 1720s the golden age of piracy was coming to an end, but it was soon followed by an increase in privateering. The Peace of Utrecht (a series of individual peace treaties) in 1713 led to a decrease in both warfare and privateering, but by 1739 privateering had again increased as many European countries fought battles and competed for control of trade in the Western Hemisphere. America at this time became one of the greatest culprits. During the American Revolution (1775–83; the American colonists' fight for independence from Great Britain) and other, shorter wars that followed, American privateers had enlarged the small American navy. And after the United States disbanded its navy in 1785, the country depended on privateers to protect its coastline. The United States was not the only country whose privateers were defending their interests at sea. Many European countries were issuing letters of marque to enlarge their naval forces during the many wars of the eighteenth century.

Anglo-French Wars

Great Britain and France had fought on opposite sides during the American Revolution, but after the war was over, a short period of relative peace ensued. But in 1792 when France had a poor harvest and needed

American privateers outside a recruiting office during the American Revolution. © NORTH WIND PICTURE ARCHIVES/ALAMY.

food to feed its people, Britain signed a treaty with Russia in March 1793 that prohibited Russia from exporting any military supplies, grain, corn or other provisions to France. Over the next few months, Great Britain signed similar treaties with many European nations. Thus, Britain and France returned to war.

On April 8, 1793, Edmund Charles Genêt (1763–1834), the French minister to America, arrived with 250 letters of marque. He wanted to use the United States as a base for privateering against the British. But two weeks later, on April 22, President George Washington (1732–1799) issued a proclamation of neutrality (a refusal to take sides in the war) that banned privateers from American ports. The United States also signed the Jay Treaty (1794), which increased its trade with Great Britain.

On July 2, 1796, France passed a decree stating it would treat neutral ships the same as warships. (Over the next six months, France would capture more than three hundred American ships in the Caribbean Sea.) Ten days later Britain responded by issuing letters of marque of its own, including one for the *Swallow*, captained by John Maciver.

Things to remember while reading "*The Swallow*, Letter of Marque against the French, Dated 12th July 1796":

- This letter of marque opens by noting that "divers injurious proceedings have lately been had in France." Before this letter was issued, several events had occurred in France that Britain considered harmful to their interests. The French had invaded the Netherlands and Spain in 1795, and these two former British allies signed treaties with France in 1796. Recent French victories in Sardinia and parts of Italy as well as harassment of British ships in the Atlantic led Britain to increase its naval power with privateers.

- The letter of marque refers to Britain's ally, the Republic of the United Provinces. Also known as the Dutch Republic, this federation consisted of seven sovereign provinces in what is now the Netherlands (Holland, Zeeland, Utrecht, Friesland, Groningen, Overijssel, and Gelderland). Although conflicting trading interests sometimes led to war between them and Britain, the countries were generally allies and, as such, Britain could take actions in support of the Dutch Republic, including issuing letters of marque against their common enemy.

- Britain asked all their allies to help John Maciver and promised to "do the like when we shall be by them thereunto desired," which meant the British would do the same for their allies when they needed it.

Elements of Letters of Marque or Reprisal

The Constitution Society web site lists the common elements found in letters of marque or reprisal. They typically include the first three items on this list, but most will also contain the last two.

1. Names person, authorizes him to pass beyond borders with forces under his command.
2. Specifies nationality of targets for action.
3. Authorizes seizure or destruction of assets or personnel of target nationality.
4. Describes offense for which commission is issued as reprisal.
5. Restriction on time, manner, place, or amount of reprisal.

"LETTERS OF MARQUE AND REPRISAL." *CONSTITUTION SOCIETY.* WWW.CONSTITUTION. ORG/MIL/LMR/LMR.HTM (ACCESSED ON JANUARY 3, 2011).

- Privateers had to give the government a performance bond, issued by an insurance company, that guaranteed they would complete their tasks. (A bond is a type of insurance in which one party gives money to another party as a guarantee that certain requirements will be followed. If these requirements are not followed, the party that issued the bond keeps the money permanently.)
- Captured ships are referred to as "prizes," a term the pirates also used to describe vessels they seized.

• • •

The Swallow, Letter of Marque against the French, Dated 12th July 1796

Presents: Documents.

Divers: Many.

Injurious: Hurtful.

Derogation: Belittling or attacking the reputation.

Republic of the United Provinces: Also known as the Dutch Republic; a federation of states in the northern Netherlands.

Vindicating: Justifying or clearing away blame, accusations, or suspicions about.

Reparation: Payment for an injury or insult.

Privy Council: The king's advisors.

Reprisals: The right to seek revenge.

Adjudication: Trying and settling a case.

Condemnation: Pronouncing as wrong or illegal.

George the Third, by the Grace of God of Great Britain, France, and Ireland, King Defender of the Faith; To all persons to whom these **presents** shall come Greeting. Whereas **divers injurious** proceedings have lately been had in France, in **derogation** of the honor of our Crown, and of the just rights of our subjects, and whereas several unjust seizures have been there made of the Ships and Goods of our subjects, contrary to the laws of nations, and to the faith of treaties. And whereas the said Acts of unprovoked hostility have been followed by an open declaration of war against us and our ally, the **Republic of the United Provinces**. We therefore, being determined to take such measures as are necessary for **vindicating** the honor of our Crown, and for procuring [obtaining] **reparation** and satisfaction for our injured subjects, did by, and with the advice of our **Privy Council**, order that general **reprisals** be granted against the Ships, Goods, and Subjects of France, so that as well our Fleets and Ships as also all other Ships and Vessels that shall be commissionated [commissioned] by Letters of Marque or general reprisals or otherwise, shall and may lawfully apprehend, seize, and take all Ships, Vessels, and Goods belonging to France, or to any persons being subjects of France, or inhabiting [inhabiting] within the Territories of France, and bring the same to judgment in our High Court of Admiralty of England, or in any of our Courts of Admiralty within our Dominions, for proceedings and **adjudication** and **condemnation** to be thereupon had according to the course of Admiralty, and the laws of Nations. And, whereas by our commission under our Great Seal of Great Britain, bearing date the Fourteenth day of February, One Thousand Seven Hundred and Ninety-three, we have willed, required, and authorized our commissioners for executing the office of Lord High Admiral of Great Britain, or any person or persons by them empowered and appointed to issue forth and grant Letters of Marque and reprisals accordingly, and with such powers and clauses to be therein inserted, and in such manner as by our said commission more at large appeareth [appears]. And, whereas our said Commissioners for executing the office of our High Admiral aforesaid, have thought John Maciver fitly qualified, who hath equipped, furnished, and **victualled** a ship called the *Swallow*, of the burthen [burden] of about *two hundred and fifty-six* tons, *British built, square stern, scroll head*, and *two* masts, mounted with *eighteen* carriage guns carrying shot of *six* pounds weight, and no swivel guns, and navigated by *thirty-five* men, of whom one third are landsmen, and belonging to the *Port of Liverpool*, whereof he the said John Maciver is commander, and that Thomas Twemlow, Peter Maciver, Samuel McDowall, and Iver Maciver, *of Liverpool, Merchants, and him the said* John Maciver are the owners. And, whereas he the said John Maciver hath given sufficient **bail with sureties** to us in our said High Court of Admiralty, according to the effect and form set down in our instructions made the Fourteenth day of February, One Thousand Seven Hundred and Ninety-three, in the Thirty-third year of our reign, a copy whereof is given to the said Captain, John Maciver. Know ye therefore, that we do by these presents issue forth and grant Letters of Marque and reprisals to, and do license and authorize the said John Maciver to set forth in a warlike manner the said ship called the "*Swallow*," under his own command, and therewith by force of arms to apprehend, seize, and take the Ships, Vessels, and Goods belonging to France, or to any persons being subjects of France, or inhabiting within any of the territories of France, excepting only within the harbours or roads of Princes and States in **amity** with us, and to bring the same to such port as shall be most convenient in order to have them legally adjudged in our said High Court of Admiralty of England or before the Judges of such other Admiralty Court as shall be lawfully authorized within our Dominions, while being finally condemned it shall and may be lawful for the said John Maciver to sell and dispose of such Ships, Vessels and Goods finally adjudged and condemned, in such sort and manner as by the Court of Admiralty hath [has] been accustomed. Provided, always, that the said John Maciver keep an exact journal of his proceedings, and therein particularly take notice of all prizes which shall be taken by him, the nature of such prizes, the times and places of their being taken, and the values of them as near as he can judge, as also of the station, motion and strength of the French as well as he or his mariners can discover by the best intelligence he can get, and also of whatsoever else shall occur unto him or any of his officers or mariners, or be discovered or declared unto him or them, or found out by examination or conference with any mariners or passengers of or in any of the Ships or Vessels taken, or by any other person or persons, or by any other ways and means whatsoever, touching or concerning the designs of the

Victualled: Supplied with food.

Bail with sureties: A performance bond, issued by an insurance company, guaranteeing the completion of assigned tasks.

Amity: Friendship or alliance.

French, or any of their Fleets, Vessels or Parties, and of their stations, ports and places, and of their intents therein, and of what Ships or Vessels of the French bound out or home, or to any other place, as he or his officers or mariners shall hear of, and of what else **material** in these cases may arrive to his or their knowledge, of all which he shall, from time to time, as he shall or may have opportunity, transmit an account to our said commissioners for executing the office of our High Admiral aforesaid, or their secretary, and keep a correspondence with them by all opportunities that shall present. And, further, providing that nothing be done by the said John Maciver, or any of his officers, mariners, or company, contrary to the true meaning of our d **aforesaid** instructions, but that the said instructions shall by them, and each and every of them, as far as they or any of them are therein concerned, in all particulars be well and truly performed and observed. And we pray and desire all Kings, Princes, Potentates, States, and Republicks [Republics], being our friends and allies, and all others to whom it shall appertain [pertain], to give the said John Maciver all aid, assistance and **succour** in their ports with his said ship, company and prizes, without doing or suffering to be done to him any wrong, trouble or hindrance, we offering to do the like when we shall be by them thereunto desired. And we will, and require all our officers whatsoever, to give him succour and assistance as occasion shall require.

In witness whereof we have caused the great seal of our High Court of our Admiralty of England to be hereunto affixed. Given at London the *Twelfth* day of *July* in the year of our Lord One Thousand Seven Hundred and Ninety-six, and in the Thirty-sixth year of our reign.

Arden,

Registrar.

• • •

What happened next . . .

French privateers continued to operate off the U.S. coast. After the French took 489 American ships between 1797 and 1798, the new president, John Adams (1735–1826), reorganized the U.S. Navy. America had disbanded its navy in 1785, a few years after the American Revolution ended. By signing the Constitution, the states had given up their right to form navies, so on July 1, 1798, a new American navy was formed to rid the seas off its coast of privateers. This action was called the Quasi-War. By 1799 the area around the Caribbean had been cleared of privateers.

Many of the French moved to the northern coast of South America. There they were welcomed by Victor Hughes (1762–1826), a governor who had formerly been tried for encouraging piracy. After being acquitted,

Material: Relevant.

Aforesaid: Previously mentioned.

Succour: Aid.

Hughes was sent back to the area in 1800 as the governor of Cayenne, the capital of French Guiana. Hughes allowed the French privateers to operate from that port until the British took over the city in 1809.

After the British blockaded many French ports, the privateers moved to the Indian Ocean. One of the most well-known French seamen of this time was Robert Surcouf (1773–1827). He had never received a letter of marque, so he was not a privateer but a pirate. Surcouf took many British prizes and then tried to convince the government to let him keep his portion. Because of his assistance, the French government agreed to split the take.

In 1802 the Treaty of Amiens halted the Anglo-French War, but hostilities broke out again in 1803. This time Surcouf was granted a letter of marque. He soon became rich enough that he could stay ashore and finance other privateers. In 1805 the French navy suffered a great defeat at Trafalgar, when it tried to invade the British Isles. Surcouf's fleet provided much assistance following the naval losses, and the French emperor Napoleon Bonaparte (1769–1821) honored him by making him a baron, or a nobleman.

Great Britain's and France's efforts to block each other's trade hurt the American economy. The British also needed more sailors for their navy, so they stopped American ships and impressed (forced into service) the crew. And after several attempts to stop impressment and regain their rights, the United States declared war on Great Britain on June 18, 1812.

In the War of 1812, Congress encouraged privateering. Within a few months, 150 privateers were supporting the U.S. Navy, which had only twenty-three ships. The number of privateers rose to 517, and they captured more than five times the ships that the navy did. They also took about thirty thousand prisoners and caused major economic damage to British trade.

Privateering continued until 1856, when Great Britain and other European countries signed the Declaration of Paris. This document made privateering illegal. The United States and Spain refused to sign. The United States said that, because they had such a small navy, they might need privateers to help them fight wars. By the end of the 1800s, after the American navy had grown larger, the United States also banned privateering. Spain forbade it in 1908.

When the countries met at the Hague Peace Conference of 1907, they agreed that armed ships, including merchant ships, had to be listed as

Robert Surcouf was a French pirate and privateer operating in the Indian Ocean. © THE ART GALLERY COLLECTION/ ALAMY.

warships. This statement is now part of international law. Each country was made responsible for any of its ships that acted in a warlike manner. Thus, privateers were no longer needed.

Did you know ...

- Article 1, section 8, of the U.S. Constitution gives Congress the power to "grant letters of marque and reprisal."

- Before a privateer could benefit from a prize, the ship had to be "condemned" in a court of law. This meant the privateer had to prove it belonged to the enemy. To do this, privateers had to show the ship's papers or get the officers, crew, or passengers to testify. Once the ship was condemned, it was sold at a court-ordered auction. About half the money from the sale went to pay taxes, duties, and the auctioneer. Investors also had to be repaid. In spite of this, most privateers made a good profit.
- If privateers made a mistake and captured a ship that later turned out not to be an enemy ship, they had to pay for damages to the cargo and give compensation for anyone they killed or injured.

Consider the following ...

- How might the results of some of the major American wars—the Revolutionary War or the War of 1812—been different if privateers had not helped the newly formed American navy?
- Sailors who joined the navy received low pay compared to privateers who brought in prizes. Most privateers could make close to a year's naval wages if they captured one or two enemy merchant ships. Why then do you think people chose to join the navy rather than become privateers?
- America had signed a treaty with France in 1778, agreeing to help protect France's territories in the Western Hemisphere. Yet when France wanted to base its privateers there during its war with Britain, America refused to allow it. Why do you think America did so? Should it have honored the treaty and helped France? Why or why not?

For More Information

BOOKS

Coggeshall, George. *A History of American Privateers and Letters of Marque Interspersed with Several Naval Battles Between American and British Ships of War.* New York: C.T. Evans, 1856; Cornell, NY: Cornell University Library, 2009.

Cordingly, David, ed. *Pirates: Terror on the High Seas from the Caribbean to the South China Sea.* North Dighton, MA: World Publications Group, 2006.

Hall, William Edward. *A Treatise on International Law.* 4th ed. Oxford: Clarendon Press, 1895.

Hill, Richard. *The Prizes of War: The Naval Prize System in the Napoleonic Wars 1793–1815.* London: Sutton, 1998.

Jameson, John Franklin, ed. *Privateering and Piracy in the Colonial Period.* New York: The Macmillan Company, 1923.

Kent, James. *Commentaries on American Law.* 12th ed. Edited by Oliver Wendell Holmes Jr. Boston: Little, Brown, and Company, 1873.

Martin, Harold Hudson, and Joseph Richardson Baker. *Laws of Maritime Warfare Affecting Rights and Duties of Belligerents.* Washington, DC: Government Printing Office, 1918.

Petrie, Donald A. *The Prize Game.* Annapolis, MD: Naval Academy Press, 1999.

Upton, Francis H. *Maritime Warfare and Prize.* New York: John Voorhies Law Bookseller and Publisher, 1863.

PERIODICALS

Anderson, G.M., and A.J. Gifford. "Privateering and the Private Production of Naval Power." *Cato Journal* 11, no. 1 (1991): 99–122.

Tabarrok, Alexander. "The Rise, Fall, and Rise Again of Privateers," *Independent Review* 11, no. 4 (Spring 2007): 565–77.

WEB SITES

"Letters of Marque and Reprisal." *Constitution Society.* www.constitution.org/mil/lmr/lmr.htm (accessed on January 3, 2011).

Maine, Henry. "International Law (1887)." *Avalon Project: Yale University* (2006). http://avalon.law.yale.edu/subject_menus/intmenu.asp (accessed on January 3, 2011).

"Privateers and Mariners in the Revolutionary War." *American Merchant Marine at War.* www.usmm.org/revolution.html (accessed on January 3, 2011).

"UK Sources for War of 1812 Privateers Service Veterans." *War of 1812: Privateers.org.* www.1812privateers.org/GB/GreatBritain.htm (accessed on January 3, 2011).

10

Pirate Surrender Document

"The Pirate Surrender Document of 1810"
  Reprinted in Pirates of the South China Coast
  Published by Stanford University Press, 1987

"We hope that you will pity the remaining life of us 'insects and ants'; save us from the flood and fire; pardon our former crimes; and open for us a new way of life from this day forward."

The earliest pirates in the South China Sea were a disorganized lot. (The South China Sea is an area of the Pacific Ocean that is surrounded by southeast China, Indochina, the Malay Peninsula, Borneo, the Philippines, and Taiwan.) They operated in small gangs, raiding along the coast. Most were driven by poverty. For example, poor fishermen would supplement their incomes with sea raiding during the off season. From the sixteenth to the eighteenth century, these pirates began to organize, building powerful pirate empires under strong leaders.

Cheng I and Cheng I Sao build pirate empire

One of those pirate leaders was Cheng I (1765–1807). During the Tay Son Rebellion (1771–1802) in Vietnam, the Tay Son rebels recruited Chinese pirates to fight their battles. By 1788 the rebels had gained control of Vietnam, but the new Tay Son emperor needed to fund the government. So he authorized Chinese pirates to raid the coasts of China, provided that they give him a share in their booty. (Booty is the goods stolen from ships or coastal villages during pirate raids or attacks on enemies in time of war.) However, the Tay Son emperor died in 1792 and within ten years the former rulers had regained control and began cracking down on piracy. In 1801, Cheng I decided to move his base of operations to China.

Chinese pirates preparing to attack. MARY EVANS PICTURE LIBRARY/EVERETT COLLECTION.

While sailing to China, he married a prostitute, who was known after the marriage as Cheng I Sao, meaning "wife of Cheng I" (1775–1844). Cheng I made his wife co-commander and they established their base in Kwangtung province.

Cheng I organized six pirate fleets that each sailed under a different colored flag—red, white, black, yellow, blue, or green. Cheng I commanded the Red Flag fleet, which began with about two hundred junks (Chinese sailboats), but quickly expanded. By 1807 the fleet included six hundred junks, about thirty thousand sea pirates, and a fighting force of about 150,000 men. Each fleet operated in a certain area and there were rules about dividing the booty. This reduced conflicts among the various groups. Within a few short years, these well-organized pirate fleets dominated the southern coast. Some say this was the largest pirate confederation in history. Cheng I's fleets threatened the coast of southern China, attacking ships and raiding villages.

During one raid, Cheng I's fleet captured Chang Pao (also known as Chang Po Tsai; died 1822), the teenage son of a fisherman. Cheng I and his wife adopted the boy, but some sources also say Chang Pao and Cheng I Sao were lovers. In any event, once he was aboard ship, Chang Pao worked his way up to positions of responsibility.

Cheng I Sao takes command

Cheng I's leadership was short-lived; he died in 1807, possibly washed overboard by a storm. After his death, his wife Cheng I Sao took command of the confederation. It was not unusual for Chinese women to sail junks. Most worked alongside their husbands onboard ship doing whatever jobs needed to be done, but Cheng I Sao took over a huge fleet. She proved herself an able leader, and she was both clever and brave.

Cheng I Sao promoted her adopted son, Chang Pao, as commander of the Red Flag fleet. Within a few years, they were married, and she later bore him a son. Cheng I Sao and Chang Pao developed a strict code of conduct that their pirates were expected to obey. Penalties for disobedience were severe. According to these regulations, going ashore without permission meant a pirate's ear was split, or sometimes cut off, the first time it happened. The second time he was beheaded. Beheading was also the punishment for disobeying orders, giving unauthorized commands, stealing from the common treasury, lying about booty, or raping female captives. Even if the woman had agreed, the pirate lost his head, and the woman's legs were tied to a weight before she was thrown overboard. Other punishments for lesser offenses included flogging or being imprisoned in irons.

To keep relations strong with the coastal villages, Cheng I Sao also established rules stating that the pirates must pay for rice, wine, and other goods. Anyone from her fleets who took these items by force was killed. This ensured that the villagers provided them with food and gunpowder as needed. Towns that did not cooperate, however, were treated brutally.

The pirate fleet plundered (robbed of goods by force) and burned houses, killed the villagers or took them prisoner. Women, especially those with bound feet—tightly wrapping women's feet was a custom in China to make their feet smaller—who could barely hobble, were often dragged back to the ship and held for ransom, or a sum of money demanded for the release of someone being held captive. Ransom was paid in money, sugar, rice, and roasted pig or some fowls. The old and sick became prisoners or were simply killed.

Demands for ransom

Instead of depending solely on booty, Cheng I Sao also required all ships on the South China Sea to pay for safe passage. Most of the time the pirates did not attack foreign ships, fearing their retaliation, but they sometimes took prisoners for ransom. British sailors who were captured by pirates told gory tales. British chief mate John Turner was taken prisoner in 1806 and held for ransom. Although he was beaten frequently during his five months of captivity, Turner described the even greater horrors that awaited officers of the Chinese imperial navy, as quoted by Janin Hunt in *The India-China Opium Trade in the Nineteenth Century*: "I saw one man … nailed to the deck through his feet with large nails, then beaten … till he vomited blood.... [Another prisoner] was fixed upright, his bowels cut open and his heart taken out, which they afterwards soaked in spirits and ate."

Another British captive, Richard Glasspoole (1788–1846), recorded his experiences aboard one of Cheng I Sao's ships in 1809. His account is reproduced in the Appendix of *History of the Pirates Who Infested the China Sea from 1807 to 1810*. At first Glasspoole and his men were chained to the guns on deck, but later he had the opportunity to see the cramped and dirty pirate quarters, which were swarming with vermin. He noted that the ship was filled with "rats in particular, which they encourage to breed, and eat them as great delicacies; in fact, there are very few creatures they will not eat. During our captivity we lived three weeks on caterpillars boiled with rice."

The pirates wanted Glasspoole's men to help ransack towns. At first Glasspoole refused, but when they learned their captors would accept a lower ransom and give them twenty dollars for every head they cut off, the British agreed. One of the captives told of seeing a pirate, sword in hand, chasing a man to lop off his head. Around the pirate's neck dangled two heads he had already severed

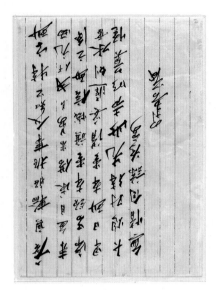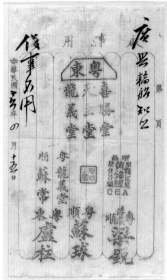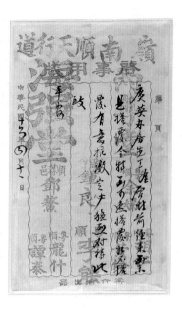

Ransom demands from Chinese pirates. Cheng I Sao's pirates sometimes took European prisoners and held them for ransom.
© NATIONAL MARITIME MUSEUM, LONDON/THE IMAGE WORKS. REPRODUCED BY PERMISSION.

Height of her empire

Within two years, Cheng I Sao had between fifty thousand and seventy thousand pirates and twelve hundred junks under her command. The Chinese government sent forces after her pirates, but Cheng I Sao always defeated them, causing the deaths of several prominent naval officers and destroying about half of the government ships. The imperial naval yards could not build ships fast enough to replace their losses, so they confiscated private fishing boats, but they were still unable to stop the pirates. Cheng I Sao's fleets moved farther inland along the Pearl River.

In August 1809 two fleets moved into place to take over more territory. The Black Flag fleet burned a customs house near Canton and threatened to attack the city if the government did not pay ransom. Meanwhile, the Red Flag fleet destroyed two forts as well as villages in several counties. The pirates defeated the government forces and left about ten thousand people dead.

In September after the pirates captured Siamese boats carrying tribute and scared off American schooners, the Chinese government leased

Cheng I Sao in battle on board a pirate ship. PRIVATE COLLECTION/PETER NEWARK HISTORICAL PICTURES/THE BRIDGEMAN ART LIBRARY INTERNATIONAL.

six men-of-war (armed warships) from the Portuguese to help blockade the pirate headquarters. But the pirates evaded the ships and sailed away.

Surrender

After numerous failures to stop Cheng I Sao's pirates, the Chinese government decided to change its tactics, offering pardons to pirates who surrendered. At the same time, rivalries were causing problems within the confederation. Some sources say the captain of the Black Flag fleet was in love with Cheng I Sao and resented Chang Pao's rise to power. On December 11, 1809, the Black Flag fleet launched an attack on the Red Flag fleet. The Black Flag fleet won the battle, and its commander turned his captives over to the government in exchange for amnesty for himself and his crew. He and his fifty-five hundred men surrendered on January 11, 1810. He was given a position in the navy and soon set out in pursuit of his former allies.

A short while later, Chang Pao decided to surrender. He met with the governor-general of Canton on February 21, but the pirates and the government could not agree on the terms. Then on April 18, Cheng I Sao took charge of the negotiations. Rather than staying aboard the boat, she bravely marched to the governor-general accompanied by a group of pirate women and children. She officially surrendered her fleet of 226 junks and 17,318 pirates on April 20, 1810.

Things to remember while reading "The Pirate Surrender Document of 1810":

- It is not certain who authored the document. Many historians believe Chang Pao, the leader of the Red Flag fleet, wrote it. Some have suggested that the staff of governor-general Pai Ling wrote it for the pirates.
- After the government lost the majority of their military force going after pirates, it was even willing to accept the surrender of pirate fleet leaders, As Dian Murray notes in *Pirates of the South China Coast: 1790–1810*, "General Pai Ling posted placards in all the ports warning pirates to 'return to allegiance' and on several occasions even dispatched emissaries [agents] to appeal to them in person."
- The document begins by reminding the government of other pirates who were pardoned in the past, perhaps hoping that the surrendering pirates would receive the same treatment.
- The pirates indicate that they are ready to leave their past lives behind and become farmers.

● ● ●

The Pirate Surrender Document of 1810

The backgrounds of heroes are different. So are the hearts of the officials, for some are **benevolent** and others have patience. Therefore, the bandits of Liang-shan were thrice pardoned for pillaging the city and became a pillar of state. The robbers of Wa-kang on several occasions resisted the soldiers, but when granted **amnesty** became cornerstones of the country. Other examples can be found in history: Kung Ming captured Ming Huo several times, and Kuan Kung thrice freed Ts'ao Ts'ao. Ma Yüan never chased a desperate enemy and Yüeh Fei never killed those who submitted. Thus, when the heroes of the world surrender, people from far and near are happy. Such events are not one-time occurrences, for their underlying principles are the same.

Now, we "ants" [the pirates' reference to themselves in humble terms] are living in a prosperous age. Originally we were good people, but we became pirates for a variety of reasons. Because some of us were not careful in making friends, we fell into a bad situation and became robbers. Others of us were unable to secure a livelihood or were captured while trading on the lakes and rivers and forced into piracy. Still others

Benevolent: Kind.

Amnesty: Pardon; forgiveness.

because of having committed some crime joined this watery empire to escape punishment. At first we **constituted** only a small number, but later we increased to a thousand and ten thousand. In addition, as a result of the **dearth** of the last several years, people had nothing with which to maintain their living, and as time went on could not help but rob in order to live. If we had not resisted the government officials, our lives would have been in danger. Therefore, we violated the laws of the empire and destroyed the merchants. This was unavoidable.

As pirates, we left our native villages. Without families, we floated upon the sea. If we encountered government patrols, their cannon and arrows frightened us. If we encountered rough seas, then we were also frightened. We fled to the east and west, and often tried to avoid the pursuit of warships. Having to live without shelter and eat the wind, we suffered all the bitterness of the sea. At those times, we wanted to leave the robbers and return to our villages, but the inhabitants would not tolerate us. We considered surrendering as a group, but did not know what the officials, with their power, would do to us, so we had to remain on the islands, just looking on and waiting with no decision. Alas! Alas!

Of course our crimes should be punished by death. It is hard to avoid the laws of the government. But our situation is extremely pitiful and if we are to survive, we must depend on men of benevolence. We are happy that you, Governor-general, have come again to Kwangtung to rule, for you regard others as yourself and love them as your sons.

We have respectfully read your proclamation several times. You advise us to surrender and take pity on our reasons for having become pirates. Your principle is to use both severity and **leniency**, and you understand the virtue of the treasure of life. In your justice you use both **extermination** and **appeasement**. Even the bird flying in the dust wants to be quiet, and how can a fish be content in boiling water? On account of this, I have gathered my entire group, and we have sent this petition with all our signatures. We hope that you will pity the remaining life of us "insects and ants"; save us from the flood and fire; pardon our former crimes; and open for us a new way of life from this day forward. We solemnly promise to "sell our swords and buy cows." In appreciation of your greatness, we burn incense and praise you in song. If we dare to act with **duplicity**, you may kill us at once.

Constituted: Made up of.

Dearth: Lack; in this case of food.

Leniency: Mercy.

Extermination: Killing off a species or group.

Appeasement: Making peace.

Duplicity: Trickery.

• • •

What happened next . . .

Of those who surrendered, 60 pirates were banished for two years, 151 were exiled, and 126 were executed. The rest received some money, and many joined the military.

Chang Pao not only received a large sum of money and a naval rank, he was also allowed to keep a fleet of about twenty to thirty junks. Cheng I Sao convinced the government to give her a rank even though the law forbade remarried widows to receive titles.

Chang Pao spent the next decade in the imperial navy erasing all traces of the former pirate empire. Along the way, he moved up the ranks. When he received a peacock feather and was promoted to second captain, people protested that a former criminal should not receive such honors. To quiet the complaints, he was transferred to Fulkien province, where he later became a lieutenant colonel. In 1815 he captured ships carrying opium, which led to the arrest of six opium dealers. Next he took command of a regiment in the Pescadores islands. Once again, complaints about his past surfaced, and a salt inspector wrote to the emperor accusing Chang Pao of smoking opium and having no manners. Chang Pao died in 1822 at age thirty-six.

Two years after her husband's death, Cheng I Sao moved to Canton, where she operated a gambling house. She died in 1844 at age sixty-nine.

Did you know ...

- Women captives were usually ransomed. Those who were not, could be bought by a pirate as a wife for forty dollars. Some women jumped overboard and drowned to avoid that fate.
- Married pirates were given a four-foot-square berth (bed) for themselves and their families, who sailed with them.
- For several centuries the Chinese practiced foot binding. Young girls' feet were wrapped tightly to keep them small. It broke the bones in the toes and often crippled them. Women with bound feet were unable to run away and so were often caught by pirates.
- Chinese names can be spelled many different ways when they are translated into English. Some alternate spellings for the pirates' names as well as other names they were known by are listed in parentheses: Cheng I (Ching Yi, Chen I, Cheng Yih, Cheng Yao-I, Cheng Wen-Hsien, Zheng Yi), Cheng I Sao (Ching Shih, Ching Hsi Kai, Ching Yih Saou, Cheng Yisao, Ching Hsi Kai, Zheng Yi Sao), and Chang Pao (Chang Paou, Cheung Po, Chang Pao Tsai, Cheung Po Tsai, Zhang Bao).
- The villain Sao Feng in the movie *Pirates of the Caribbean: At World's End* is based on myth and facts about Chang Pao.

Consider the following . . .

- Chinese pirates kept their wives and children with them as they traveled. What do you think life on the high seas, particularly during battle, was like for the children?
- Pirates grew used to life on the open seas and faced many dangers and adventures. What adjustments do you think would be most difficult for them if they lived the rest of their lives as farmers or government officials?
- Do you think the government made a wise choice in offering amnesty to the pirates and offering some of them positions in the government and military? Why or why not?

For More Information

BOOKS

Carpenter, John Reeve. *Pirates: Scourge of the Seas.* New York: Sterling, 2006.

"Ching Shih (fl. 1807–1810)." In *Women in World History: A Biographical Encyclopedia*, edited by Anne Commire and Deborah Klezmer. Vol. 3. Detroit: Yorkin, 2000.

Glasspoole, Richard. "A brief Narrative of my captivity and treatment amongst the Ladrones" Appendix of *History of the Pirates Who Infested the China Sea from 1807 to 1810*, translated by Karl Friedrich Neumann. London: J.L. Cox, 1931, p. 128.

Janin, Hunt. *The India-China Opium Trade in the Nineteenth Century.* Jefferson, NC: McFarland, 1999, p. 135.

Lorimer, Sara. *Booty: Girl Pirates on the High Seas.* San Francisco: Chronicle Books, 2001.

Murray, Dian. "Cheng I Sao in Fact and Fiction." In *Bandits at Sea*, edited by C.R. Pennell. New York: New York University Press, 2001.

———. *Pirates of the South China Coast: 1790–1810.* Stanford, CA: Stanford University Press, 1987, p. 137.

Weatherly, Myra. *Women of the Sea: Ten Pirate Stories.* Greensboro, NC: Morgan Reynolds. 2005.

PERIODICALS

Murray, Dian H. "Pirates of the South China Coast 1790–1810," *Journal of the Economic and Social History of the Orient* 33, no. 2 (1990): 234–6.

11

The Corsair

Excerpt from *The Corsair*
By Lord George Gordon Byron
Originally published in 1814
Reprinted in The Works of Lord Byron, *Volume 3*
Published by Charles Scribner's Sons, 1900

"Far as the breeze can bear, the billows foam, / Survey our empire, and behold our home! / These are our realms, no limits to their sway— / Our flag the sceptre all who meet obey."

As the golden age of piracy came to a close in the first three decades of the eighteenth century, many people were still drawn to the swashbuckling heroes and tales of adventures on the high seas. Pirate biographies and autobiographies went into second or even third printings, because customers snapped them up as soon as they were printed. Many authors also wove this popular topic into their works, and several of these became classics. One author to do so was George Gordon, usually referred to as Lord Byron (1788–1824), who penned a poem about a pirate captain who is saved by a slave in a Turkish harem. (A harem is the area of a Muslim household historically reserved for wives, concubines, and female relatives.) When *The Corsair* was released in London in 1814, the publishing world was stunned; the poem sold out its first run of ten thousand copies in just one day. By this time the threat of pirates had diminished, so the harder truths about the trials and tribulations of a corsair, or a pirate of the Barbary Coast, had been replaced by a romanticized account of life at sea. (The Barbary Coast is an area in the Mediterranean Sea roughly encompassing the present-day countries of Morocco, Algeria, Tunisia, and northwest Libya.)

About the author

Lord Byron was a Romantic poet who lived a scandalous life. (Romantic poets celebrated nature.) Born to John Byron and the Scottish heiress

George Gordon, Lord Byron.
STOCK MONTAGE/ARCHIVE
PHOTOS/GETTY IMAGES.

Catherine Gordon on January 22, 1788, Byron was christened George Gordon. He was born with a clubfoot, a deformity in which the foot is twisted inward or outward. His clubfoot caused him to limp, and Byron was ashamed of this his entire life. After his father died in 1791, Byron's mother had to sell her land and title to pay her husband's debts. Catherine took her young son back to her homeland, and they settled in Aberdeen, Scotland, where Byron was raised until the age of ten.

Life in England In 1798 the young Byron inherited a title and an estate, Newstead Abbey, in Nottinghamshire, England, when his great-uncle died. From 1801 to 1805 he attended Harrow School, in London, where he did well at oratory (public speaking) and wrote poetry. He then went on to attend Cambridge University's Trinity College. In 1806 he self-published his first collection of poetry, *Fugitive Pieces*, but he withdrew it from circulation at the advice of his friend, the Reverend John Thomas Becher (1770–1848), who expressed shock at some of the subject matter. Byron self-published another volume, *Poems on Various Occasions*, with the objectionable content deleted, in 1807. He later added to the book and called it *Hours of Idleness*.

After graduating with a master's degree in 1808, Byron traveled with his friend, John Cam Hobhouse, to parts of Europe and to the Mediterranean. When he returned in 1811, he took his seat in the House of Lords and, though he made only three speeches, those he gave supported the rights of the oppressed. (The House of Lords is the upper house of Parliament, Great Britain's legislature. Membership is attained by inheritance, as was the case for Byron, or appointment.) He also expressed his views in political poems.

Byron became involved in several love affairs, with both men and women. Some of his passions, such as that for his distant cousin Mary Chaworth, inspired poetic works. From 1812 to 1816 Byron published several epic tales, including *The Corsair*. On January 2, 1815, he married Anne Isabella (Annabella) Milbanke, and in December they had a daughter, Augusta Ada. The marriage was short-lived, and the couple separated in 1816. Byron left England and never returned.

Life abroad Byron settled in Switzerland near Percy Bysshe Shelley (1792–1822) and his wife, Mary Wollstonecraft Godwin (1797–1851). There he had an affair with Godwin's stepdaughter, Claire Clairmont, with whom he had a child, Clara Allegra, in 1817. Allegra died at age five. While Byron was in Switzerland, he wrote part of *Childe Harold's Pilgrimage* (1816), one of his most famous works.

Next he visited Italy, where he studied Armenian culture and language, and wrote *Don Juan* as well as other works. He also joined the *Carbonari*, a secret society that planned to free Italy from Austrian rule. In April 1823 he moved to Greece to help the Greeks in their struggle for independence from the Ottoman Empire and even paid to have a fleet fitted for the cause. However, early the next year, he became ill and died on April 19, 1824, in Missolonghi, Greece. The Greeks hailed him as a national hero, and a suburb of Athens was named for him. Some say that if he had lived, Byron might have been crowned the king of Greece.

Byron's legacy Although the famous Danish sculptor Bertel Thorvaldsen (177–1844) created a memorial statue of Byron after he died, none of the museums in England would accept it, because they considered Byron's morals unacceptable. For more than a century after Byron's death, his dog had a larger monument than he did. Not until 1969, 145 years after Byron's death, was a memorial placed in Westminster Abbey in England.

Byron left behind a large collection of works, including satire, dramatic monologue, narrative verse, and many other forms of poetry. Some of his most famous works were the narrative poems *Childe Harold's Pilgrimage* and *Don Juan*, and the shorter poems "She Walks in Beauty," "So, We'll Go No More a-Roving," and "When We Two Parted."

Byron was also known for creating the Byronic hero. The heroes of Byron's poems share similar characteristics, which have earned them this special classification in literature. Because Byron exhibited these characteristics, many believe he modeled his characters after himself.

The Byronic hero is driven by passion and talent, but he is haunted by secret guilt. This idealized, but flawed, character is arrogant, overconfident, and self-destructive. Rebellion against society and a lack respect for social status are two other marks of Byron's heroes, who find society's rules and morals a hindrance to love and, thus, are outcasts.

About *The Corsair*

The first of the three related narrative poems with pirate heroes, the *Bride of Abydos*, was published on November 29, 1813. A few weeks later Byron wrote *The Corsair*. He began the poem on December 18 and completed it in ten days, then possibly spent several days copying it out. The final draft arrived at the printer by January 12, 1814. It became an instant hit with the public.

The cantos Like many of Byron's long narrative poems, *The Corsair* was divided into sections called cantos. This romantic tale of pirates had three cantos. The first canto begins on an island, where readers meet the pirate Conrad and his wife, Medora. Conrad intends to fight Seyd [pronounced Seed], the pasha (Turkish ruler), but his wife begs him to stay home with her. Nevertheless, Conrad sets sail for the pasha's palace.

In the second canto Conrad disguises himself and enters the palace to distract the pasha, while his crew surrounds the building. The pirates are winning the battle, when the women in the harem cry out because the building is on fire. Conrad orders his men to save the women. Meanwhile Seyd rallies his forces, and they capture Conrad and kill most of his crew. Because Conrad has saved her, the pasha's favorite harem slave, Gulnare, whose name means "flower of the pomegranate," tries to rescue him.

An illustration of a scene from The Corsair *in which Conrad's wife Medora reacts to the news that he intends to fight the pasha Seyd.* © LEBRECHT MUSIC AND ARTS PHOTO LIBRARY/ALAMY.

The third canto tells of Gulnare's attempts to free Conrad. She suggests to the pasha that he let Conrad go to gain his pirate's treasure, then recapture him. But the pasha is suspicious of her motives and threatens Gulnare's life.

Gulnare sneaks a knife to Conrad, but he refuses to kill the pasha unless it is a fair fight. (The pirate code demands that duels be held face to face.) Gulnare kills the pasha instead. Then she and Conrad escape to the pirates' island, where Conrad discovers his wife has died of grief after she received the mistaken news that Conrad had been killed.

The poem ends on a mysterious note. Conrad has disappeared. The only clue his crew has to his whereabouts is a broken boat chain, but no one ever sees him again. The pirates erect a monument for Medora, but not for Conrad. The final lines of *The Corsair* read:

> For him they raise not the recording stone—
> His death yet dubious, deeds too widely known;
> He left a Corsair's name to other times,
> Linked with one virtue, and a thousand crimes.

Things to remember while reading the excerpt from *The Corsair*:

- Many scholars call this an autobiographical poem because the hero of the poem, the pirate Conrad, has many of Byron's personality traits, and at times the events in the poem seem similar to things that happened to Byron. For example, in Canto I Byron describes Conrad as the "man of loneliness and mystery," a good description of Byron's own life. Both Byron and Conrad traveled to distant lands and both ended up with another woman after passionate relationships ended in tragedy. Byron may also have seen himself as the noble outlaw, a role he gave Conrad, because he himself was living abroad after society condemned his morals.

- Byron, like many people of his time, had a romantic view of pirates. He wrote of their thrilling adventures and camaraderie, or group friendship, but the reality of pirate life was quite different. Life on the high seas was often difficult. Storms, lack of food and water, being hunted down by authorities, and fighting with shipmates were only some of the hardships pirates faced.

- Byron included a note at the beginning of the poem that said the Aegean Islands were only a few hours from the Greek mainland, so they could be reached in the time frame that he uses in the poem.

- Conrad does not join in the pirates' entertaining meals ("jovial mess") nor does he drink wine ("the purpling cup"). McGill University literary scholar Tom Mole compares Byron's eating habits with those of Conrad in an article for *Romanticism*. He points out that Byron was on a strict diet when he wrote *The Corsair*. Because he wanted to look stylish, Byron tried to keep his weight down and often went days without eating much. Perhaps that is why Conrad also ate little.

• • •

The Corsair

Canto the First

I

O'er the glad waters of the dark blue sea,
Our thoughts as boundless, and our souls as free,
Far as the breeze can bear, the billows foam,
Survey our empire, and behold our home!
These are our realms, no limits to their sway—
Our flag the **sceptre** all who meet obey.
Ours the wild life in **tumult** still to range
From toil to rest, and joy in every change.
Oh, who can tell? not thou, luxurious slave!
Whose soul would sicken o'er the heaving wave;
Not thou, vain lord of **wantonness** and ease!
Whom slumber soothes not—pleasure cannot please—
Oh, who can tell, **save** he whose heart hath tried,
And danced in triumph o'er the waters wide,
The exulting sense—the pulse's maddening play,
That thrills the wanderer of that trackless way?
That for itself can woo the approaching fight,
And turn what some deem danger to delight;
That seeks what **cravens** shun with more than zeal,
And where the feebler faint can only feel—
Feel—to the rising bosom's inmost core,
Its hope awaken and its spirit soar?
No dread of death if with us die our foes—
Save that it seems even duller than repose:
Come when it will—we snatch the life of life—
When lost—what recks it but disease or strife?

Sceptre: A staff or a rod carried by a king to show his power and authority.

Tumult: Disorder, commotion.

Wantonness: Uncontrolled, reckless, or excessive behavior.

Save: Except.

Cravens: Cowards.

II
Such were the notes that from the Pirate's isle
Around the kindling watch-fire, rang the while:
Such were the sounds that thrill'd the rocks along,
And unto ears as rugged seem'd a song!
In scatter'd groups upon the golden sand,
They game—**carouse**—converse—or what the brand:
Select the arms—to each his blade assign,
And careless eye the blood that dims its shine,
Repair the boat, replace the helm or oar,
While others straggling **muse** along the shore:
For the wild bird the busy **springes** set,
Or spread beneath the sun the dripping net:
Gaze where some distant sail a speck supplies,
With all the thirsting eye of Enterprise:
Tell o'er the tales of many a night of toil,
And marvel where they next shall seize a spoil:
No matter where—their chief's allotment this;
Theirs, to believe no prey nor plan amiss.
But who that CHIEF? his name on every shore
Is famed and fear'd—they ask and know no more.
With these he mingles not but to command;
Few are his words, but keen his eye and hand.
Ne'er seasons he with mirth their jovial **mess**,
But they forgive his silence for success.
Ne'er for his lip the **purpling cup** they fill,
That goblet passes him untasted still—
And for his fare—the rudest of his crew
Would that, in turn, have pass'd untasted too;
Earth's coarsest bread, the garden's homeliest roots,
And scarce the summer luxury of fruits,
His short repast in humbleness supply
With all a hermit's board would scarce deny.
But while he shuns the grosser joys of sense,
His mind seems nourish'd by that **abstinence**.
'Steer to that shore!'—they sail. 'Do this!'—'tis done:
'Now form and follow me!'—the spoil is won.
Thus prompt his accents and his actions still,
And all obey and few inquire his will;
To such, brief answer and **contemptuous** eye
Convey **reproof**, nor further **deign** reply. . . .

Carouse: Have loud, drunken parties.

Muse: Think reflectively.

Springes: Traps or snares.

Mess: Meal.

Purpling cup: Wine glass.

Abstinence: Fasting or not partaking of something, such as food or drink.

Contemptuous: Scornful.

Reproof: Criticism.

Deign: Lower one's dignity or stoop to.

What happened next ...

After the book was published, Byron wrote in his diary on March 10, 1814, that his friend Hobhouse had said many people believed Byron actually had been a corsair. Byron responded that people sometimes got close to the truth and hinted that no one knew what he had done during the year after he traveled in the Levant, the countries along the eastern Mediterranean Sea from Turkey to Egypt. Though most doubt that Byron spent time as a pirate, a book published in 1825, the *Life, Writings, Opinions, and Times of the R.H. George Gordon Noel Byron*, indicated that Byron had spent time in the company of a pirate a few years before the book came out. Other scholars say that Byron's ideas most likely came from the time he spent traveling in Greece from 1809 to 1811. He would have heard many stories of Lambros Katzones, a Greek pirate sailing under the Russian flag who fought off the coast of the Morea, a peninsula in southern Greece, where Byron's story was also set. It is even possible that Byron met this famous Greek raider. In whatever way he obtained his knowledge of pirates, one thing is certain—Byron admired pirates. He wrote in his diary of his negative feelings about governments, so for him pirates, who were a law unto themselves, appealed to him.

Byron ended *The Corsair* with a long note about a story of pirates that had appeared in an American newspaper. In Barataria, a bayou in Louisiana just south of New Orleans, two brothers, Jean and Pierre Lafitte headed a group of pirates. On November 24, 1813, the governor offered a $500 reward for the capture of Jean Lafitte (c. 1776–c. 1823). The pirate countered by offering a reward of $15,000 for the governor's head. The governor sent forces to burn the pirate's property. But when the captain approached Lafitte's island, a whistle brought armed men to surround him. Lafitte tried to bribe the man to join them, but when he did not, Lafitte allowed him to leave. The governor soon realized that he could not take the pirates by land, so he sent naval forces. Lafitte's ships, however, sent the small navy into retreat. The military requested reinforcements to overthrow the pirates. Although they subdued pirate activity, they never caught the Lafitte brothers.

The romanticism of pirates attracted many book buyers. *The Corsair* not only sold ten thousand copies the first day it came out, it continued to sell well. Within a few months, twenty-five thousand copies had sold. Some scholars claim that Byron and his publisher manipulated the public to increase sales. Some volumes of the book included an eight-line poem,

Eugène Delacroix

Many artists immortalized pirates in their paintings, depicting a life few people had ever seen. Some artists based their pictures on tales created by authors who had only imagined life on the high seas. Lord Byron's poems inspired the paintings of Eugène Delacroix (1798–1863), a French Romantic painter who was known for expressive brushstrokes, use of color and movement, and dramatic subject matter.

One of Delacroix's most famous oils was *Liberty Leading the People*, painted between October and December 1830. It showed the French citizens, including a young boy with a gun, following Lady Liberty in a march for freedom and equal rights. When Delacroix exhibited *Liberty* in Paris, in 1831, he also entered a watercolor based on *The Corsair*. This painting, titled *Episode from "The Corsair" by Lord Byron*, showed Gulnare visiting the pirate Conrad in his prison cell.

Byron's works were the subject of several of Delacroix's artworks during the 1820s. Delacroix's *Combat of the Giaour and the Hassan* (1813) and *Combat of the Giaour and the Pasha* (1827), showing two men on horseback engaged in battle; both came from Byron's narrative poem *The Giaour: A Fragment of a Turkish Tale*. Delacroix's 1827 *Death of Sardanapalus* depicts the Assyrian king watching as all his possessions and concubines are destroyed. Rather than basing his painting on the accepted classical story, Delacroix used Byron's contemporary drama to create his fiery,

A self-portrait of Eugène Delacroix. © MASTERPICS/ ALAMY

swirling masterpiece, which resulted in government threats to cut off the artist's commissions if he continued to paint in this style.

Like Byron, Delacroix was moved by the Greek civil war. In 1826 he showed *Marino Faliero Decapitated on the Giant's Staircase of the Ducal Palace* and *Greece Lamenting on the Ruins of Missolonghi* as his way of honoring the patriots. (Byron died in Greece, where he had hoped to support the Greeks in their struggle for independence.)

"To a Lady Weeping," about English princess Charlotte (1796–1817) crying after her father criticized his former political supporters. People were curious about the poem, and, when critics denounced it, that stirred even more interest. Customers bought the book to read this controversial poem.

Byron dedicated *The Corsair* to his friend, Irish poet Thomas Moore (1779–1852). In the dedication, Byron announced that this would be the last poem he would write for many years. So crowds flocked to buy what they thought would be his final work. *The Corsair* sold so briskly, the publisher had to reprint it eight times within the first year. The ninth edition of three thousand copies came out in early 1815. Although Byron had claimed it would be his last book, he wrote a sequel called *Lara*, also starring a pirate, that was released in August 1814. In addition to inspiring other writers as well as artists, such as painter Eugène Delacroix (1798–1863), Byron's work so appealed to the people that he became the most popular poet of his lifetime.

Did you know ...

- No poet was as popular during his or her own lifetime as Byron was during his. Many poets only become famous after their deaths, but Byron was not only well known during his life but sold many books, something many poets never did, especially while they were alive.
- In Byron's day women were thought of as the weaker sex, but in *The Corsair* the Turkish slave woman Gulnare performs the daring deed of killing the pasha. However, Byron does not completely depart from the usual beliefs of his time, because he writes that after the murder, Gulnare loses her femininity in Conrad's eyes.
- One of the women who had an affair with Byron, Lady Caroline Lamb (1785–1828), called him "mad, bad, and dangerous to know."
- Some people believe Byron had a daughter with his half-sister, Augusta Leigh. The baby was born on April 14, 1814, soon after *The Corsair* was published, and she was named Elizabeth Medora after the pirate's wife, Medora.

Consider the following ...

- Byron often felt like an outcast because society frowned on his morals. What parallels might there be between his life and that of a pirate?
- Most artists at this time painted classical subjects like the myths of ancient Greece and Rome, but Eugène Delacroix chose to illustrate scenes from Bryon's poems. Why do you think the artist Delacroix found Byron's contemporary poems so inspiring?
- Judging by what he wrote in the poem, how likely do you think it was that Byron spent time as a pirate or spent time with one?

For More Information

BOOKS

Byron, Lord George Gordon. *Byron's Letters and Journals*, edited by Leslie A. Marchand. 12 vols. Cambridge, MA: Harvard University Press, 1973–82.

Coleridge, Ernest Hartley. *The Works of Lord Byron*. Volume 3. New York: Charles Scribner's Sons, 1900.

Ford, Talissa. "Byron Under a Black Flag." In *Romantic Border Crossings*, edited by Jeffrey Cass and Larry Peer. Burlington, VT: Ashgate, 2008.

Smiles, Samuel. *A Publisher and His Friends: Memoir and Correspondence of the Late John Murray, with an Account of the Origin and Progress of the House, 1768–1843*. 2 vols. London: Murray, 1891; New York: AMS Press, 1973.

St. Clair, William. "The Impact of Byron's Writings: An Evaluative Approach." In *Byron: Augustan and Romantic*, edited by Andrew Rutherford. New York: St. Martin's, 1990.

PERIODICALS

Albergotti, Dan. "Playing the Audience; or, How Byron and Murray Sold *The Corsair*," *Postscript: The Journal of the Philological Association of the Carolinas* 13, no. 6 (1996): 57–66. Available online at www2.unca.edu/postscript/postscript13/ps13.6.pdf (accessed on January 3, 2011).

Jeffrey, Francis. "Review of *The Bride of Abydos* and *The Corsair*, by Lord Byron," *Edinburgh Review* 23 (April 1814): 198–229.

Mole, Tom. "'Nourished by that Abstinence': Consumption and Control in *The Corsair*," *Romanticism* 12, no. 1 (2006) 26–34. Available online at http://muse.jhu.edu/journals/romanticism/v012/12.1mole.html (accessed on January 3, 2011).

WEB SITES

Elsie, Robert. "1809–1810 Lord Byron: Letters on Albania." *Texts and Documents of Albanian History*. www.albanianhistory.net/texts19/AH1809_1.html (accessed January 3, 2011).

"Episode from *The Corsair* by Lord Byron," *J. Paul Getty Trust*. www.getty.edu/art/gettyguide/artObjectDetails?artobj=112010 (accessed on January 3, 2011).

"Jean Lafitte," *Jean Lafitte National Historical Park and Preserve*. www.nps.gov/jela/upload/Jean%20Lafitte%20pirate%20site%20bulletin.pdf (accessed on January 3, 2011).

Jones, Steven. "'The Corsair,' Lord Byron's Best-Seller." *NPR*. www.npr.org/templates/story/story.php?storyId=4487368 (accessed on January 3, 2011).

"Lord George Gordon Byron." *The Literature Network*. www.online-literature.com/byron/ (accessed on January 3, 2011).

Sevareid, Karen. "Summary of *The Corsair*." *University of Michigan-Dearborn*. www.umd.umich.edu/casl/hum/eng/classes/434/charweb/sevareid2.htm (accessed on January 3, 2011).

12

Treasure Island

Excerpts from *Treasure Island*
  By Robert Louis Stevenson
  Published in 1883

"A lion's nothing alongside of Long John! I seen him grapple [wrestle] four, and knock their heads together—him unarmed."

Treasure Island, a novel by Scottish author Robert Louis Stevenson (1850–1895), is a rollicking adventure of pirates and buried treasure. It has become one of the most influential pieces of pirate literature. This book introduced many of the myths that surrounded pirate lore for centuries to come. Because the golden age of piracy, which began at the end of the seventeenth century and spanned the first three decades of the eighteenth century, was over by the time Stevenson wove his tale, he invented romantic lives for the pirates that were often far from reality. A stirring narrative of pirates paired with striking illustrations conjured up positive images of piracy that still linger in readers' minds today.

Pirate myths exposed

First published under the title *The Sea Cook*, the story of *Treasure Island*, appealed to young and old alike and is behind many of today's well-known myths about pirates. As David Cordingly wrote in *Under the Black Flag: The Romance and the Reality of Life among the Pirates*, "The effect of *Treasure Island* on our perception of pirates cannot be overestimated. Stevenson linked pirates forever with maps, black schooners, tropical islands, and one-legged seamen with parrots on their shoulders. The treasure map with an *X* marking the location of the buried treasure is one of the most familiar pirate props." Stevenson also enshrined the pirate chantey, "Yo-ho-ho and a bottle of rum," and walking the plank. Though

Illustrating Pirates

Stevenson was not alone in creating the pirate myths that sprang up after the publication of *Treasure Island*. The artists who illustrated his works with dramatic scenes of adventure added to the romantic visions many people held of pirates. Theatrically lit figures caught at the height of action wearing swirling capes, boots or buckled shoes, and plumed hats or kerchiefs tied around their heads, brandishing swords and pistols, came to life on the pages of *Treasure Island* and other pirate tales. Art from two of the most famous illustrators of that time, Howard Pyle (1853–1911) and N.C. Wyeth (1882–1945), graced the early editions of Stevenson's swashbuckling tales.

Howard Pyle, born in Wilmington, Delaware, moved to New York City to work in magazine illustration when he was in his twenties and illustrated many classic children's books. Pyle spent summers at the beach with his family, hearing local legends of pirates, which inspired his artwork. He believed in sketching on location, so he even traveled to Jamaica to make his pirate illustrations more authentic. Pyle also wrote many pirate stories to go with his paintings. A prolific illustrator and writer, Pyle created more than thirty-three hundred published illustrations and two hundred texts.

In 1900 Pyle opened an art school and selected only twelve of the hundreds of talented artists who applied for admission. One of those students, N.C. Wyeth, later went on to paint illustrations for *Treasure Island*. Born in Needham, Massachusetts, Wyeth was the first of three generations of great artists, and his body of work included more than three thousand paintings and 112 books.

Wyeth's art is different from his mentor's, but both share the same classic style and striking, realistic compositions paired with emotional complexity and, for their pirate illustrations, a sinister feel. Each chose to depict moments in the story that were not elaborated on in the text, thus adding richness and depth to the story. The two artists' styles differed, though, in that Pyle's finely rendered paintings contained exquisite detail, whereas Wyeth's menacing shadows and moody backgrounds were executed with looser strokes. But both of these painters are responsible for originating many of the visual images people have of pirates.

many of his facts were correct, he invented others, which have nonetheless survived as part of pirate lore.

Pirates fought with swords, pistols, and cannonballs. Many pirates lost limbs during fights or battles. Added to that is the fact that often ships' doctors were not skilled in the fine art of surgery, so limbs were just as likely to be amputated as to be repaired. This meant that one-armed pirates and peg-legged sea robbers were not unusual.

Some pirates did catch parrots, either for pets or to sell, and marooning, or stranding an individual on a deserted island or shore with few provisions, was a common punishment. Walking the plank, though, was not. A few scattered instances of this were reported, but pirates usually preferred to shoot their victims or toss them overboard.

Some of the other famous characteristics of pirates were purely fictional. Stevenson made up the "Yo-ho-ho" song—although pirates did drink quite a bit of rum on sea voyages—and he invented the treasure map with an *X* marking the location of buried treasure. Pirates had short life spans, so most spent their money as soon as they got it, rather than burying it. Nevertheless, Stevenson's portrayal of pirate behavior lives on.

About the author

Born in Scotland, Robert Louis Stevenson lived in Edinburgh for twenty-nine years. Later he often returned to the city, both in person and in his imagination. Many of his stories were set there, and it was in Edinburgh that he experienced his first writing successes. When he was six years old, he won a writing contest his uncle put on. As a teenager, he completed a book that his father published. His first articles were printed by *Edinburgh University Magazine* when he was in his early twenties.

During childhood Stevenson attended various schools and was also tutored, but tuberculosis (a disease that affects the lungs) made him sickly, so he frequently missed school. He went on to study lighthouse engineering and then switched to law, but his first love was always writing. He was unable to make a living from writing, so his father often financially supported him and, later, his family. In 1880 Stevenson married Fanny Osbourne, who had two children from a previous marriage. When *Treasure Island* was published in 1883, it brought him fame and money. Three years later he published two of his other most well known books, *The Strange Case of Dr. Jekyll and Mr. Hyde* and *Kidnapped*.

Stevenson traveled frequently during his lifetime, but in 1887 he left Europe, never to return. After cruises to the Pacific islands, he settled in Samoa, where he died on December 3, 1894, a few weeks after his forty-fourth birthday.

The plot of *Treasure Island*

The story of *Treasure Island* is narrated by the character of young Jim Hawkins, who helps his parents run the Admiral Benbow Inn in England. After Jim discovers a treasure map in a dead lodger's sea chest, he gathers

Robert Louis Stevenson, author of Treasure Island.
© LEBRECHT MUSIC AND ARTS PHOTO LIBRARY/ALAMY.

an unlikely crew and sets off to find it. Most of the crew is hired by a one-legged pirate, Long John Silver, who serves as a cook. Along the way, the crew plans a mutiny (open rebellion against the ship's officers), and Jim overhears these plans and reports them to the captain.

When the ships lands on Treasure Island, Jim hides from the pirates in the forest, but sees Long John Silver kill a man who refuses to join his group. Later Jim meets Ben Gunn, one of the pirates that originally buried the treasure. Gunn, marooned on the island, has already dug up the treasure and hidden it elsewhere, but he offers to share it if Jim will let him sail back with them.

Meanwhile, the captain has taken his faithful crew members to a fort on the island, but a fight soon breaks out between the ship's officers and the mutineers. Jim helps the officers defend the fort. He also sneaks away and takes back the ship that two of the pirates have taken over. But when he helps Israel Hands, who is wounded, Hands throws a knife that pins Jim's shoulder to the mast. Jim then shoots and kills him.

By the time Jim returns to the fort, his friends have been captured. After being taken hostage by the pirates, Jim accompanies them as they search for the treasure. When they cannot locate it, the pirates turn on Silver. Several honest crew members then ambush them, killing two of the pirates and capturing Silver. Then Jim and his loyal crew load the treasure onto the ship. They plan to take Silver back to England for trial, but when they stop at a port for supplies, Silver escapes with one of the money bags, and that is the last they see of him.

Things to remember while reading the excerpts from *Treasure Island*:

- The first excerpt is from the tenth chapter of the book, titled "The Voyage." This section describes Long John Silver, who is also known by the nickname "Barbecue."
- Long John Silver named his parrot after Captain Flint, who buried his treasure on an island, then killed all six of the crew members who had assisted him.
- The second excerpt is from the eleventh chapter, "What I Heard in the Apple Barrel." In this chapter Jim Hawkins overhears plans for mutiny while hiding inside an apple barrel. A much-disliked crew member has disappeared overboard (no mention is made of whether he was swept overboard in a storm or was pushed), and the crew must decide who to promote in his place. This discussion sparks the conversation about mutiny.
- Early in the story, Jim is warned by Billy Bones, the lodger from whom he took the map, about a dangerous one-legged pirate. That pirate turns out to be Long John Silver, the leader of this mutinous group.

Long John Silver. © LEBRECHT MUSIC AND ARTS PHOTO LIBRARY/ALAMY.

- The ship is captained by Alexander Smollett. One of the crew, Israel Hands, dislikes Smollett and is anxious to start the mutiny, but Silver urges the men to be cautious and wait for the right moment.

Treasure Island

The Voyage

... And so the mention of his name leads me on to speak of our ship's cook, **Barbecue**, as the men called him.

Aboard ship he carried his crutch by a **lanyard** round his neck, to have both hands as free as possible. It was something to see him wedge the foot of the crutch against a **bulkhead**, and, propped against it, yielding to every movement of the ship, get on with his cooking like someone safe ashore. Still more strange was it to see him in the heaviest of weather cross the deck. He had a line or two rigged up to help him across the widest spaces—Long John's earrings, they were called; and he would **hand himself** from one place to another, now using the crutch, now trailing it alongside by the lanyard, as quickly as another man could walk. Yet some of the men who had sailed with him before expressed their pity to see him so reduced.

"He's no common man, Barbecue," said the coxswain to me. "He had good schooling in his young days, and can speak like a book when so minded; and brave—a lion's nothing alongside of Long John! I seen him **grapple** four, and knock their heads together—him unarmed."

All the crew respected and even obeyed him. He had a way of talking to each, and doing everybody some particular service. To me he was unweariedly kind; and always glad to see me in the **galley**, which he kept as clean as a new pin; the dishes hanging up **burnished**, and his parrot in a cage in one corner.

"Come away, Hawkins," he would say; "come and have a **yarn** with John. Nobody more welcome than yourself, my son. Sit you down and hear the news. Here's Cap'n Flint—I calls my parrot Cap'n Flint, after the famous buccaneer—here's Cap'n Flint predicting success to our v'yage. Wasn't you, cap'n?"

And the parrot would say, with great rapidity, "**Pieces of eight**! pieces of eight! pieces of eight!" till you wondered that it was not out of breath, or till John threw his handkerchief over the cage. ...

What I Heard in the Apple Barrel

[Long John Silver is the speaker] "Here it is about gentlemen of fortune. They lives rough, and they risk swinging [hanging], but they eat and drink like fighting-cocks, and when a cruise is done, why, it's hundreds of **pounds** instead of hundreds of **farthings** in their pockets. Now, the most

Barbecue: A nickname for Long John Silver.

Lanyard: Cord, strap, or piece of rope.

Bulkhead: A wall on a ship.

Hand himself: Pull himself along using the ropes.

Grapple: Wrestle.

Galley: The area of a ship where food is prepared.

Burnished: Polished and shiny.

Yarn: Story.

Pieces of eight: Spanish silver dollar coins.

Pound: The British unit of currency; one pound is equal to 100 pence, or pennies.

Farthing: A British coin worth one-quarter of a penny.

TREASURE ISLAND.

BY

ROBERT LOUIS STEVENSON.

Illustrated Edition.

TWENTY-FIRST THOUSAND.

CASSELL & COMPANY, LIMITED:

LONDON, PARIS, NEW YORK & MELBOURNE.

1886.

[ALL RIGHTS RESERVED.]

The title page of the 1886 edition of Treasure Island. © WORLD HISTORY ARCHIVE/ ALAMY.

goes for rum and a good **fling**, and to sea again in their shirts. But that's not the course I lay. I puts it all away, some here, some there, and none too much anywheres, by reason of suspicion. I'm fifty, mark you; once back from this cruise, I set up gentleman in earnest. Time enough, too, says you. Ah, but I've lived easy in the meantime; never denied myself o' nothing heart desires, and slep' soft and ate dainty all my days, but when at sea. And how did I begin? Before the mast, like you!" . . .

Fling: Time with a prostitute.

"Gentlemen of fortune . . . usually trusts little among themselves, and right they are, you may **lay to** it. But I have a way with me, I have. When a mate brings a **slip on his cable**—one as knows me, I mean—it won't be in the same world with old John. There was some that was feared [afraid] of Pew, and some that was feared of Flint; but Flint his own self was feared of me. Feared he was, and proud. They was the roughest crew afloat, was Flint's; the devil himself would have been feared to go to sea with them. Well, now, I tell you, I'm not a boasting man, and you seen yourself how easy I keep company; but when I was **quartermaster**, *lambs* wasn't the word for Flint's old buccaneers. Ah, you may be sure of yourself in old John's ship."

"Well, I tell you now," replied the lad, "I didn't half a quarter like the job till I had this talk with you, John; but there's my hand on it now."

"And a brave lad you were, and smart, too," answered Silver, shaking hands so heartily that all the barrel shook, "and a finer figure head for a gentleman of fortune I never clapped my eyes on."

By this time I had begun to understand the meaning of their terms. By a "gentleman of fortune" they plainly meant neither more nor less than a common pirate, and the little scene that I had overheard was the last act in the corruption of one of the honest **hands**—perhaps of the last one left aboard. But on this point I was soon to be relieved, for Silver giving a little whistle, a third man strolled up and sat down by the party [group].

"Dick's square," said Silver.

"Oh, I know'd Dick was square," returned the voice of the **coxswain**, Israel Hands. "He's no fool, is Dick." And he turned his **quid** and spat. "But, look here," he went on, "here's what I want to know, Barbecue: how long are we a-going to stand off and on like a blessed **bumboat**? I've had a'most enough o' Cap'n Smollett; he's **hazed** me long enough, by thunder! I want to go into that cabin, I do. I want their pickles and wines, and that."

"Israel," said Silver, "your head ain't much account, nor ever was. But you're able to hear, I reckon; leastways, your ears is big enough. Now, here's what I say: you'll **berth forward**, and you'll live hard, and you'll speak soft, and you'll keep sober, till I give the word; and you may lay to that, my son."

"Well, I don't say no, do I?" growled the coxswain. "What I say is, when? That's what I say."

"When! by the powers!" cried Silver. "Well, now, if you want to know, I'll tell you when. The last moment I can manage; and that's when. Here's a first-rate seaman, Cap'n Smollett, sails the blessed ship for us. Here's this squire and doctor with a map and such—I don't know where it is, do I? No more do you, says you. Well, then, I mean this squire and doctor shall find the stuff, and help us to get it aboard, **by the powers**. Then we'll see. If I was sure

Lay to: Believe.

Slip on his cable: Wrong or tricky action.

Quartermaster: The officer in charge of provisions and other supplies.

Hand: Deckhand; a member of the crew who performs manual labor.

Coxswain: The crewman in charge of navigation and steering.

Quid: A wad, most likely of chewing tobacco.

Bumboat: A small boat that ferries supplies back and forth to a larger ship.

Hazed: Persecuted or harassed, often by assigning difficult, meaningless, or humiliating jobs.

Berth forward: Sleep in the front of the ship, where the common sailors berthed.

By the powers: A mild curse similar to "By God!"

of you all, sons of double Dutchmen, I'd have Cap'n Smollett navigate us half-way back again before I struck.''

''Why, we're all seamen aboard here, I should think,'' said the lad Dick.

''We're all **forecastle hands**, you mean,'' snapped Silver. ''We can steer a course, but who's to set one? That's what all you gentlemen split [disagree] on, first and last. If I had my way, I'd have Cap'n Smollett work us back into the trades [tradewinds] at least; then we'd have no blessed miscalculations and a spoonful of water a day. But I know the sort you are. I'll finish with 'em at the island, as soon's the **blunt**'s on board, and a pity it is. But you're never happy till you're drunk. Split my sides, I've a sick heart to sail with the likes of you!''

''Easy all, Long John,'' cried Israel. ''Who's a-crossin' of you?''

''Why, how many tall ships, think ye, now, have I seen laid aboard? And how many brisk lads drying in the sun at **Execution Dock**?'' cried Silver, ''And all for this same hurry and hurry and hurry. You hear me? I seen a thing or two at sea, I have. If you would on'y [only] lay your course, and a p'int [point] to windward, you would ride in carriages, you would. But not you! I know you. You'll have your mouthful of rum to-morrow, and go hang.''

''Everybody know'd you was a kind of a **chapling**, John; but there's others as could hand and steer as well as you,'' said Israel. ''They liked a bit o' fun, they did. They wasn't so high and dry, nohow, but took their fling, like jolly companions every one.''

''So?'' says Silver. ''Well, and where are they now? Pew was that sort, and he died a beggar-man. Flint was, and he died of rum at Savannah. Ah, they was a sweet crew, they was! on'y, where are they?''

''But,'' asked Dick, ''when we do **lay 'em athwart**, what are we to do with 'em, anyhow?''

''There's the man for me!'' cried the cook, admiringly. ''That's what I call business. Well, what would you think? Put 'em ashore like **maroons**? That would have been England's way. Or cut 'em down like that much pork? That would have been Flint's, or Billy Bones's.''

''Billy was the man for that,'' said Israel. '''Dead men don't bite,' says he. Well, he's dead now hisself; he knows the long and short on it now; and if ever a rough hand come to port, it was Billy.''

''Right you are,'' said Silver, ''rough and ready. But mark you here, I'm an easy man—I'm quite the gentleman, says you; but this time it's serious. Dooty [Duty] is dooty, mates. I give my vote—death. When I'm in **Parlment**, and riding in my coach, I don't want none of these sea-lawyers in the cabin a-coming home, unlooked for, like the devil at prayers. Wait is what I say; but when the time comes, why let her rip!''

Forecastle hands: Ordinary sailors rather than officers. The forecastle is the front of a ship's upper deck where the sailors' living quarters are.

Blunt: Money.

Execution Dock: The place in London where pirates were hanged; their bodies were often displayed to discourage others from turning to piracy.

Chapling: Chaplain; a clergyman assigned to minister to the crew.

Lay 'em athwart: Oppose them.

Maroons: Sailors abandoned on deserted islands.

Parlment: Parliament; Britain's legislature.

Jim Hawkins hides in an apple barrel while Long John Silver and other crew members plan a mutiny. © LEBRECHT MUSIC AND ARTS PHOTO LIBRARY/ ALAMY.

• • •

What happened next ...

Desire for the map, the symbol that started the whole voyage, and the treasure it represented, sparked greed and resulted in many deaths. Yet, as

All Because of a Map

The inspiration for *Treasure Island* was a map. Who made the map has been the subject of debate. Stevenson's stepson Lloyd Osbourne (1868–1947) claimed he drew the map when he was twelve years old. According to Lloyd, as quoted in the introductory notes to *Treasure Island*, Stevenson came in and started naming places on the map. Lloyd said, "I shall never forget the thrill of Skeleton Island, Spy-Glass Hill, nor the heart-stirring climax of the three red crosses! And the greater climax still when he wrote down the words 'Treasure Island' at the top right-hand corner!" Stevenson told Lloyd about buried treasure and a man marooned on an island, and the boy begged for a story about it. Stevenson obliged, writing fifteen chapters, one each day from late August into September 1881. He finished the book later in the year and published it as a serial in the magazine *Young Folks*, using the pen name Captain George North.

According to Stevenson in his essay, "My First Book: 'Treasure Island,'" however, he and Lloyd had been painting together, when "I made the map of an island. . . . The shape of the map took my fancy beyond expression; it contained harbours that pleased me like sonnets."

No matter who drew the map, it sparked a pirate story that became a classic. Stevenson continued, "As I paused upon my map of Treasure Island, the future characters of the book began to appear there visibly among the imaginary woods; and their brown faces and bright weapons peeped out upon me from unexpected quarters, as they passed to and fro, fighting and hunting treasure," Stevenson recalled. Unfortunately, the map itself has been lost. It was sent to the book publisher, but never arrived.

the pirates discovered, it was a worthless piece of paper, because the gold had already been dug up. Gunn, who had located the treasure, had no use for it while he was on the island. Unless he found someone to rescue him and take him back to a society that valued gold, the coins were worthless.

Once he returned to England, Jim discovered that the treasure held no appeal for him. In fact, the treasure was responsible for his nightmares: "Oxen and wain-ropes would not bring me back again to that accursed island; and the worst dreams that ever I have are when I hear the surf booming about its coasts, or start upright in bed, with the sharp voice of Captain Flint still ringing in my ears: 'Pieces of eight! pieces of eight!'"

Did you know . . .

- Six of the ten best-selling books in the United States between 1875 and 1895 were children's books, and two of them were Stevenson's: *Treasure Island* and *A Child's Garden of Verses*.
- In addition to his children's books, Stevenson was also known for his travel articles and books.
- After he started *Treasure Island*, Stevenson wrote to his friend, poet W.E. Henley (1849–1903), that he thought his project would be a moneymaker, but he had one problem, as quoted by editor Emma Letley in the introduction to the 1985 edition of *Treasure Island*: "If this don't fetch the kids, why, they have gone rotten since my day. . . . Two chapters are written, and have been tried on Lloyd [his twelve-year-old stepson] with great success; the trouble is to work it off without oaths

[profanity]. Buccaneers without oaths [are like] bricks without straw."

- In Scottish author J.M. Barrie's (1860–1937) play *Peter Pan* (1911), it says the only person the old Sea-Cook (a nickname for Long John Silver) was afraid of was Captain Hook. It also mentions Captain Flint and his ship, the *Walrus*. (For more information see **Peter Pan.**)
- Long John Silver was modeled after Stevenson's friend W.E. Henley, who had his leg amputated due to tuberculosis of the bone.
- Stevenson mentions five actual pirates in the book: Blackbeard (c. 1680–1718), Howell Davis (c. 1690–1718), William Kidd (c. 1645–1701), Edward England (d. 1720), and Bartholomew Roberts (1682–1722).

Consider the following ...

- Stevenson selected young Jim Hawkins as the first-person narrator for the story. What do you think his reasons are for this choice?
- Marooning was a common punishment for sailors who mutinied. They were left on a deserted island with a little water, a weapon, and some ammunition. Ben Gunn had been marooned on Treasure Island for three years. How likely would he have been to survive if this were real life rather than fiction?
- Why do you think the title of this story was changed from *The Sea-Cook* to *Treasure Island*? Was it a wise choice? Why or why not?

For More Information

BOOKS

Balfour, Graham. *The Life of Robert Louis Stevenson*. Volume 1. New York: Charles Scribner's Sons, 1901.

Berlatsky, Noah, ed. "Introduction to Piracy on the High Seas." In *At Issue: Piracy on the High Seas*. Detroit: Greenhaven Press, 2010.

Cordingly, David. *Under the Black Flag: The Romance and the Reality of Life among the Pirates*. Westminster, MD: Random House, 1996.

Furnas, J.C. *Voyage to Windward: The Life of Robert Louis Stevenson*. New York: Sloane, 1951.

Jolly, Roslyn. *Robert Louis Stevenson in the Pacific: Travel, Empire, and the Author's Profession*. Burlington, VT: Ashgate Publishing, 2009.

Kellman, Steven, ed. "Stevenson, Robert Louis." In *Magill's Survey of World Literature*. Vol. 6. Pasadena, CA: Salem Press, 2009.

Letley, Emma, ed. "Introduction." In *Treasure Island* by Robert Louis Stevenson. Oxford World Classics, 1985, p. vii.

Stevenson, Robert Louis. "My First Book: 'Treasure Island.'" In *Essays in the Art of Writing*. 1905. First published in *Idler* (August 1894). Available online at http://ebooks.adelaide.edu.au/s/stevenson/robert_louis/s848aw/part5.html (accessed on January 3, 2011).

Terry, R.C., ed. *Robert Louis Stevenson: Interviews and Recollections*. Iowa City: University of Iowa Press, 1996.

PERIODICALS

Byrd, Max. "This Is Not a Map," *The Wilson Quarterly* 33, no. 3 (Summer 2009): 26–32.

Hayes, Timothy S. "Colonialism in R.L. Stevenson's South Seas Fiction: 'Child's Play' in the Pacific," *English Literature in Transition 1880–1920* 52, no. 2 (Spring 2009): 160–68.

WEB SITES

"Robert Louis Stevenson." *The Literature Network*. www.online-literature.com/stevenson/ (accessed on January 3, 2011).

Robert Louis Stevenson. www.robert-louis-stevenson.org/ (accessed on January 3, 2011).

Scott, Patrick, Roger Mortimer, and Bruce Bowlin. "Robert Louis Stevenson, 1850–1894." *University of South Carolina*. www.sc.edu/library/spcoll/britlit/rls/rls.html (accessed on January 3, 2011).

13

Peter Pan

Excerpt from *Peter Pan, or The Boy Who Would Not Grow Up*
  By J.M. Barrie
  Originally published in 1928
  Reprinted by Charles Scribner's Books, 1928, 1956

> "Most of all I want their captain, Peter Pan. 'Twas he cut off my arm. I have waited long to shake his hand with this [hook]. . . . Oh, I'll tear him!"

Two decades after Robert Louis Stevenson (1850–1895) published *Treasure Island*, another author began a pirate tale that was also destined to become a classic. (For more information see **Treasure Island**.) Scottish author J.M. Barrie (1860–1937) plotted out the tale of a group of children, who with the help of some magic, defeated a band of pirates. The leader of the young fighters, Peter Pan, became the hero of a play, several novels, and numerous films. Many of *Treasure Island*'s imaginary details about pirates found their way into Barrie's play *Peter Pan, or The Boy Who Would Not Grow Up* and later into his novels, establishing pirate lore that would last into the next century.

Genesis of the story

Peter Pan was first mentioned in five chapters of a novel Barrie wrote for adults, *The Little White Bird* (1902). Then from 1903 to 1904, Barrie worked on a play starring Peter Pan. He later indicated in the dedication to the novel *Peter Pan* (1911) that he did not really remember writing the story and credits five young boys with being his inspiration: "I made Peter by rubbing the five of you violently together, as savages with two sticks produce a flame. Peter Pan is the spark I got from you." The boys were the children of his friends, Sylvia and Arthur Llewellyn Davies.

Barrie and his wife, Mary, had no children of their own, and he doted on the Davies boys. They often spent the summers at Black Lake Cottage,

Who Was Captain Hook?

Many pirates sailed the high seas, so Captain Hook could have been based on any of them. He was alleged to be Blackbeard's boatswain (the officer in charge of the sails and rigging, as well as supervision of the deck crew) and the only man Long John Silver ever feared. Blackbeard (Edward Teach; c. 1680–1718) was an actual pirate with a reputation for cruelty. Long John Silver was fiction, invented by Robert Louis Stevenson in *Treasure Island*.

Some scholars think Hook resembles Christopher Newport (1561–1617), the English captain of the *Susan Constant*, the ship that carried settlers to Jamestown in 1607. Newport was noted for his bravery in attacking more Spanish ships and settlements than any other privateer (private ship commissioned by a state or government to attack the merchant ships of an enemy nation) who sailed for Queen Elizabeth I of England (1533–1603). He, too, had a metal hook for a hand. Another similarity is that he brought two baby crocodiles back from his travels for King James I (1566–1625). This might have given Barrie his idea for the crocodile who swallowed Hook's hand.

Other people point to British explorer Captain James Cook (1728–1779), whose name is similar to Captain James Hook. Cook, an eighteenth-century explorer who sailed around the world twice, claimed Australia and mapped parts of New Zealand. He was killed by Hawaiian natives, who may have been the inspiration for the Lost Boys in *Peter Pan*.

Yet Hook's elegant clothes and manners bring to mind the Welsh pirate Bartholomew Roberts (1682–1722), who reluctantly became a pirate after his ship was captured in 1719. In just three years Roberts, also known as Black Bart, captured more prizes than any other pirate during the golden age of piracy, which began at the end of the seventeenth century and spanned the first three decades of the eighteenth century. Yet, Roberts was known for his gentlemanly ways and educated speech, traits Hook seems to share.

In a speech Barrie gave called "Captain Hook at Eton," he indicated that Hook had attended the prestigious boys' school, loved poetry, and was good at sports and schoolwork. But in Chapter 14 of the novel *Peter Pan*, Barrie declined to say who had inspired the infamous captain because "to reveal who he really was would even at this date set the country in a blaze."

the Barries' country house, where they acted out stories that they made up. In 1901, Barrie even chronicled their make-believe with a photo book titled *The Boy Castaways of Black Lake Island*. He made only two copies of this book, which describes the boys being shipwrecked on an island, where they met pirates and wild animals. This sparked the idea for Barrie's play *Peter Pan*. At first Peter Pan was the villain in the tales, but Barrie added some acts so the scenery could be changed. The new villain was a pirate named Captain Hook. The idea for making him a one-armed character came straight out of Barrie's own childhood in Scotland, where the postman, called Hookie, had a hook for his right hand.

Peter Pan and the Darling children flying through London on their way to Never Land in the 1953 Disney animated film Peter Pan.
© WALT DISNEY PICTURES/COURTESY EVERETT COLLECTION.

Peter Pan onstage

Peter Pan was first performed at the Duke of York's Theatre in London, England, on December 27, 1904, and ran for 145 performances. In 1905 the play first appeared on Broadway in New York City. For half a century, the play was put on every year in London at Christmas time. Later it was adapted as a pantomime, or a traditional Christmas entertainment, that is still staged across the United Kingdom in December and early January.

To allow the children to fly, George Kirby, a stage carpenter, developed a pendulum system that lifted them into the air. The actors wore a special leather garment around their chests that attached to wires above the stage. An actress played the role of Peter Pan, a tradition that continued unbroken for almost fifty years. Nana, the Newfoundland dog who serves as the children's nanny, was played by an actor in costume. The children's father, Mr. Darling, played the role of Captain Hook, and the maid, Liza, doubled as the Indian princess, Tiger Lily. Originally, Barrie had planned to have Mrs. Darling play Captain Hook, but Gerald du Maurier (1873–1934), the actor playing Mr. Darling convinced Barrie to give him the part. The fairy Tinker Bell was a beam of light from offstage.

In 1908 Barrie wrote a new scene, "When Wendy Grew Up: An Afterthought," which is sometimes added to the play. This scene became the final chapter when Barrie's popular story of Peter Pan was published in 1911 as the novel *Peter and Wendy* (later published as *Peter Pan and Wendy*). *Peter Pan* moved to the silent screen in 1925. The script of the play was published in 1928, and the following year Barrie gave the copyright to a London children's hospital, Great Ormond Street Hospital. The hospital received all of the royalties (fees paid to rights holders for the use of their work) whenever the play was produced. After his death several adaptations of *Peter Pan* were released, including a 1953 animated Disney film, several stage musicals, the movies *Hook* (1991) and *Peter Pan* (2003), and a novel sequel *Peter Pan in Scarlet* (2006) by Geraldine McCaughrean (1951–). The authors of many other books and movies were also inspired by Barrie's characters, particularly Peter, who never wants to grow up.

The life of J.M. Barrie

The ninth of ten children, James Matthew Barrie was born on May 9, 1860, at Kirriemuir, Forfarshire, Scotland. When he was six years old, an older brother died in a skating accident. Overwhelmed by grief, his mother closed herself off from her children. James's loneliness was compounded when he did not grow very tall. He did not reach five feet, and often felt isolated from his schoolmates.

After graduating from Edinburgh University, he became a journalist, but soon began publishing stories, plays, and novels for adults. In 1894 he married actress Mary Ansell and gave her a St. Bernard puppy named Porthos. They also owned a Newfoundland named Luath, which would later inspire the character Nana in *Peter Pan*. When Barrie was walking the dogs in the park one day, he met the three oldest Davies boys.

Later he met their parents at a dinner party and soon began spending a great deal of time with the family. The family soon grew to include five boys. Barrie enjoyed making up stories and plays with them. The boys

J.M. Barrie, author of Peter Pan. © LEBRECHT MUSIC AND ARTS PHOTO LIBRARY/ ALAMY.

were orphaned in 1910 after the death of the mother. (Their father had died three years earlier.). Barrie, whose wife, Mary, had left him by then, adopted the five boys and raised them.

In 1913 Barrie was knighted and became rector of St. Andrews University. (A knight is a man granted a rank of honor by the monarch for his personal merit or service to the country.) In 1922 he received the Order of Merit. When he died on June 19, 1937, he left behind a great legacy of literature, one of the most beloved of which was *Peter Pan.*

The story of *Peter Pan*

Peter Pan begins in the Bloomsbury home of the Darling family. Peter Pan has been sneaking outside the window to listen to Mrs. Darling tell bedtime stories to her three children, Wendy, Michael, and John. Once, Peter is almost caught, but he escapes, leaving his shadow behind. When he returns with the fairy Tinker Bell to get it, Wendy wakes. After she discovers Peter can fly, she begs him to teach her and her brothers. Then they all fly off with Peter to Never Land.

Never Land is a place where children never grow older. Wendy takes over mothering the Lost Boys who live there. They have many adventures with mermaids, Indians, fairies, and pirates. The leader of the pirates, Captain Hook, has one goal in mind. He is determined to get back at Peter for chopping off his hand. As he and his crew search for Peter, the Lost Boys hide, except for Nibs, who is spotted by Hook.

Things to remember while reading the excerpt from *Peter Pan, or The Boy Who Would Not Grow Up*:

- This excerpt is from the play, so the author has included stage directions for the actors in italics. Setting and information about characters are also in italics. The director and the cast read these sections to find out how to stage the play. They learn about the characters' emotions, background, motivation, and physical appearance. The introductions also give stage managers a general idea of the props they need.

- Never Land is an island Barrie created where children never grow older. The children flew there by using pixie dust or thinking happy thoughts. On this island they had many adventures, including fighting pirates.

- Barrie notes that Captain Hook dresses like the dandies (men who wore the latest fashions) during the reign of King Charles II (1630–1685; ruled 1660–85) and he looks like the "ill-fated Stuarts." Charles II was one of the Stuarts, a succession of kings

Dustin Hoffman as Captain Hook in the 1991 film Hook. *Captain Hook is portrayed as a dandy from the time of the Stuarts.*
© TRISTAR PICTURES/COURTESY EVERETT COLLECTION.

and queens who ruled England and Scotland from 1603 until 1714. Many were executed, exiled, driven from the throne, or simply disliked. Charles II's father, Charles I (1600–1649), was executed, and Charles II spent most of his life in exile. But during Charles II's reign, dandies spent a lot of time and money on looking fashionable, which is what Captain Hook was known for. Some also say Hook resembles the real-life Welsh pirate Bartholomew Roberts, who dressed in fine clothes before battle. Roberts preferred silks, velvet, and satin clothes with ruffled shirts, sashes, buckled shoes, and a plumed hat. When Captain Hook is pictured, he wears similar clothing.

• Tiger Lily was the princess of a tribe of Indians who were fighting the pirates for control of Never Land. Many people object to

Barrie's naming the tribe Piccaninny (a derogatory or degrading term for small African American children), calling the tribe "red-skins," and portraying them as savages. But at the time Barrie wrote *Peter Pan* many of his readers would have shared his views. These stereotypes gradually changed over time.

- Smee called his cutlass (a short, heavy, single-edged sword) "Johnny Corkscrew," because after he stuck it into a victim, he wiggled or twisted it around in the wound. He wants go after Nibs and kill him with his cutlass.

- Hook orders his men to search for the Lost Boys. His order is communicated by the boatswain's call, or boatswain's pipe. This is a long pipe with a hole in it. The boatswain (the officer in charge of the sails and rigging, as well as supervision of the deck crew) blew into it and could vary the pitch by opening and closing a hand over the hole, thus signaling the crew what to do. The piercing call of the boatswain's pipe could be heard over the noise of the crew or when storms drowned out shouted commands. Pirates and sailors never called it a whistle, though.

• • •

Peter Pan, or The Boy Who Would Not Grow Up

Act II

. . . A sound is heard that sends them [the Lost Boys] scurrying down their holes: in a second of time the scene is **bereft** *of human life. What they have heard from near-by is a verse of the dreadful song with which on the Never Land the pirates stealthily trumpet their approach—*

> Yo ho, yo ho, the pirate life,
> The flag of skull and bones,
> A merry hour, a hempen rope,
> And hey for **Davy Jones**!

Bereft: Lacking.

Davy Jones: The bottom of a sea; the resting place of drowned sailors.

Execution Dock: The place in London where pirates were hanged; their bodies were often displayed to discourage others from turning to piracy.

Gao: A city in North Africa.

The pirates appear upon the frozen river dragging a raft, on which reclines among cushions that dark and fearful man, CAPTAIN JAS HOOK. *A more villainous-looking brotherhood of men never hung in a row on* **Execution dock**. *Here, his great arms bare, pieces of eight [coins] in his ears as ornaments, is the handsome* CEECO, *who cut his name on the back of the governor of the prison at* **Gao**. *Heavier in the pull is the gigantic black who has had many names since the first one terrified dusky children on the banks of the Guidjo-mo.* BILL JUKES *comes next, every inch of him tattooed, the same* JUKES *who got six dozen on the Walrus from* FLINT. *Following* these are COOKSON, *said to be* BLACK MURPHY'S *brother (but this was never proved); and* GENTLEMAN STARKEY, *once an usher in a school; and* SKYLIGHTS *(Morgan's Skylights); and* NOODLER, *whose hands are fixed on backwards; and the spectacled* **boatswain**, SMEE, *the only* **Nonconformist** *in* HOOK'S *crew; and other ruffians long known and feared on the* **Spanish main**.

Cruelest jewel in that dark setting is HOOK *himself,* **cadaverous** *and* **blackavised**, *his hair dressed in long curls which look like black candles about to melt, his eyes blue as the forget-me-not [flower] and of a profound* **insensibility**, *save when he* **claws**, *at which time a red spot appears in them. He has an iron hook instead of a right hand, and it is with this he claws. He is never more sinister than when he is most polite, and the elegance of his* **diction**, *the distinction of his* **demeanour**, *show him one of a different class from his crew, a solitary among uncultured companions. This courtliness impresses even his victims on the high seas, who note that he always says 'Sorry' when prodding them along the plank. A man of* **indomitable** *courage, the only thing at which he flinches is the sight of his own blood, which is thick and of an unusual colour. At his public school they said of him that he 'bled yellow.' In dress he apes [imitates] the* **dandiacal** *associated with Charles II, having heard it said in an earlier period of his career that he bore a strange resemblance to the ill-fated Stuarts. A holder of his own* **contrivance** *is in his mouth enabling him to smoke two cigars at once. Those, however, who have seen him in the flesh, which is an inadequate term for his* **earthly tenement**, *agree that the* **grimmest** *part of him is his iron claw. They continue their distasteful singing as they disembark—*

> Avast, belay, yo ho, heave to,
> A-pirating we go,
> And if we're parted by a shot
> We're sure to meet below!

NIBS, *the only one of the boys who has not sought safety in his tree, is seen for a moment near the lagoon, and* STARKEY'S *pistol is at once up-raised. The captain twists his hook in him.*

STARKEY (*abject* [sad]). Captain, let go!

HOOK. Put back that pistol, first.

STARKEY. 'Twas one of those boys you hate; I could have shot him dead.

HOOK. Ay, and the sound would have brought Tiger Lily's redskins on us. Do you want to lose your scalp?

SMEE (*wriggling his cutlass pleasantly*). That is true. Shall I after him, Captain, and tickle him with Johnny Corkscrew? Johnny is a silent fellow.

HOOK. Not now. He is only one, and I want to **mischief** all the seven. Scatter and look for them. (*The boatswain whistles his instructions, and the men disperse on their frightful errand. With none to hear save* SMEE, HOOK *becomes confidential.*) Most of all I want their captain, Peter Pan. 'Twas he cut off my arm. I have waited long

Boatswain: The officer in charge of the sails and rigging, as well as supervision of the deck crew.

Nonconformist: A British citizen who was not a member of the national Anglican Church.

Spanish Main: The Spanish colonies around the Caribbean Sea and the Gulf of Mexico.

Cadaverous: Looking like a corpse.

Blackavised: Having a dark complexion.

Insensibility: Incapable of feeling; indifferent.

Claws: Attacks, as if with claws.

Diction: Pronunciation and choice of words.

Demeanour: Demeanor; behavior toward others.

Indomitable: Unbeatable.

Dandiacal: Paying excessive attention to elegance and style in clothing.

Contrivance: Making or invention.

Earthly tenement: Earlthly dwelling; the human body.

Grimmest: Most ghastly or sinister.

Mischief: Harm or injure.

to shake his hand with this. (*Luxuriating* [enjoying himself]) Oh, I'll tear him!

SMEE (*always ready for a chat*). Yet I have oft heard you say your hook was worth a **score** of hands, for combing the hair and other homely uses.

HOOK. If I was a mother I would pray to have my children born with this instead of that (*his left arm creeps nervously behind him. He has a galling remembrance*). Smee, Pan flung my arm to a crocodile that happened to be passing by.

SMEE. I have often noticed your strange dread of crocodiles.

HOOK (*pettishly*). Not of crocodiles but of that one crocodile. (*He lays bare a* **lacerated** *heart.*) The brute liked my arm so much, Smee, that he has followed me ever since, from sea to sea, and from land to land, licking his lips for the rest of me. . . .

• • •

What happened next . . .

Hook tries to get his revenge on Peter but is unsuccessful until his men are tying a captive Tiger Lily and her Indians to rocks at the Mermaid Lagoon, where Peter and the Lost Boys were trying to catch a mermaid to show Wendy. By imitating Captain Hook's voice, Peter gets the pirates to free the Indians. But his own life is in jeopardy when Hook shows up, claws Peter with his hook, and strands him on a rock as the tide is rising. Peter assumes he is going to die, but a bird gives him her nest so he can sail home.

As Wendy is telling the Lost Boys a story, she thinks of home and decides to take the Lost Boys back to England with her. But she and the boys are captured by Captain Hook and the pirates, who leave poison for Peter. Tinker Bell drinks the poison to save Peter's life and almost dies. Peter rushes to the ship to save everyone. Along the way he hears the ticking crocodile— the one who ate Hook's hand and swallowed a clock. Peter imitates the ticking sound and frightens Hook, who is deathly afraid of that crocodile.

In the panic that follows Peter sneaks into one of the ship's cabins to get the keys and free the Lost Boys. He lures the pirates into the cabin one by one with a strange noise. Then he frees Wendy, who is tied to the mast and takes her place, wrapping a cloak around himself so Hook will not know. When Hook comes to get Wendy, Peter confronts the pirate, and they battle. Peter is gentlemanly throughout, and even allows Hook to pick up his dropped weapon. In the end Peter kicks Hook off the ship and into the mouth of the waiting crocodile.

Score: Twenty.

Lacerated: Jaggedly torn.

Captain Hook falling overboard, into the mouth of the crocodile. © BLUE LANTERN STUDIO/CORBIS.

Peter takes control of the ship and sails it to London. Wendy decides to stay at home, and her mother agrees to adopt the Lost Boys—all but Peter, who flies back to Never Land so he can remain young forever. He promises to return for Wendy every spring.

The original play ended with Wendy asking Peter not to forget, but the final act that Barrie wrote later and included in the novel had a different ending. When Peter returns for Wendy, she is grown and has a child of her own. Peter's heart is broken, but Wendy's daughter, Jane, agrees to go to Never Land with him. In the novel Jane also grows up, and when Peter returns, it is Jane's daughter, Margaret, who goes with him, a cycle that will continue as long as children are "innocent and heartless."

Did you know . . .

- Captain Hook's first name was James, which was also Barrie's first name.
- Barrie made up the name Wendy. He got the idea from Scottish poet W.E. Henley's (1849–1903) four-year-old daughter Margaret, who could not pronounce her *r*'s, so she called Barrie "fwendy" or "fwendy-wendy."
- Both Barrie and Robert Louis Stevenson were friends with W.E. Henley, which may account for Barrie's mentions of Stevenson's *Treasure Island* characters in *Peter Pan*. Furthermore, Stevenson wrote to American author and critic Henry James (1843–1916) that Barrie, James, and Rudyard Kipling (1865–1936) were his muses, or literary inspiration.
- Barrie originally titled his play *Peter Pan, or The Boy Who Hated Mothers*. The producer, Charles Frohman, suggested he change it.
- The movie *Finding Neverland* (2004) is based on Barrie's relationship with Sylvia Llewellyn Davies and her children, although it differed from the true story in several major ways.

Consider the following . . .

- If you were stage director of *Peter Pan*, what props, costumes, and actors would you use to make the pirates seem real?
- The pirates in *Peter Pan* are imaginary, as is the story of Captain Hook. What things in the story seem as if they could have actually happened, and what could only occur in fiction?
- Why do you think Barrie used fictional characters from *Treasure Island* in his story, and how do you think Robert Louis Stevenson felt about his including them?
- Which of the two endings Barrie created for the play is most effective and why?

For More Information

BOOKS

Birkin, Andrew. *J.M. Barrie and the Lost Boys: The Real Story Behind Peter Pan.* New Haven, CT: Yale University Press, 2005.

Dunbar, Janet. *J.M. Barrie: The Man Behind the Image.* New York: HarperCollins, 1970.

Green, Roger Lancelyn. *Fifty Years of Peter Pan.* London: P. Davies, 1954.

Hanson, Bruce K. *The Peter Pan Chronicles: The Nearly 100-Year History of the "Boy Who Wouldn't Grow Up"*. Secaucus, NJ: Carol Publishing Group, 1993.

PERIODICALS

Evezich, Lois. "How Peter Pan Came to Life More than 100 Years Ago," *Orange County Register* (September 15, 2010). Available online at www.ocregister.com/articles/peter-263860-years-ago.html (accessed on January 3, 2011).

Raw, Laurence. "Second Star to the Right: Peter Pan in the Popular Imagination," *The Journal of Popular Culture* 42, no. 5 (October 2009): 962–64.

Springer, Heather. "Barrie's Peter Pan," *The Explicator* 65, no. 2 (Winter 2007): 96–8.

WEB SITES

Barrie, J.M. "Dedication to Peter Pan." *J.M. Barrie.co.uk*. www.jmbarrie.co.uk/jmb/?mode=peterpandedication (accessed on January 3, 2011).

Ellacott, Nigel. "Peter Pan." *It's Behind You Ltd*. www.its-behind-you.com/storypeterpan.html (accessed on January 3, 2011).

"Peter Pan Copyright." *Great Ormond Street Hospital for Children*. www.gosh.org/about-us/peter-pan/peter-pan-copyright/ (accessed on January 3, 2011).

Merriman, C.D. "James M. Barrie." *The Literature Network*. www.online-literature.com/barrie/ (accessed on January 3, 2011).

Schmidt, Robert. "Tiger Lily in *Peter Pan*: An Allegory of Anglo-Indian Relations." *Blue Corn Comics*. www.bluecorncomics.com/tigerlil.htm (accessed on January 3, 2011).

Ullrich, T. Leigh. "Boatswain's Call Instructions." *Chesapeake Picaroons*. www.chesapeakepicaroons.org/Boatswain_pipe/BoatswainsPipe.html (accessed on January 3, 2011).

14

United Nations Convention on the Law of the Sea

Excerpt from *United Nations Convention on the Law of the Sea*

December 10, 1982

Available online at: www.un.org/Depts/los/convention_agreements/texts/
unclos/unclos_e.pdf

Accessed on January 3, 2011

"On the high seas, or in any other place outside the jurisdiction of any State, every State may seize a pirate ship or aircraft, or a ship or aircraft taken by piracy and under the control of pirates, and arrest the persons and seize the property on board."

During the early centuries BCE, piracy, or robbery at sea, was generally an accepted way of life. Over time that view changed, and pirates became the villains of the sea. Most countries tried, often unsuccessfully, to curb piracy. In time, nations began working together, establishing treaties that set down agreed-upon maritime (sea) practices. In 1982 the United Nations Conference on the Law of the Sea (UNCLOS) collected the regulations from existing treaties relating to the world's oceans into a single law.

Fighting piracy throughout history

International efforts to eradicate piracy have faced many challenges. At the same time that countries were working to end piracy, many governments were outfitting privateers in times of conflict or war. (Privateers are private ships or ship owners commissioned by a state or government to attack the merchant ships of an enemy nation.) These privateers protected their homelands and often served as additions to the country's navy. But the countries whose ships they attacked considered them to be no better than pirates. And when wars ended, privateers often continued to raid vessels, hoping to make their fortunes. Sea robbers reached their peak during the golden age of piracy, which began at the end of the seventeenth century and spanned the first three decades of the eighteenth century. During that time many nations instituted stiff penalties for piracy, and Great Britain issued a declaration that made aiding and abetting pirates a crime. Fearful of prosecution, many people captured and turned pirates in for the rewards.

The 1700s and early 1800s witnessed many wars between nations. Battles occurred between European nations for the control of territory in the New World, and the American colonists fought for independence from Britain in the American Revolution (1775–83). Privateering grew as nations increased their navies with private citizens. After America won its independence, the leaders of the country disbanded the navy. As new battles arose, the country depended on privateers to supplement a new navy. After peace had been restored, many European countries met to sign the 1856 Declaration of Paris, making privateering illegal. The United States refused to sign, because it had such a small navy and needed privateers for defense. Spain also declined to sign. But in 1907 when the countries gathered for the Hague Peace Conference, all the participants, including Spain and the United States, decided that any armed ships, including merchant ships, had to be listed as warships. This made each country responsible for any of its ships that acted in a warlike manner and put an end to privateering. Following World Wars I (1914–18) and II (1939–45), the countries again met to set international maritime policies at the 1958 Geneva Convention on the High Seas in Switzerland, the First United Nations Conference on the Law of the Sea (UNCLOS).

The First and Second UNCLOS

From February 24 to April 27, 1958, eighty-six countries met in Geneva, Switzerland, with the goal of setting new laws for the high seas to curb piracy. They first agreed on a definition of the high seas, which were, according to *Convention on the High Seas 1958*, "all parts of the sea that are not included in the territorial sea or in the internal waters of a State." (Territorial sea, also referred to as territorial waters, are the waters surrounding a nation over which that nation exercises sole authority.) The First UNCLOS also granted the following freedoms of the high seas to all nations:

1. Freedom of navigation;
2. Freedom of fishing;
3. Freedom to lay submarine cables and pipelines;
4. Freedom to fly over the high seas.

The convention gave water access to landlocked countries and decided that each nation would be responsible for setting laws for licensing ships and preventing pollution. They forbade piracy and the transporting of slaves and gave all nations the right to capture and prosecute pirates.

Participating nations had until October 31, 1958, to sign the agreement, which had a clause that stated that after five years any country signing the agreement could request a revision to the terms of the convention.

This convention, however, left one major question unresolved: how far from a country's borders would their water rights extend? These boundaries also affected fishing rights. Twelve miles (19.2 kilometers) was suggested, but failed to get the two-thirds majority vote it needed to pass. This became one of the main items at the Second UNCLOS, again held in Geneva two years later. The participating nations, who met from March 16 to April 26, 1960, proposed limits from 3 to 200 miles (4.8 to 320 kilometers). Without a majority vote, the issue remained unsettled, but the convention went into effect on September 30, 1962.

Third UNCLOS

By the middle of the twentieth century, concerns such as pollution and overfishing emerged, making it imperative that some agreement be reached between countries to preserve ocean life and ensure all nations' rights. In 1945 the United States had been the first to expand its territory to its coastal shelf, and other countries had gradually been doing the same. (The coastal shelf is the part of a continent that is under water and slopes down to the ocean bottom.) Prior to that, most nations had only claimed an area about 3 nautical miles (5.7 kilometers) from their coastlines. (A nautical mile is a unit of distance used for sea navigation. One nautical mile equals 6,080 feet or 1.9 kilometers.) But now some countries wanted areas as large as 200 nautical miles (380 kilometers). Oil exploration and mining that began in the 1960s expanded the territorial waters of many countries. Concerned about conflicting claims on the ocean and the devastation to natural resources and ocean life, Arvid Pardo (1914–1999), Malta's ambassador to the United Nations, in 1967 called on the nations to come together to establish an international policy.

More than 160 countries met from 1973 through 1982 and set policies on the joint use of the ocean. One hundred fifty-eight nations signed the law. The United States signed, but did not ratify, the agreement at that time. Other nations that did not ratify the treaty included North Korea, Iran, and Syria. The law went into effect in 1994.

Things to remember while reading the excerpt from *United Nations Convention on the Law of the Sea*:

- Many of the discussions and articles at this third convention were similar to the ones discussed at the second convention. Some of the areas the convention covered included defining each country's sea territory, giving landlocked countries access to the sea, protecting and preserving the living resources of the ocean, balancing scientific research with nations' territorial rights, and settling disputes peacefully.
- The convention also addressed piracy beginning with Article 100.
- Warships are not subject to the laws or authority of any country except the nation whose flag they fly.
- The continental shelf is the sea bed about 330–660 feet (100–200 meters) in depth that juts out around the edge of each continent before the land drops steeply to the ocean floor.

• • •

United Nations Convention on the Law of the Sea

Part VII

High Seas

Section 1. General Provisions
Article 86
Application of the provisions of this Part
The provisions of this Part apply to all parts of the sea that are not included in the exclusive economic zone, in the territorial sea or in the internal waters of a State, or in the **archipelagic** waters of an archipelagic State. This article does not entail any abridgement of the freedoms enjoyed by all States in the exclusive economic zone in accordance with article 58.
Article 87
Freedom of the high seas

Archipelagic: Belonging to a chain or group of islands.

1. The high seas are open to all States, whether coastal or **land-locked**. Freedom of the high seas is exercised under the conditions laid down by this Convention and by other rules of international law. It comprises, **inter alia**, both for coastal and land-locked States:

a. freedom of navigation;
b. freedom of overflight;
c. freedom to lay submarine cables and pipelines, subject to Part VI;
d. freedom to construct artificial islands and other installations permitted under international law, subject to Part VI;
e. freedom of fishing, subject to the conditions laid down in section 2;
f. freedom of scientific research, subject to Parts VI and XIII.

2. These freedoms shall be exercised by all States with due regard for the interests of other States in their exercise of the freedom of the high seas, and also with due regard for the rights under this Convention with respect to activities in the Area.

Article 88
Reservation of the high seas for peaceful purposes

The high seas shall be reserved for peaceful purposes.

Article 89
Invalidity of claims of **sovereignty** over the high seas

No State may validly **purport** to subject any part of the high seas to its sovereignty.

Article 90
Right of navigation

Every State, whether coastal or land-locked, has the right to sail ships flying its flag on the high seas.

Article 91
Nationality of ships

1. Every State shall fix the conditions for the grant of its nationality to ships, for the registration of ships in its territory, and for the right to fly its flag. Ships have the nationality of the State whose flag they are entitled to fly. There must exist a genuine link between the State and the ship.

2. Every State shall issue to ships to which it has granted the right to fly its flag documents to that effect. . . .

Article 95
Immunity of warships on the high seas

Warships on the high seas have complete immunity from the jurisdiction of any State other than the flag State.

Article 96
Immunity of ships used only on government non-commercial service

Land-locked: Having no borders on an ocean or sea.

Inter alia: Among other things.

Invalidity: Having no legal force; unable to be enforced.

Sovereignty: Authority or control.

Puport: Convey or claim, often falsely.

Ships owned or operated by a State and used only on government non-commercial service shall, on the high seas, have complete immunity from the jurisdiction of any State other than the flag State. . . .

Article 99
Prohibition of the transport of slaves

Every State shall take effective measures to prevent and punish the transport of slaves in ships authorized to fly its flag and to prevent the unlawful use of its flag for that purpose. Any slave taking refuge on board any ship, whatever its flag, shall **ipso facto** be free.

Article 100
Duty to cooperate in the repression of piracy

All States shall cooperate to the fullest possible extent in the repression of piracy on the high seas or in any other place outside the jurisdiction of any State.

Article 101
Definition of piracy

Piracy consists of any of the following acts:

a. any illegal acts of violence or detention, or any act of **depredation**, committed for private ends by the crew or the passengers of a private ship or a private aircraft, and directed:

   i.   on the high seas, against another ship or aircraft, or against persons or property on board such ship or aircraft;
   ii. against a ship, aircraft, persons or property in a place outside the jurisdiction of any State;

b. any act of voluntary participation in the operation of a ship or of an aircraft with knowledge of facts making it a pirate ship or aircraft;

c. any act of **inciting** or of intentionally facilitating an act described in subparagraph (a) or (b).

Article 102
Piracy by a warship, government ship or government aircraft whose crew has **mutinied**

The acts of piracy, as defined in article 101, committed by a warship, government ship or government aircraft whose crew has mutinied and taken control of the ship or aircraft are **assimilated** to acts committed by a private ship or aircraft.

Article 103
Definition of a pirate ship or aircraft

A ship or aircraft is considered a pirate ship or aircraft if it is intended by the persons in dominant control to be used for the purpose of committing one

Ipso facto: By that fact itself.

Depredation: Destructive act of preying upon, such as raiding or plundering.

Inciting: Stirring up.

Mutinied: Risen up against authority; taken over a vessel from its captain or leader.

Assimilated: Made similar to.

of the acts referred to in article 101. The same applies if the ship or aircraft has been used to commit any such act, so long as it remains under the control of the persons guilty of that act.

Article 104
Retention or loss of the nationality of a pirate ship or aircraft

A ship or aircraft may retain its nationality although it has become a pirate ship or aircraft. The retention or loss of nationality is determined by the law of the State from which such nationality was derived.

Article 105
Seizure of a pirate ship or aircraft

On the high seas, or in any other place outside the jurisdiction of any State, every State may seize a pirate ship or aircraft, or a ship or aircraft taken by piracy and under the control of pirates, and arrest the persons and seize the property on board. The courts of the State which carried out the seizure may decide upon the penalties to be imposed, and may also determine the action to be taken with regard to the ships, aircraft or property, subject to the rights of third parties acting in good faith.

Article 106
Liability for seizure without adequate grounds

Where the seizure of a ship or aircraft on suspicion of piracy has been effected without adequate grounds, the State making the seizure shall be liable to the State the nationality of which is possessed by the ship or aircraft for any loss or damage caused by the seizure.

Article 107
Ships and aircraft which are entitled to seize on account of piracy

A seizure on account of piracy may be carried out only by warships or military aircraft, or other ships or aircraft clearly marked and identifiable as being on government service and authorized to that effect. . . .

Article 110
Right of visit

1. Except where acts of interference derive from powers conferred by treaty, a warship which encounters on the high seas a foreign ship, other than a ship entitled to complete immunity in accordance with articles 95 and 96, is not justified in boarding it unless there is reasonable ground for suspecting that:

    a. the ship is engaged in piracy;
    b. the ship is engaged in the slave trade;
    c. the ship is engaged in unauthorized broadcasting and the flag State of the warship has jurisdiction under article 109;
    d. the ship is without nationality; or
    e. though flying a foreign flag or refusing to show its flag, the ship is, in reality, of the same nationality as the warship.

2. In the cases provided for in paragraph 1, the warship may proceed to verify the ship's right to fly its flag. To this end, it may send a boat under the command of an officer to the suspected ship. If suspicion remains after the documents have been checked, it may proceed to a further examination on board the ship, which must be carried out with all possible consideration.

3. If the suspicions prove to be unfounded, and provided that the ship boarded has not committed any act justifying them, it shall be compensated for any loss or damage that may have been sustained.

4. These provisions apply **mutatis mutandis** to military aircraft.

5. These provisions also apply to any other duly authorized ships or aircraft clearly marked and identifiable as being on government service.

Article 111

Right of hot pursuit

1. The hot pursuit of a foreign ship may be undertaken when the competent authorities of the coastal State have good reason to believe that the ship has violated the laws and regulations of that State. Such pursuit must be commenced when the foreign ship or one of its boats is within the internal waters, the archipelagic waters, the territorial sea or the **contiguous** zone of the pursuing State, and may only be continued outside the territorial sea or the contiguous zone if the pursuit has not been interrupted. It is not necessary that, at the time when the foreign ship within the territorial sea or the contiguous zone receives the order to stop, the ship giving the order should likewise be within the territorial sea or the contiguous zone. If the foreign ship is within a contiguous zone, as defined in article 33, the pursuit may only be undertaken if there has been a violation of the rights for the protection of which the zone was established.

2. The right of hot pursuit shall apply *mutatis mutandis* to violations in the exclusive economic zone or on the continental shelf, including safety zones around continental shelf installations, of the laws and regulations of the coastal State applicable in accordance with this Convention to the exclusive economic zone or the continental shelf, including such safety zones.

3. The right of hot pursuit ceases as soon as the ship pursued enters the territorial sea of its own State or of a third State.

4. Hot pursuit is not deemed to have begun unless the pursuing ship has satisfied itself by such practicable means as may be available that the ship pursued or one of its boats or other craft working as a team and using the ship pursued as a mother ship is within the limits of the territorial sea, or, as the case may be, within the contiguous zone or the exclusive economic zone or above the continental shelf. The pursuit may only be commenced after a visual or auditory signal to stop has been given at a distance which enables it to be seen or heard by the foreign ship.

Mutatis mutandis: With all necessary changes having been made.

Contiguous: Touching, connected, or neighboring.

Pirates Through the Ages: Primary Sources

5. The right of hot pursuit may be exercised only by warships or military aircraft, or other ships or aircraft clearly marked and identifiable as being on government service and authorized to that effect.

6. Where hot pursuit is effected by an aircraft:

a.   the provisions of paragraphs 1 to 4 shall apply *mutatis mutandis*;

b.   the aircraft giving the order to stop must itself actively pursue the ship until a ship or another aircraft of the coastal State, summoned by the aircraft, arrives to take over the pursuit, unless the aircraft is itself able to arrest the ship. It does not suffice to justify an arrest outside the territorial sea that the ship was merely sighted by the aircraft as an offender or suspected offender, if it was not both ordered to stop and pursued by the aircraft itself or other aircraft or ships which continue the pursuit without interruption.

7. The release of a ship arrested within the jurisdiction of a State and escorted to a port of that State for the purposes of an inquiry before the competent authorities may not be claimed solely on the ground that the ship, in the course of its voyage, was escorted across a portion of the exclusive economic zone or the high seas, if the circumstances rendered this necessary.

8. Where a ship has been stopped or arrested outside the territorial sea in circumstances which do not justify the exercise of the right of hot pursuit, it shall be compensated for any loss or damage that may have been thereby sustained.

• • •

What happened next ...

UNCLOS made some changes to the laws of the second convention. It gave countries economic rights over a 200-nautical-mile-wide (380-kilometer) zone along their shores. A 12-nautical mile (22.8-kilometer) territorial-sea limit was adopted to protect countries from attack. Before the convention many nations had differing limits, some were as close as 4 miles (6.4 kilometers), others as far as 200 miles (320 kilometers). Countries that did not have large navies preferred to have a wide protected zone around their land, but gradually everyone agreed on this new limit. States were also given an area of 24 nautical miles (45.6 kilometers) for policing the area around their coastlines. This "contiguous zone" allowed the coast guard to arrest smugglers, illegal immigrants, or other lawbreakers within that vicinity.

Along with defining piracy, the document stated that all nations have a duty to help curb piracy on the high seas. The laws gave

U.S. forces capture a suspected Somali pirate ship in the Gulf of Aden. UNCLOS grants member nations the right to seize ships suspected of piracy. AP IMAGES/US NAVY, PETTY OFFICER 1ST CLASS ERIC BEAUREGARD.

member nations the right to seize ships suspected of piracy but at the same time set limits so vessels would not be unlawfully or unfairly captured. If a nation mistakenly takes over a ship, that nation must pay for any losses the takeover causes. Other articles allowed a country to enter another nation's contiguous zone if the former were in continuous hot pursuit of a pirate.

For an act to be declared piracy, however, it must be for "private ends" and be committed outside the jurisdiction, or authority, of a state. Two difficulties arose with this definition. First, by making piracy only for "private ends," it eliminated any acts done for political reasons. Second, with the new definitions of territorial waters, each nation must police the area 12 nautical miles (22.8 kilometers) from its coastline. Thus, prosecuting pirates within that 12-nautical mile radius is left up to the nation that has control over those waters. Because many pirate attacks occur fairly close to shore, this can be a problem in areas where governments do not enforce regulations against piracy.

Another problem is that most of the countries involved in piracy have no interest in signing an international law that curtails their freedom to take ships and prisoners. Thus, piracy continues to be an ongoing problem in several areas of the world.

Did you know ...

- The United States wanted to keep mining rights in international areas of the sea, but the other convention members requested that it reconsider this position. To handle these rights more fairly, the convention formed the International Seabed Authority to regulate mining and deep sea-bed activity.
- The first day, December 10, 1982, 119 countries signed the convention, and it went into force on November 16, 1994. By September 2010, 161 countries had signed.

Consider the following ...

- What might nations do to help curb piracy in countries that have not signed the convention and/or do not have any policies in place for prosecuting pirates?
- When the convention announced the new rules, it mentioned that some countries had signed even though they were not completely satisfied with everything that had been decided. Why do you think the unsatisfied states signed?
- If you were the ruler of a nation, would you have ratified the convention? Why or why not?
- What proposals would you make for the convention to consider the next time it meets?

For More Information

BOOKS

Alexander, Yonah, and Tyler B. Richardson, eds. *Terror on the High Seas: From Piracy to Strategic Challenge.* Santa Barbara, CA: Praeger, 2009.

Guilfoyle, Douglas. *Shipping Interdiction and the Law of the Sea.* New York: Cambridge University Press, 2009.

Klein, Natalie. *Dispute Settlement in the UN Convention on the Law of the Sea.* New York: Cambridge University Press, 2005.

PERIODICALS

Birnie, P.W. "Piracy: Past, Present, and Future," *Marine Policy* 11, no. 3 (July 1987): 163–83.

Borgeson, Scott. *The National Interest and the Law of the Sea.* Council on Foreign Relations Special Report no. 46 (May 2009). Available online at www.cfr.org/content/publications/attachments/LawoftheSea_CSR46.pdf (accessed on January 3, 2011).

Hudson, Manley O. "Present Status of the Hague Conventions of 1899 and 1907," *The American Journal of International Law* 25, no.1 (January 1931): 114–17.

Jones, Ashby. "Who's a Pirate? Turns Out, the Answer's Not So Simple," *The Wall Street Journal* (August 16, 2010). Available online at http://blogs.wsj.com/law/2010/08/16/whos-a-pirate-turns-out-the-answers-not-so-simple/ (accessed on January 3, 2011).

Kraska, James. "Piracy, Policy, and Law," *U.S. Naval Institute Proceedings Magazine* 134, no. 12 (December 2008). Available online at www.usni.org/magazines/proceedings/2008-12/piracy-policy-and-law (accessed on January 3, 2011).

Lowe, A.V. "The Laws of War at Sea and the 1958 and 1982 Conventions," *Marine Policy* 12, no. 3 (July 1988): 286–96.

WEB SITES

The Avalon Project. "The Laws of War." *Yale Law School: Lillian Goldman Law Library.* http://avalon.law.yale.edu/subject_menus/lawwar.asp (accessed on January 3, 2011).

"Chronological Lists of Ratifications of, Accessions and Successions to the Convention and the Related Agreements as at 01 March 2010," *Oceans and Law of the Sea, Division for Ocean Affairs and the Law of the Sea.* www.un.org/Depts/los/reference_files/chronological_lists_of_ratifications.htm (accessed on January 3, 2011).

United Nations. *Convention on the High Seas 1958.* http://untreaty.un.org/ilc/texts/instruments/english/conventions/8_1_1958_high_seas.pdf (accessed on January 3, 2011).

15

Pirates Hijack a Tanker in the Strait of Malacca

Excerpt from "Dark Passage"

By Peter Gwin

Published by National Geographic, *October 2007*

Available online at: http://ngm.nationalgeographic.com/2007/10/malacca-strait-pirates/pirates-text.html

Accessed on January 3, 2011

"It is very hard for Indonesian seamen. We all need money."

– John Ariffin, pirate

The Strait of Malacca, a 550-mile (885-kilometer) channel separating the Indonesian island of Sumatra from the Malay Peninsula, has provided pirates with riches for centuries. Ships laden with gold, gems, spices, mahogany, rubber, tin, gunpowder, opium, and slaves passed through the waterway. With hundreds of mangrove islands, inlets, and waterways, this sea lane offers many places for pirates to hide. In the 1990s, the Malacca Strait was a piracy hot spot and well-organized pirate gangs launched coordinated attacks on merchant vessels. Efforts to curb Strait of Malacca piracy in the early 2000s were successful, and other hot spots emerged.

Strait of Malacca piracy

As early as 414 CE, a Buddhist monk from Ceylon (present-day Sri Lanka) wrote of the hazards of traveling through the Malacca Strait. Fear of typhoons as well as of the pirates who hid in the mangrove-covered inlets of the numerous islands made the trip treacherous. Later, in the fourteenth century Wang Ta-yuan of China noted that the inhabitants of Temasek (present-day Singapore) were "addicted to piracy," as quoted by Robert C. Beckman, Carl Grundy-War, and Vivian L. Forbes in *Maritime Briefing: Acts of Piracy in the Malacca and Singapore Straits.* When they reached the entrance to the Singapore Strait, which connects the Strait of Malacca to the South China Sea, most sailors donned armor and set up padded screens to protect themselves from the arrows of the pirates who chased them in *prahus* (swift Malaysian sailboats). Sailors who did not escape were killed, and their cargo was stolen.

Piracy increased in the sixteenth century when Europeans attempted to control the trade flowing through the Straits of Singapore and Malacca. The colonizers put many local traders and sailors out of work. The only advantage the *orang laut* (sea people) had was their knowledge of the many islands and channels. They used these skills to defend their sultan (ruler)'s legitimate ownership to the seas surrounding their islands.

The founding of Singapore in 1819 and the signing of the Anglo-Dutch Treaty of London on March 1824 split the strait between Malaysia and Singapore. Several months later Great Britain signed a treaty with the sultan that gave Britain the island of Singapore and all rights within 10 miles (16 kilometers) of its coast. This new boundary line divided the lands of the local sea lords, who then could not conduct their business, leaving many little choice but to live by piracy.

The Malays themselves, at least the *orang laut*, did not consider themselves pirates; they believed that they were only protecting what was rightfully theirs. Another type of pirate existed—the *perompak*—who were part of bands of outlaws with no fixed home. Britain, who retained control over the area until the mid–1900s, tried to suppress piracy, but was never entirely successful.

The bounty passing through this area increased along with world trade. About seventy thousand ships yearly use the strait, which serves as the main shipping channel between the Indian and Pacific Oceans. A large proportion of the world's trade goods and oil shipments make their way through this passageway.

By the late 1990s, the International Maritime Bureau (IMB) had labeled this area one of the most active piracy zones in the world. Piracy had evolved from small gangs who robbed ships to include crime syndicates that stole the ships and cargo, and armed kidnappers who seized people or goods for ransom, or a sum of money demanded for the release of someone being held captive. Each of these types of pirate operate differently.

Jumping squirrels

Small pirate gangs known as jumping squirrels go on "shopping trips," which means they find small, older ships with little or no security and swarm aboard. They take the cash—most ships pay their crews in cash—and any

Pirates practicing with bamboo rods, which they climb to board a ship. © MICHAEL S. YAMASHITA/CORBIS.

other goods they can find, including expensive navigation equipment. Their *pancungs*, or heavy wooden boats, allow them to get close to the ship they have targeted. Then they board and force the captain to turn over money and goods.

Jumping squirrels train until they can swiftly board a ship. They must catch the crew by surprise. If they are too slow, they risk being spotted and shot or captured. To board ships, the gang waits until after dark, then the *tekong*, or boat pilot, moves alongside the larger ship they plan to attack.

Quietness and speed are important, so the jumping squirrels use a long bamboo stalk to get into the boat. Because of its firmness and natural joints, bamboo is much easier and faster to climb than a rope. The jumping squirrels sneak up behind the sailors, grab them, and hold a *parang* blade to their victims' throats, then demand whatever valuables the boat holds. In heists like these, the pirates often net as much as ten thousand to twenty thousand dollars. Jumping squirrels are usually on and off the targeted boat in less than an hour, so after they take their cut, they have made a huge profit for just a few hours of time, but the risks are great.

Crime syndicates and kidnappers

When whole ships and their cargo are hijacked, most often it is an inside job. The pirates need to know the ship's route and what is on board. In as many as 75 percent of these thefts, the captain or a crew member passes that information on to the pirates. The hijackers board the ship at a prearranged time, sail it to a safe harbor, dump or kill the crew, repaint the boat, and give it false identification. The boats are either sold for profit or converted to pirate ships called phantom ships. These phantom ships take the pirates and their smaller vessels out to sea so they can capture other ships. Crew members who betray their ship to pirates can never work for the same shipping company again, so they change their names and use faked passports to get other employment.

Occasionally, the pirates do not steal the ship. Instead they steer it to a safe harbor and unload the cargo onto their own ships. Many ships that pass through the Strait of Malacca carry oil or other expensive goods, so stealing cargo is lucrative. These hijackings are often done by crime syndicates. Shipping companies often do not report these thefts in order to avoid losing their insurance.

Pirates who seize passengers, crew, or goods for ransom usually demand one hundred thousand dollars or more, but usually settle for ten thousand to twenty thousand dollars. Most of the time the kidnapped crew members are released unharmed. Experts say, though, that by paying a ransom, the shipping companies are rewarding the pirates and encouraging others to attempt the same crimes.

Things to remember while reading the excerpt from "Dark Passage":

- Many pirates and their accomplices cannot afford the training to become licensed sailors. Instead, using aliases and counterfeit licenses, they often have to resort to piracy to make money.
- Peter Gwin, the author of the excerpt, is a reporter for *National Geographic* magazine. He interviewed John Ariffin, also known as John Palembang, who along with nine others hijacked the *Nepline Delima* in the Strait of Malacca in June 2005. They had a contact on the ship who gave them the inside information they needed to take over this tanker filled with diesel fuel worth three million dollars.

• • •

Dark Passage

The Strait of Malacca. Pirates haunt it. Sailors fear it, Global trade depends on it.

Batam: An island and city in Indonesia known for smugglers, pirates, and gangsters.

... The plot was hatched in a **Batam** coffee shop, Ariffin says, when a Malaysian shipping executive approached an Indonesian sailor named

Lukman and inquired whether he could organize a crew to hijack the tanker. Ariffin, who went to sea in his teens and rose through the maritime ranks to become a mechanic, had served with Lukman on a few crews. Lately both of them had struggled to find work, and Lukman asked if he wanted in on the heist. It would be an easy job, he promised, because a member of the tanker's crew was in on the plan.

As a young crewman, Ariffin says he was once on a ship attacked by pirates. They waved parangs (machete-like knives), threatened to kill everyone, and took cash and food. He smiles wryly at the irony. "It is very hard for Indonesian seamen. We all need money." He told Lukman he was in. "All we had to do was board the tanker, tie up the crew, and sail to open sea," Ariffin says. They would meet a tanker coming from Thailand, transfer the fuel, and abandon the *Nepline Delima*. Lukman promised Ariffin $10,000 for manning the tanker's engines.

The plan began smoothly. Posing as tourists, Ariffin, Lukman, and two other seamen from Batam pretended to snap photos as they rode a ferry up the strait to the Malaysian port of Pinang. There they met six other men Lukman had recruited from Aceh, Sumatra's northernmost province. "They weren't seamen," said Ariffin. "We needed their muscles."

At a nearby beach, they stole a fiberglass speedboat, painted it blue, and loaded it with gasoline, water and food, two cell phones, a GPS, and five freshly sharpened parangs. In addition, each man brought a ski mask, a change of clothes, some cash, and a passport. After midnight, they slipped into the strait. Meanwhile, the **turncoat** crew member was sending text messages from the tanker, updating the ship's position, course, and speed. Most important, Ariffin said, "he told us when he would man the watch."

A few hours later, the pirates, wearing ski masks and **wielding** parangs, commanded the *Nepline Delima*'s bridge. The tanker's distress signal had been disabled, and 16 of its 17 crew lay bound and blindfolded in a locked cabin, some of them bleeding. The pirates set a new course for the Thai tanker on the open sea. By the next evening the gang would be on their way back to what Batam pirates call "happy happy," a blur of **hedonism**, ranging from extravagant amounts of crystal meth and ecstasy to marathon sessions with prostitutes. Or, if Ariffin is to be believed, home to his family.

The problem was the 17th crewman. Soon after the pirates had boarded the tanker, Ariffin, guarding the speedboat, heard one of the sailors yell: "**Lanun**!" **Bedlam** erupted on the ship's decks as the pirates tried to round up the frightened crew. Lukman and two others were on the bridge. They switched on the public address system and started beating the captain until his shouts for the crew to surrender blared over the ship's loudspeakers. "Please, they are killing me," he cried. Sixteen crewmen eventually gave up. Each was asked his name, then bound and blindfolded. "We had a copy of the **ship's manifest**," said Ariffin, "we knew one was missing."

Turncoat: Person who switches to an opposing side; traitor.

Wielding: Carrying.

Hedonism: Pursuit of pleasure.

Lanun: Pronounced lah-NOON; pirate.

Bedlam: Uproar and confusion.

Ship's manifest: The list of cargo and/or passengers on board a ship.

Meanwhile, the sea had picked up. Ariffin tied the speedboat to the tanker's railing and scrambled aboard to find the engine room. It was there, an hour later, that he got a frantic call from Lukman on the bridge. The missing crewman had escaped in their speedboat, stranding them on the tanker. Ariffin ran the *Nepline Delima*'s engines at full throttle trying to reach international waters, but even at top speed the tanker could make only about 12 miles an hour (19 kilometers). Within a few hours the Malaysian marine police had cut off their escape. Ariffin went up on the deck and lit a cigarette. "There was nothing to do," he said. "Allah [God] had his hand on that sailor."

• • •

What happened next . . .

Ariffin was arrested along with nine others and sent to prison for seven years. Once they are released from prison, pirates often return to a life of crime, because they have no way to earn an honest living. With the many antipiracy organizations and the increased patrols in the Malacca Strait area, however, piracy may no longer be a worthwhile option.

Several initiatives were begun to reduce piracy in the Malacca Strait in the 1990s and early 2000s. In October 1992 IMB's Piracy Reporting Centre opened in Kuala Lumpur, Malaysia, to collect information on pirate attacks around the world. Several years later, however, the 1997 Asian financial crisis became a major setback to the war on piracy, because people in desperate situations turned to illegal means to make a living. At the same time governments in crisis had no time or resources to pursue criminals. Although foreign countries offered to assist them, none of the countries around the Malacca Strait wanted to give up their sovereignty, or control, over their territory.

Piracy reached an all-time high in 2000, and continued to climb. By 2004 the areas around the Malacca Strait accounted for 40 percent of the pirate attacks worldwide. That year several organizations formed to curb piracy. The first, the Trilateral Coordinated Patrol, or MALSINDO, began in July as the navies of Malaysia, Indonesia, and Singapore each began patrolling their coasts. But because they each wanted to maintain sovereignty over their territorial waters, each navy could only pursue pirates in its own seas.

Five months later a tsunami devastated coastlines along the Indian Ocean. Indonesia experienced the worst destruction; about 70 percent of the people in Aceh in northern Sumatra died. Almost half the people lost their jobs. Aceh had been a pirate haven, and, following the tsunami, hijacking in the Malacca Strait ceased. The tsunami also brought an end

Naval ships from Indonesia, Singapore, and Malaysia sail during a ceremony to launch the Trilateral Coordinated Patrol in 2004.
© SUPRI/REUTERS/CORBIS.

to decades of conflict between two groups in the area, both of which had also been suspected of pirating. The rivals came together to plan disaster relief and signed a peace deal in 2005.

In 2005 the countries around the Strait of Malacca started Eyes in the Sky (EiS), a joint air patrol that watches the seas for pirates. After that, the number of attacks fell dramatically. Compared with 2004, piracy declined more than 60 percent in 2005. By comparison, IMB statistics for that year showed a 10 percent increase in piracy worldwide.

In 2006 EiS and MALSINDO joined to form the Malacca Strait Patrols. Funding and resources continued to be an ongoing problem. The group wanted to run seventy patrols a week, but was only able to manage eight. Nevertheless, those eight patrols were a deterrent. Many of the other nations in Southeast Asia offered support for the Regional Cooperation Agreement on Anti-Piracy (ReCAAP). By 2010, sixteen countries had signed this agreement to help each other by sharing information and reports on pirate attacks. Malaysia and Indonesia have not signed the agreement.

Statistics from the IMB showed only four attempted attacks in 2007; three of them were successful. In the first quarter of 2010, no incidents were reported in the Malacca Strait. Some attributed this decrease to ships not reporting unsuccessful attacks in order to keep insurance costs down, but others saw it as a result of the antipiracy measures.

Some experts believe that the countries around the Strait of Malacca have not been given enough credit for the strides they have made in combating piracy. As Catherine Zara Raymond points out in "Piracy and Armed Robbery in the Malacca Strait: A Problem Solved?": "Lessons learned in the fight against piracy in the Malacca Strait should be applied to other regions to make these waters more secure. No longer should there be a false perception that the Malacca Strait is a 'Dark Passage.' Rather, it is time for it to be held up as an example to the rest of the world of how piracy can successfully be reduced."

Although measures in the Malacca Strait appear successful, piracy still continues in nearby areas, such as the shipping lane in the South China Sea that feeds into the Malacca Strait. Between February to September 2010, for example, the IMB recorded twenty-six attacks in that area. Thus, ongoing vigilance is necessary.

Did you know ...

- According to the United Nations Convention on the Law of the Sea (UNCLOS), piracy takes place on the high seas, or the open waters of the ocean that are outside the limits of any country's territorial authority. UNCLOS defines this area the waters bordering the country's coast up to 12 nautical miles (22.8 kilometers) from land. (A nautical mile is a unit of distance used for sea navigation. One nautical mile equals 6,080 feet [1.9 kilometers].) Because most attacks and some hijackings occur in the waters close to the shores of the countries that border the Malacca Strait, these crimes cannot officially be called piracy. Any heists that take place within a country's territorial waters would actually be armed robbery. But most sources classify all attacks against ships and their crew or passengers as pirate attacks. (For more information on UNCLOS, see **United Nations Convention on the Law of the Sea**.)
- The IMB Piracy Reporting Centre in Kuala Lumpur, Malaysia, is open twenty-four hours a day and is usually the first to receive the report of pirate attacks anywhere in the world. The center then radios out an alert to ships and organizations around the world.

- With only 114 naval ships, Indonesia has trouble patrolling its seventeen thousand islands, and only 25 percent of its boats are believed to be usable.

Consider the following ...

- Should the *orang laut*'s attacks against British ships be classified as piracy? Why or why not?
- Many events occurred in the first decade of the 2000s that had an impact on the countries surrounding the Strait of Malacca. Which of these do you think had the greatest impact on piracy in that area?
- What effects might a shipping company's decision not to report a pirate attack have on everyone involved?
- How might Malaysia's insistence on maintaining its sovereignty interfere with stopping piracy?

For More Information

BOOKS

Beckman, Robert C., Carl Grundy-War, and Vivian L. Forbes. *Maritime Briefing: Acts of Piracy in the Malacca and Singapore Straits.* Vol. 1, No. 4. Durham, UK: International Boundaries Research Unit Press, 1994, p. 1.

Eklöf, Stefan. *Pirates in Paradise: A Modern History of Southeast Asia's Maritime Marauders.* Copenhagen: Nordic Institute of Asian Studies, 2006.

Elleman, Bruce A. *Waves of Hope: The U.S. Navy's Response to the Tsunami in Northern Indonesia.* Newport Paper 28. Newport, RI: Naval War College Press, 2007.

Wu, Shicun, and Keyuan Zou, eds. *Maritime Security in the South China Sea.* Burlington, VT: AshgatePublishing, 2009.

PERIODICALS

Bateman, Sam, Joshua Ho, and Mathew Mathai. "Shipping Patterns in the Malacca and Singapore Straits: An Assessment of the Risks to Different Types of Vessel," *Contemporary Southeast Asia* 29, no. 2 (August 1, 2007): 309–32.

Marshall, Andrew. "The Malacca Strait: Waterway to the World." *Time* (July 31, 2006). Available online at www.time.com/time/asia/2006/journey/strait.html (accessed on January 3, 2011).

Raymond, Catherine Zara. "Piracy and Armed Robbery in the Malacca Strait: A Problem Solved?" *Naval War College Review* 62, no. 3 (Summer 2009).

WEB SITES

"Anti-Piracy Drive in Malacca Straits," *BBC News.* http://news.bbc.co.uk/2/hi/3908821.stm (accessed on January 3, 2011).

"Royal Malaysian Navy Thwarts Pirate Attack." *International Chamber of Commerce, Commercial Crime Services.*. www.icc-ccs.org/index.php?option=com_content&view=article&id=324:royal-malaysian-navy-thwarts-pirate-attack&catid=60:news&Itemid=51 (accessed on January 3, 2011).

ReCAAP Agreement, Regional Cooperation Agreement on Combating Piracy and Armed Robbery against Ships in Asia. www.recaap.org/about/pdf/ReCAAP%20Agreement.pdf (accessed on January 3, 2011).

16

Interview with a Somali Pirate

Excerpt from "I'm Not a Pirate, I'm the Saviour of the Sea"

By Jay Bahadur

Published by Times Online, *April 16, 2009*

Available online at: www.timesonline.co.uk/tol/news/world/africa/
article6100783.ece

Accessed on January 3, 2011

"If they do [attack] . . . that's OK. We believe in God. Force alone cannot stop us. . . . We don't care about death."

– Boyah, Somali pirate

In the 1990s and early 2000s Somalia developed into a piracy hot spot. Several factors have made this African nation an ideal location for piracy. Political unrest has led to a weak government that cannot police its waters. War, drought, and foreign incursion on local fishing have left the people impoverished. Furthermore, the country is located near one of the most important maritime (sea) trade routes in the world.

Political and economic unrest

Piracy first became a major problem in Somalia in the 1990s, around the time the civil war began. In 1991 Somalia's dictator was ousted and rival factions struggled to gain power. In the violence that followed thousands of Somalis faced death, starvation, and dislocation. A temporary government, the Transitional Federal Government, was formed in 2004. But the government was weak and had no resources to police its waters, where many of its people made their living by fishing. Large commercial trawlers (fishing vessels) from other countries took advantage of the situation to harvest the fish, using equipment that destroyed the ecosystem. Somalis believed these nations owed them compensation. A small group of Somalis

An abandoned fishing boat at the Port of Barbera, Somalia. Many Somalis made their living by fishing until commercial trawlers from other countries began harvesting fish in the region, destroying the ecosystem. © AURORA PHOTOS/ALAMY.

began to stop the foreign fishing vessels, demanding that they pay to fish in Somali waters. This later escalated into piracy.

Given the extreme poverty in Somalia, it is understandable that many young men are lured by the wealth that can be made through piracy. Almost three-fourths of the population lives on an income of less than two dollars a day. With yearly wages averaging six hundred dollars, capturing one ship that will bring each pirate ten thousand dollars or more is often irresistible. Even those who do not make the pirate attack often benefit. The pirates are usually a small group of six to ten, but accomplices onshore or those who guard captive vessels also get a share of the money. With the rate of ransom payments between $300,000 and $1.5 million, even the guards can make good money. (A ransom is a sum of money demanded for the release of someone being held captive.)

Somalia is situated on the Horn of Africa (the easternmost projection of Africa). The Indian Ocean it located off the nation's eastern coast and its northern coastline runs along the Gulf of Aden, an arm of the Arabian Sea that connects the Red Sea to the Indian Ocean. More than twenty thousand ships travel the Gulf of Aden each year. This area has been called "pirate alley," because of the large number of pirate attacks. Although Somali pirates took only about one out of every one thousand vessels that passed through the gulf, total losses for ship owners in 2009 totaled millions of dollars. Insurance on the many ships that use this route skyrocketed. According to the International Maritime Bureau (IMB), the number of pirate attacks dropped in 2010, but pirates had moved farther from shore and broadened their range to include the Indian Ocean and the southern Red Sea.

Somali pirate economy

Piracy has become intricately tied to the economy of many towns along the Somali coast. Most have investors who equip the pirates with skiffs (small, easy-to-maneuver boats) containing assault rifles, pistols, grenades, rope ladders for boarding ships, binoculars, fuel, and provisions. In exchange for their investment, these financiers receive one-third of the profit from each hijacked ship.

The pirates operate in groups of about six to twelve, divided between two or three skiffs. They spend extended time at sea, watching for passing ships to seize. Once they capture a ship, they usually ransom the ship and passengers. Each of the pirates receives a share of the ransom. Any pirates who have donated a skiff or weapons receive a larger share.

In addition to the pirates involved in the attack, accomplices are needed on land to assist once a ship has been captured. Volunteers guard prisoners who are being held for ransom and serve as scouts to protect the pirates. Local men, women, and children work as cooks, accountants, boat-builders, and mechanics, or provide other needed services. All of these people receive a share of the profit, even if only a small amount. This money helps many Somalis survive. So piracy is very much tied up with the community's economy. Ending piracy would mean a return to poverty for most in a pirate town.

Things to remember while reading the excerpt from "I'm Not a Pirate, I'm the Saviour of the Sea":

- Journalist Jay Bahadur interviewed a Somali pirate named Boyah for the British newspaper *The Times*. Boyah does not see himself as a pirate, and believes that he is protecting his country.

An armed Somali pirate keeping watch along the coastline. MOHAMED DAHIR/AFP/GETTY IMAGES.

- Boyah is from Eyl, a town on the eastern coast of Somalia. Eyl is a pirate haven, or a safe place for pirates to harbor and repair their ships, resupply, and organize raiding parties. Somali pirate havens are mainly found in two regions: the province of Puntland in northeastern Somalia, where Eyl is located, and the Mudug region in north-central Somalia.

- Many pirates claim they are taking taxes from the foreign companies who have been illegally fishing off their shores. Because several groups are fighting for control of the country, the Somali government is in no position to collect taxes or to protect their shores from these commercial vessels that have done great damage to the offshore regions, including dumping toxic waste.

- Giving away a lot of their money has turned Boyah's pirates into a "merry band into Robin Hood figures." In English folktales Robin Hood robbed from the rich and gave to the poor, and these

Somali pirates see themselves as helping others, because their piracy provides income for others in their community.

• • •

I'm Not a Pirate, I'm the Saviour of the Sea

Boyah is a pirate. One of the original "Old Boys", he quietly pursued his trade in the waters of his coastal home town of Eyl, years before it **galvanised** the world's imagination as Somalia's infamous "pirate haven". Boyah is dismissive of the recent **posers**, the headline-grabbers who have bathed in the international media spotlight and it shows; he **exudes** a self-assured superiority.

Pirates are easy to spot on the streets of Garowe, the regional capital: their Toyota 4×4s cluster around equally new white-washed mansions on the edge of town. But to approach them, I am warned, is to invite kidnapping or robbery. In Somalia, everything is done through connections, be they clan, family, or friend, and Mohamed, my interpreter, was on and off the phone for almost a week to coax his network into producing Boyah.

Our meeting takes place at a virtually deserted farm 15 km [9 miles] outside Garowe. Mohamed is the son of the newly elected president of Puntland and does not want to be seen in public **cavorting** with pirates. Moreover, Boyah has recently contracted **tuberculosis** and Mohamed insists that we meet him in an open space.

As we step out of our vehicles, I catch my first glimpse of Boyah. Immensely tall and disconcertingly menacing, he is wearing a ma'awis, the traditional robe of a clan elder, and a cimaamad, a decorative shawl. On his feet is a pair of shiny onyx [black] leather sandals. He weaves his way around the tomato plants and lemon trees, before settling in a shady clearing, where he squats down. Other than the farm's owners, there is no one near by, yet the two **AK-47**-toting police escorts, who accompany me wherever I go, stand guard with an amusing military **officiousness**.

Asking my first question through my interpreter, I hesitate to use the word "pirate". Somali pirates are aware enough of themselves in the international media that the word has become part of their **vernacular** but its closest Somali translation is *burcad badeed*, which means "ocean robber", a political statement I am anxious to avoid. Boyah likes to refer to him[self] and his comrades as *badaadinta badah*, "saviours of the sea", a term that is most often translated in the English-speaking media as "coastguard". Boyah jokes that he is the "Chief of the Coastguard", a title he evokes with pride. To him, his actions have been about protecting his sea; his hijackings, a

Galvanised: Stimulated; spelled *galvanized* in American English.

Poseurs: People who pretend to be part of a group, in this case those who pretend to be pirates to get attention.

Exudes: Gives off or radiates.

Cavorting: Associating.

Tuberculosis: A disease that affects the lungs.

AK-47: An automatic assault rifle.

Officiousness: Aggressiveness and intrusion.

Vernacular: Everyday language.

legitimate form of taxation levied **in absentia** on behalf of a defunct government that he represents in spirit, if not in law.

His story is typical of many who have turned to piracy since the onset of the civil war. Fourteen years ago, he was still working as a lobster diver in Eyl—"one of the best", he says. Since then, according to Boyah, these reefs off Eyl have been devastated by foreign fishing fleets—mostly Chinese, Taiwanese and Korean—using steel-pronged dragnets. He says that there are no longer lobsters to be found locally, a claim partially **corroborated** by a 2005 UN Development Project report into the depletion of local stocks.

From 1995 to 1997, Boyah and others captured three foreign fishing vessels, keeping the catch and ransoming the crew. He boasts that he received an $800,000 bounty for one ship. When the foreign fishing fleets entered into protection contracts with local warlords, making armed guards and anti-aircraft guns fixtures on ships, Boyah and his men went after commercial shipping vessels instead.

Boyah says that there are about 500 pirates operating in the area, over whom he serves as "chairman". Eyl's pirate groups function as a loose confederation, and Boyah is a key organiser, recruiter, financier and mission commander, rather than a traditional crime boss, but he claims that all applicants for the position of Pirate (Eyl Division) must come to him. Boyah's sole criteria for a recruit are that he has to own a gun, and that he must "[be] a hero, and accept death"—qualities that grace the **CV**s of many local youth.

Turnover in Boyah's core group is low; when I ask if his men ever use their new-found wealth to leave Somalia, he laughs: "The only way they leave is when they die." He adds that a member of his band departed last night, dying in his sleep of undisclosed reasons.

When it comes to targets, Boyah's standards are not very exacting. He says that his men go after any ship that wanders into their sights. He separates his prey into "commercial" and "tourist" ships. The commercial ships, identifiable by the cranes on their decks, are slower and easier to capture. Boyah has gone after too many of these to remember. He claims to employ different tactics for different ships, but the basic strategy is that several skiffs will approach from all sides, swarming like a waterborne wolfpack. If brandishing their weapons fails to frighten the ship's crew into stopping, they fire into the air. If that doesn't do it, and if the target ship is incapable of outperforming the 85 to 150 horsepower engines on their skiffs, they pull alongside their target, toss hooked rope ladders on to the decks and board the ship. Resistance is rare.

Boyah guesses that 20 to 30 per cent of attempted hijackings succeed. Speedy prey, technical problems, and foreign naval or domestic coastguard intervention account for the high rate of failure.

In absentia: In the absence.

Corroborated: Confirmed by others.

CV: *Curriculum vitae,* literally, "course of life" one's résumé or life history.

Captured ships are steered to Eyl, where guards and interpreters are brought to look after the hostages during the **ransom** negotiation. Once secured, the money—often routed through banks in London and Dubai and parachuted directly on to the deck of the ship—is split: half goes to the hijackers, a third to the investors who fronted cash for the ships and weapons, and 20 per cent to everyone else, from the guards to the translators (occasionally high school students on a summer break). Some money is also given as charity to the local poor; such **largesse**, Boyah tells me, has turned his merry band into Robin Hood figures.

When I ask where his men have obtained their training, he **pithily** responds that it comes "from famine". This isn't the whole truth. Beginning in 1999, the government of Puntland launched a series of ill-fated attempts to establish an (official) regional Coastguard, efforts that each time ended with the **dissolution** of the contracting company and the dismissal of its employees. The new generation of Somali pirates—better trained, more efficiently organised and possessing superior equipment—can be traced in part to these failed experiments. When pressed, Boyah confirms that some of his men are former coastguard recruits, and he reveals another detail of the interwoven dynamic between pirates, coastguards and fishermen. He claims that the Puntland Coastguard of the late 1990s and early 2000s worked as a private militia for the protection of commercial **trawlers** in possession of official "fishing licences", alienating local fishermen. Sometimes the situation escalated into confrontation, and Boyah recounts that in 2001 his men seized several fishing vessels "licensed" by President **Abdullahi Yusuf** and protected by his coastguard force. Almost a decade before the rise in pirate hijackings hit the Gulf of Aden, the conditions for the coming storm were already recognisable.

Boyah's moral compass, like his body, seems to be split between sea and shore. "We're not murderers," he says, "we've never killed anyone." He warns me, half-jokingly, not to run into him in a boat, but assures me that he is quite harmless on land. He insists that he is not a criminal but that he knows what he is doing is wrong.

Boyah hasn't been on a mission for more than two months, for which he has a two-pronged explanation: "I got sick and became rich." He has called for an end to hijackings albeit from a position of luxury that most do not enjoy. I ask him whether his ceasefire was motivated by the recent deployment to the region of a NATO [North Atlantic Treaty Organization] task force. "No," he says, "it has nothing to do with that. It's a moral issue. We realised that we didn't have public support." That support, according to Boyah, took a plunge last summer [2008] when a delegation of clan and religious leaders visited Eyl and declared that dealing with pirates is haram— religiously forbidden. NATO deliberations regarding possible missile strikes on Eyl, though, do not worry Boyah: "Only civilians live there, it would be

Ransom: A sum of money demanded for the release of someone being held captive.

Largesse: Generosity.

Pithily: Concisely, or to the point.

Dissolution: Dissolving or breaking up.

Trawlers: Fishing boats that use nets.

Abdullahi Yusuf: Abdullahi Yusuf Ahmed (1937–), president of Puntland (1998–2004) and president of Somalia (2004–8).

illegal for them to attack. If they do ... that's OK. We believe in God. Force alone cannot stop us," he says **vehemently**, "we don't care about death."

Throughout our interview, Boyah has looked uninterested but when I ask him to recount his most exhilarating raid, he brightens up, launching into the story of the *Golden Nori*. In October 2007, he captured the Japanese chemical tanker about eight **nautical miles** off the northern Somali coast, only to be surrounded by the US Navy. Boyah recalls seven naval vessels encircling him. He recites **by rote** the identification numbers marking the sides of four of the vessels: 41, 56, 76, and 78 (the last being the destroyer USS *Porter*). Fortunately for them, the *Golden Nori* was carrying volatile chemicals, including the extremely flammable compound **benzene**.

The stand-off dragged on for months and he claims that they "almost abandoned the ship so we wouldn't start eating the crew." Eventually, Boyah ordered the ship into the harbour at Bosasso, Puntland's big port and most populous city. In case the *Nori*'s explosive cargo proved an insufficient deterrent, Boyah added the defensive screen provided by the presence of the city's civilian population.

His perseverance paid off. After extensive negotiations, a ransom of $1.5 million was secured for the ship and its crew. The US military guaranteed Boyah and his team safe passage off the hijacked ship and Puntland's security forces could only watch as US gunships escorted the pirate skiffs to land and allowed them to disembark. Why did he and his men trust the Americans? "Because that was the agreement," Boyah says. But I already know the real answer. Like many Western nations, the Americans wouldn't have known what to do with Boyah and his men if they had captured them. According to international law—to the extent that international law has any meaning in an utterly **failed state**—the Americans were not even supposed to be in Somali **territorial waters**. . . .

Boyah may have accumulated a small fortune, but how long his current state of **affluence** will last is unclear—he announces with pride how he has given his money away to his friends, to the poor and how he didn't build a house or a hotel like many of his more **parsimonious** co-workers. When asked about his future plans, Boyah is evasive. "That is up to the international community," he says, "they need to solve the problem of illegal fishing, the root of our troubles. We are waiting for action."

• • •

What happened next . . .

Boyah gave several other interviews besides this one, including one a month later in which he declared that he was giving up piracy for good. As he mentioned in the article, local religious leaders had begun using moral pressure on the pirates. Many mosques (Muslim places of worship)

Vehemently: Strongly.

Nautical mile: A unit of distance used for sea navigation. One nautical mile equals 6,080 feet (1.9 kilometers).

By rote: From memory.

Benzene: A colorless liquid found in gasoline, paint, glue, and pesticide that burns easily.

Failed state: A state without a functioning government above the local level.

Territorial waters: Waters surrounding a nation over which that nation exercises sole authority.

Affluence: Wealth.

Parsimonious: Thrifty or stingy.

U.S. Marines approach the Magellan Star *as they prepare to board the ship, which was captured by Somali pirates. Increased patrols have significantly reduced the rate of successful pirate hijackings.* CHRISTOPHER NODINE/U.S. NAVY VIA GETTY IMAGES.

preached against piracy. Sheiks (village or family leaders), government leaders, and even townspeople began campaigns to exclude any "burcad badeed," or sea bandits, in their community.

In addition many nations banded together to fight piracy. Antipiracy coalitions such as the Contact Group on Somali Piracy gathered volunteers and helped to coordinate the efforts of various groups working to increase security in the seas around Somalia. With more patrols and better protection for foreign ships, the number of Somali hijackings in the Gulf of Aden for the first half of the year (January to June), according to IMB, slipped from 86 in 2009 to 33 in 2010.

Local Somali officials began cooperating with NATO in 2009 and within a year had arrested dozens of pirates. Kenya, which borders Somalia, took on the responsibility for many of the trials, and opened a special court near its port city of Mombasa. Seychelles and Tanzania also offered to assist with prosecution. Some pirates were taken to Amsterdam, the Netherlands; Paris, France; or New York City for trial. In many cases, however, it is not easy to get evidence, so captured pirates are often disarmed and released.

One year later Boyah again made headlines. On May 20, 2010, the newspapers announced the arrest of a notorious pirate on the U.S. Wanted List: forty-four-year-old Abshir Abdillahi, also known as Andirizaq Abdillahi Boyah or Abshir Boyah. Somali security forces also arrested eleven other pirates in Puntland. The governor of the region, Abdi Hirsi Qarjab, insisted that although Boyah claimed he was not a pirate, Boyah had helped begin the piracy trade in the area and also served as an investor.

When Boyah tried to flee in his car, he was captured and sent to a prison in the town of Bossaso, where almost four hundred pirates are housed. The security team also seized two pistols and $29,500 in cash from his car, not much money for a pirate responsible for ransoming twenty-five ships.

That may have been because the United States Treasury Department had frozen the bank accounts of several suspected Somali Islamist militants, including Boyah, a month before the arrest. Another reason may have been that Boyah gave away some of his profits. When questioned about the money, Boyah said that poor people who suddenly become wealthy do not always make wise decisions about spending their money.

Several months after his arrest, Boyah had not been charged. As a member of the same subclan as Puntland's president, some suspect he never will be. (A clan is a family group.)

Many experts warn that an end to Somali piracy will not be achieved by naval attacks. The only way to end piracy is to work within the traditional clan structure rather than imposing other countries' political systems on Somalia. Until the country has a stable government and poverty is erased, piracy will continue.

Did you know . . .

- The International Maritime Bureau's Piracy Reporting Centre stated that in 2009 Somali pirates were involved in 217 acts of piracy. They hijacked 47 ships and took 867 crew hostage.
- According to Jeffrey Gettleman's article in "Somali Pirates Tell Their Side," in the *New York Times*, one pirate claimed that they treated their prisoners well because "killing is not in our plans. We only want money so we can protect ourselves from hunger."
- Some sources estimate that each year foreign ships illegally take about $300 million in tuna, shrimp, and lobster from the waters off the Somali coast, whereas Somalis net about $100 million yearly from piracy.

Consider the following . . .

- Boyah views himself as a heroic figure, calling himself a "savior of the sea." How does he justify this view? Do you think other members of his community see him as a hero or a criminal?

- Knowing the situation in Somalia, what would you recommend as the best way to stop the piracy?
- Pirates are often tried in nearby countries rather than in the country whose ships they boarded. Do you think this practice would result in fairer trials? Why or why not? What advantages and disadvantages might there be to handling trials in this manner?

For More Information

BOOKS

Cawthorne, Nigel. *Pirates of the 21st Century: How Modern-day Buccaneers Are Terrorising the World's Oceans.* London: John Blake, 2010.

Hanley, Gerald. *Warriors: Life and Death Among the Somalis.* London: Eland, 2004.

Murphy, Martin N. *Somalia: The New Barbary? Piracy and Islam in the Horn of Africa.* New York: Columbia University Press, 2010.

PERIODICALS

Gettleman, Jeffrey. "For Somali Pirates, Worst Enemy May Be on Shore," *New York Times* (May 8, 2009). Available online at www.nytimes.com/2009/05/09/world/africa/09pirate.html (accessed on January 3, 2011).

———. "Somalia's Pirates Flourish in a Lawless Nation," *New York Times* (October 31, 2008). Available online at www.nytimes.com/2008/10/31/world/africa/31pirates.html (accessed on January 3, 2011).

———. "Somali Pirates Tell Their Side: They Want Only Money," *New York Times* (September 30, 2008): A6. Available online at www.nytimes.com/2008/10/01/world/africa/01pirates.html (accessed on January 3, 2011).

Kontorovich, Eugene. "International Legal Responses to Piracy off the Coast of Somalia," *American Society of International Law* 13, no. 2 (February 6, 2009). Available online at www.asil.org/insights090206.cfm (accessed on January 3, 2011).

Menkhaus, K. "State Collapse in Somalia: Second Thoughts," *Review of African Political Economy* 97 (2003): 407–20.

Møller, Bjørn. *Piracy, Maritime Terrorism and Naval Strategy.* Danish Institute for International Studies Report (November 16, 2008). Available online at www.diis.dk/graphics/Publications/Reports2009/DIIS_Report_2009-02_%20Piracy_maritime_terrorism_and_naval_strategy.pdf (accessed on January 3, 2011).

Siegelbaum, D.J. "Piracy Sparks High-Tech Defenses," *Time* (April 18, 2008). Available online at www.time.com/time/business/article/0,8599,1732125,00.html (accessed on January 3, 2011).

Sörenson, Karl. *State Failure on the High Seas—Reviewing the Somali Piracy.* FOI Somalia Papers: Report 3. Swedish Defence Research Agency (November 2008). Avaiable online at www.foi.se/upload/projects/Africa/FOI-R–2610.pdf (accessed on January 3, 2011).

WEB SITES

"Piracy." *Foreign & Commonwealth Office.* www.fco.gov.uk/en/global-issues/conflict-prevention/piracy/ (accessed on January 3, 2011).

Harper, Mary. "Life in Somalia's Pirate Town," *BBC News.* http://news.bbc.co.uk/2/hi/africa/7623329.stm (accessed on January 3, 2011).

"International Response: Contact Group on Piracy off the Coast of Somalia." *U.S. State Department, Office of Electronic Information, Bureau of Public Affairs.* www.state.gov/t/pm/ppa/piracy/contactgroup/index.htm (accessed on January 3, 2011).

Maggi, Robert W. "Countering Piracy: International Partnership Achieves Steady Progress." *DIPNote: U.S. Dept of State Official Blog* (August 24, 2010). http://blogs.state.gov/index.php/site/entry/piracy_international_partnership_progress (accessed on January 3, 2011).

Middleton, Roger. "Piracy Symptom of Bigger Problem." *BBC News.* http://news.bbc.co.uk/2/hi/africa/8001183.stm (accessed on January 3, 2011).

"Piracy off the Coast of Somalia and the Response by the United States and the International Community." *U.S. State Department, Office of Electronic Information, Bureau of Public Affairs.* www.state.gov/t/pm/ppa/piracy/index.htm (accessed on January 3, 2011).

17

Interview with Captain Richard Phillips

Excerpt from "Captain Richard Phillips and the Pirates: What's Ahead for the Vermont Captain"

By Mel Allen

Published in Yankee, *March/April 2010*

Available online at: www.yankeemagazine.com/issues/2010-03/features/captain

Accessed on January 3, 2011

You have to keep the pirates off the ship. Once they get on, it's over."

– Captain Richard Phillips

On April 8, 2009, the *Maersk Alabama*, a ship loaded with food to aid the hungry, was attacked by pirates off the coast of Somalia. Although the crew tried to evade the smaller ship, the smooth water allowed the pirates to get close enough to board. The four pirates captured Captain Richard Phillips (1963–) and several crew members. The captain offered himself as a hostage in exchange for the release of the ship and the crew. Television cameras watched as events played out, bringing international attention to the problem of piracy in Somalia.

Pirates spotted

Although the crew of twenty knew the risks involved in sailing the waters around Somalia, they believed they had prepared themselves well for emergencies as they headed to Mombasa, Kenya, to deliver their cargo. When they saw a suspicious small boat heading toward them, they began evasive maneuvers. The small ship could not handle the choppy water and gave up.

But the next morning the skiff returned with four pirates onboard. (A skiff is a small, easy-to-maneuver boat.) This time the water was still,

Captain Richard Phillips. AP IMAGES/STEVE HELBER.

and the pirates tried to board the *Maersk Alabama.* Phillips's crew executed their plans. Chief Engineer Mike Perry kept swinging the boat from side to side to swamp the pirates' boat and stop them from boarding. Perry did flood their boat, but the pirates still managed to board the ship. Most of the crew had gone to safety in the engine room, but four people were captured by the armed pirates: Captain Phillips, Third Mate Colin Wright, Able Bodied Seaman (AB) ATM Reza, and AB Clifford Lacon.

The pirates demanded that the captain call the rest of the crew, but no one responded. Fourteen of the crew had already hidden in a special, secure room. Meanwhile, Perry set to work disabling the ship, so that the pirates could not steal it. He turned off the engine and the lights, and then, in a daring move, climbed up to the main deck to disable the emergency generator. In the distance he saw a pirate holding Phillips at gunpoint but was unable to get close enough to help.

Down below, the hidden crew members had no fresh air, water, or light, and the temperature in the room had risen to 125°F (52°C). Perry did not enter the room to hide. Instead he slipped back to the dark engine room to gather nylon zip ties, hoping that he might have a chance to tie up some of the pirates. He heard voices and hid as Phillips entered with one of pirates. Phillips convinced the pirate that no one was in the room and they left.

A short while later, two shadows approached with a flashlight. One was a pirate; the other was Reza. Perry tried to hide, but the pirate saw him and chased him. Perry ran down a corridor, turned down a corner and, when the pirate got there, he grabbed the pirate's wrists and held a knife to the man's neck. Reza helped Perry tie up the pirate. Then the two shipmates took the man, who turned out to be the pirate leader, Abduwali Abdukhadir Muse (c. 1990–), to the secure room. That left three pirates on deck and three crew members captive.

Anxious now to get away, the other pirates decided to use the lifeboat for their escape. They agreed to exchange Captain Phillips for their leader. Meanwhile the crew secretly made plans to get the ship up and running as soon as the pirates had left. When Perry gave the signal that the pirates had gone overboard, the men came tumbling out of the safe room. They collapsed with heat exhaustion but soon forced themselves to do what was needed.

Attempt prisoner exchange

That night under the full moon, the crew let Muse climb down the ladder into the lifeboat. Then they waited for Captain Phillips to climb up, but the pirates refused to let him go. The *Maersk Alabama* followed the lifeboat, hoping for a chance to rescue Phillips but also fearing that the pirates would call their mother ship, a large stolen vessel that carried the small skiffs out to sea. The mother ship could have as many as fifty pirates on board.

The Maersk Alabama *docked in Mombasa, Kenya.* REUTERS/ ANTHONY NJUGNA/LANDOV.

The *Alabama* crew had radioed for help, and that evening a navy search plane flew overhead. Then the USS *Bainbridge* arrived around midnight. The next morning an armed eighteen-member team boarded the *Maersk Alabama*. Although the crew was safe, Captain Phillips still remained a prisoner on the lifeboat. The crew did not want to leave, but they were ordered to go on to Kenya. They obeyed orders, leaving Captain Phillips behind.

Things to remember while reading the excerpt from "Captain Richard Phillips and the Pirates":

- Somalia is a country torn by civil war, and most of its people are extremely poor. Many Somali pirates are young boys who feel that piracy in their only option. Muse, the leader of the group who attacked the *Maersk Alabama*, was in his teens.
- Somali pirates often use a mother ship as their base of operations at sea. (A mother ship is a large ship that carries a smaller vessel that operates independently from it.) Skiffs are launched from the mother ship and return after an attack. Mother ships allow the pirates to extend their range, because small skiffs cannot carry enough fuel or supplies for long distances.

• • •

Captain Richard Phillips and the Pirates: What's Ahead for the Vermont Captain

[Phillips:] "Pirates are like a pack of hyenas on the hunt. Usually these are 25- to 30-foot fishing boats [with] high-powered engines on the back. They go fast, and they're very maneuverable. They've got four or five guys in a boat who all live on the mother ship. The mother ship can be a tugboat, a fishing boat, a yacht, [or] just something they've stolen. Forty or more guys are living on it, and they either tow their boats or they put them on the deck if it's a big enough ship, and they go [hundreds of miles] out and they just sit there and drift and wait for a target . . .

"You have to keep the pirates off the ship. Once they get on, it's over. I've said that before and I say that now. I think ships should be armed [with] specially trained Special Forces types. Give us ways to protect ourselves. Had the mother ship made it to the *Maersk Alabama*, it would have been over. Then they can put 20 people [on board] with guns and they can just comb through the ship and find everyone. So it's imperative [that] the pirates do not get on the ship. . . .

"They were trying to call Somalia, to get the mother ship there, and had they [succeeded], I'd probably still be in Somalia with the whole crew. But they didn't know how to operate the radar, because I'd disabled it; they were trying to talk on the **VHF**, but I'd changed channels on them and they didn't realize it, and they just couldn't reach the mother ship. They did try and use communications on the sat [satellite] phone, but they didn't know how to use it properly, and they would even check to make sure I dialed the right number, but I [made sure] it didn't work. I just told them it was poor coverage on their cell phones. . . .

"[The pirates] were skinny and underfed. The one I called [in my book] Leader was very mean. Said "Shut up" a lot. A good leader, though. Intelligent. Capable. Ran a tight ship. [There were] two tall guys who were very good seamen, I'll give them that; they knew a lot of knots, very hard knots to tie, let alone untie. [And the fourth] was a crazy young guy [with] **Charlie Manson eyes**. He had no problem just clicking the gun at me frequently and smiling as he did it. . . .

"Once they got aboard, they were very quick up to the **bridge**. So me and two of my crew were taken hostage up on the bridge. I knew where [my] men were, because when the pirates were boarding and shooting, they were going from the initial safe room to a backup safe room. [The pirates] wanted me to call everyone else up, but I didn't give a secret word, so no one paid attention to me. I was also able to cue my mike to let them hear what was going on up on the bridge.

VHF: Very High Frequency; often used for mobile two-way radio communication.

Charlie Manson eyes: Manson was a cult leader and mass murderer in the 1960s and early 1970s known for his crazed stare.

Bridge: The upper deck where a ship is steered and the captain stands.

"The pirates went through the rooms a couple of times ... and they just couldn't find anybody. They told us they would shoot us in two minutes unless everybody was up there. And I was prepared for that ... But I saw nothing to be gained from my side to give my crew up. Once they get the crew up there, they could just shoot all of us. It's for the safety of the many against the hazards of the few. And that's something I knew and accepted.... A captain's duty is to take care of your ship, your crew, and your cargo. Everything derives from this."

The pirates lost their leader when he was captured by Phillips's men as he was searching for the ship's crew. With the crew hidden, the *Maersk Alabama* shut down by its engineers, and the Somalis' own high-speed skiff swamped by waves, the three other pirates looked for a way to **extricate** themselves. Phillips helped them see the advantages of leaving the ship with him. They agreed that they would exchange him for their leader. Once they were all safe in the enclosed lifeboat, however, the pirates said no deal, and Phillips became their hostage.

"I'd been taught that the captain has to be the last one off the ship, but in my situation I knew that the best thing for my ship was for me to get off the ship and take the pirates with me, even though that goes against all the training I've ever had.... I told the chief engineer, 'You have the boat ready to go as soon as they're in the water. Leave me. Don't worry about it.' Because my concern at that time was other pirates....

"I told the pirates that they wouldn't get any **ransom** for me; I told them we'd [all] die here. And I didn't expect any ransom to take place, because that's pretty much the way we are. If you pay the ransom, basically for every dollar you pay, you've just enlisted three pirates. I was just their shield, and I saw that they had no **qualms** about killing me. No qualms at all.... I was afraid and fearful for the majority of the time, but I just had to sit that down in the seat next to me and just take care of what's ahead, and deal with what's right now, what's five minutes away, and not worry about tomorrow.... You've got to hold fast—don't give in....

"I had a chance to settle my affairs, getting ready to die. I was just saying goodbye to [his wife] Andrea and [to] Mariah and Danny [his children]. I was just apologizing for the 4 A.M. phone call [saying I was dead].... I was thinking about people who had died: my father, and a neighbor who had died just before I left. I said, 'I'll get to see them, and Frannie, my nutcase dog who never came when I called the whole time she was alive.' And then I would think about my daughter and my son. It still gets to me. I can hear it in my voice. I did pray for strength so that I could know when to try to escape. So that I wouldn't be too weak when it was time. I always felt there would be a time; that's what I prayed for, and to give me patience."

The Navy destroyer *Bainbridge* moved into position several hundred yards distant early on Thursday. Phillips waited for a chance to escape.

Extricate: Get out of a situation.

Ransom: A sum of money demanded for the release of someone being held captive.

Qualms: Misgivings, doubts, or worries.

"I'd been on there for over 24 hours. I was in an enclosed lifeboat with no ventilation. The heat was second only to having a gun right in your face or hearing it click behind your head. Because I live in Vermont, the heat was unbearable.... They had two guys with **AK-47s** on me all the time. The forward guy would be sleeping or awake, and the last guy, usually the leader, would be up in the cockpit. I couldn't wait them out. I had to outwit them. I knew I had to get away before I got to land.

"One of the guys walked forward, and he lay down. Now there were two people snoring up there, and the young guy steps out for a call of nature. I'm mad at myself because I'm a wimp for not escaping yet. I'm not tied up, and I could see [the Navy ship] out the back door. So I got up and pushed him in the water, and I had a chance to go for the gun, but I didn't know how to use it, so I just dove in. It was just my chance....

"I got probably 50 feet. I popped up and took a look around. The moon was fully out, and it was very light. I said, 'Oh s—,' because they'd see my head. I went right back down. I could see them spinning around and yelling, and they were seeing me, and I started doing the crawl toward the Navy ship as fast as I could...."

The pirates moved to where Phillips was swimming. He tried to hide beneath the boat.

"I went back underwater and [the pirates and the lifeboat] are doing circles, and I went from going side to side up and down in the water to listening to footsteps. I was underneath the boat [holding on] by the cooling tubes.... I could hear talking, yelling, and arguing, people running around the boat, so when I heard them coming, I'd go to the other side, and I'd hear them come [and] go back to the other side ... I was hoping they'd give up. Eventually I popped up, and there was a guy right there, and he took a shot at my head and I said, 'Okay, okay, you got me.' They were irate, screaming, swearing. They kicked, hit, slapped, whacked me with the **revolver**...."

As the hours stretched into days, tensions aboard the lifeboat intensified. The pirates' leader, sensing impending trouble, arranged to be taken aboard the *Bainbridge* "to negotiate." President Obama had authorized the Navy to use whatever force necessary to free Phillips if his life was in imminent danger. On Sunday, April 12, a gunshot rang out in the lifeboat. The Navy saw an AK-47 aimed at the captain's back. Three concealed Navy SEAL snipers were ready.

"There was animosity building [among the pirates]. Then a shot went off, and the young crazy guy went up to the **cockpit**, just disgusted, and the other two went up to assure the Navy that everything was all right, no problem. They did something then that they'd never done. And that was the first time, unbeknownst to one another, [that] all of a sudden they were

AK-47: An automatic assault rifle.

Revolver: A handgun.

Cockpit: The area of a boat where the steering controls are.

all seen. The military took its chance and gratefully so. . . . I was lucky. I could have died. But I'm alive. . . .

* * *

What happened next . . .

Captain Phillips had been a prisoner on the lifeboat from Wednesday evening until Sunday evening. After the USS *Bainbridge* had sent the *Maersk Alabama* on its way to Mombasa, plans got under way to rescue Phillips. At night U.S. Navy SEALs parachuted into the ocean close to the USS *Halyburton*, which was en route to join the rescue efforts. The SEALs later boarded the *Bainbridge*. They had been authorized to use force if Phillips's life seemed to be in danger.

The Somali pirates had run out of fuel and were drifting, when the *Bainbridge* offered to tow them. They started with a 200-foot (60-meter) rope, but gradually drew the lifeboat closer. That kept the pirates in range of the snipers onboard the *Bainbridge*. The pirates had tried to get accomplices to assist them, but no one came. Most likely the U.S. warship frightened them away. One young pirate, Muse, gave up completely and jumped into the boat that brought food to the lifeboat. He wanted medical attention for his cut hand, and he also tried to work out a deal.

Negotiations had not gone well for the pirates. They had demanded $2 million, but the United States refused. Then Muse offered Phillips in exchange for freedom for himself and his crew, but that was also turned down.

The turning point came after one of the pirates on the lifeboat fired at the warship on Sunday evening. Another pirate had his assault weapon trained on the back of Phillips's head and looked ready to shoot. The *Bainbridge*'s captain decided that Phillips's life was in danger and ordered the SEALs to take out the pirates. Using their night sights, the three snipers fired at the same time, each aiming for a different pirate. They killed all three pirates, then pulled themselves along the tow rope to the lifeboat to rescue Phillips.

Muse, who had surrendered, was taken in shackles to Metropolitan Correctional Center in Manhattan, New York. Initially there was some confusion about Muse's age. His father claimed he was fifteen but later admitted his son was around eighteen or nineteen. A judge had already ruled, however, that Muse would be tried as an adult.

Muse's mother claimed that Muse had been tricked into going with the pirates. But testimony revealed that he had been the leader of the group. In fact, charges were later added for two other hijackings he had participated in during the spring of 2009. Muse was charged on April 21, 2009, with piracy and other counts, including conspiracy to commit hostage-taking. But when he pled guilty, four of the six counts against him were dropped, including piracy, which carries a mandatory life sentence.

The trial angered many Somalis, particularly the pirates, some of whom threatened the United States. A pirate from Eyl claimed the Somalis would take their revenge on foreign captives to get back at America. They insisted that the Americans should have negotiated with the Somali pirates rather than killing them. Even Somali officials criticized the United States for not sending Muse back to Somalia to stand trial. The United States countered by citing international piracy laws, which allow countries to prosecute pirates who attack their ships on the high seas.

Did you know ...

- The destroyer that rescued Captain Phillips was named after William Bainbridge, captain of the frigate *Philadelphia*, which was captured by pirates off the coast of Africa in 1803. Bainbridge and his crew were held hostage for nineteen months in Tripoli.
- Although many news reports said that the attack on the *Maersk Alabama* was the first pirate attack on a U.S. ship since the 1800s, several U.S. ships had been attacked by Somali pirates between 2006 and 2008. Phillips was the only crew member captured during that time.
- On November 18, 2009, seven months after this event, Somali pirates once again went after the *Maersk Alabama*, which had been put back into service. Guards on the *Maersk Alabama* fired guns and used a high-decibel noise device to scare off their attackers.
- On the day the pirates boarded the *Maersk Alabama*, the International Maritime Bureau reported that 14 ships and 260 crewmen were already being held by Somali pirates.

Consider the following ...

- Do you think Captain Phillips made the right choice in going with the pirates? Why or why not?

The USS Bainbridge, *the destroyer that rescued Captain Phillips, was named after William Bainbridge (pictured).* © NORTH WIND PICTURE ARCHIVES/ALAMY.

- The crew had many emergency procedures already in place that helped them avoid capture. Are there any other things they could have done to stay safe?
- What do you think of Captain Phillips's statement that "for every dollar you pay, you've just enlisted three pirates"? Should countries pay ransom money if there is no other way to get the prisoners and ship back?

- The Somali government wanted Muse returned to their country for trial. What do you think would have happened if the pirate had been returned to Somalia?

For More Information

BOOKS

Hanley, Gerald. *Warriors: Life and Death Among the Somalis.* London: Eland, 2004.

Murphy, Martin N. *Somalia: The New Barbary? Piracy and Islam in the Horn of Africa.* New York: Columbia University Press, 2010.

Phillips, Richard, and Stephan Talty. *A Captain's Duty: Somali Pirates, Navy SEALS, and Dangerous Days at Sea.* New York: Hyperion, 2010.

U.S. Government. *2009 Rescue at Sea: Maersk-Alabama Captain Richard Phillips, Snipers on USS Bainbridge Attack Pirates Off the Coast of Somalia.* Washington, DC: Progressive Management, 2009.

PERIODICALS

Gettleman, Jeffrey. "Somalia's Pirates Flourish in a Lawless Nation." *New York Times* (October 31, 2008). Available online at www.nytimes.com/2008/10/31/world/africa/31pirates.html (accessed on January 3, 2011).

———. "Somali Pirates Tell Their Side: They Want Only Money," *New York Times* (September 30, 2008): A6. Available online at www.nytimes.com/2008/10/01/world/africa/01pirates.html (accessed on January 3, 2011).

Marine Engineers' Beneficial Association. "Don't Give Up the Ship!" *Marine Officer* (Summer 2009). Available online at www.meba.us/MarineOfficer/Summer_2009/The_Real_Story_of_the_MAERSK_ALABAMA.pdf (accessed on January 3, 2011).

McGreal, Chris. "Three Shots Brought Down Pirates Who Took *Maersk Alabama* Captain Hostage," *Guardian* (April 13, 2009). Available online at www.guardian.co.uk/world/2009/apr/13/us-navy-maersk-alabama-bainbridge (accessed on January 3, 2011).

Møller, Bjørn. *Piracy, Maritime Terrorism and Naval Strategy.* Danish Institute for International Studies Report (November 16, 2008). Available online at www.diis.dk/graphics/Publications/Reports2009/DIIS_Report_2009-02_%20Piracy_maritime_terrorism_and_naval_strategy.pdf (accessed on January 3, 2011).

Weiser, Benjamin. "Pirate Suspect Charged as Adult in New York," *New York Times* (April 21, 2009). Available online at www.nytimes.com/2009/04/22/nyregion/22pirate.html (accessed on January 3, 2011).

———. "Somali Man Is Charged in 2 More Ship Hijackings," *New York Times* (January 13, 2010). Available online at www.nytimes.com/2010/01/13/nyregion/13pirate.html (accessed on January 3, 2011).

WEB SITES

"Captain Freed after Snipers Kill Somali Pirates," *NBC News.* www.msnbc.msn.com/id/30178013/ (accessed on January 3, 2011).

"Somalia Criticises US for Putting Pirate on Trial." *BBC News.* www.bbc.co.uk/news/10126248 (accessed January 3, 2011).

Middleton, Roger. "Piracy Symptom of Bigger Problem." *BBC News.* http://news.bbc.co.uk/2/hi/africa/8001183.stm (accessed on January 3, 2011).

18

Country Watch List

Excerpt from the *2010 Country Watch List*
  Published by the Congressional International Anti-Piracy Caucus, 2010

"According to industry analysis using watermarks, there has been a 700% increase in identified camcorded copies sourced from Mexico since 2005."

S ome pirates sail the high seas; others surf the Internet and hack online information or steal copyrighted products. Instead of capturing ships, these pirates hijack intellectual property (IP). (Intellectual property is a product of someone's intellect and creativity that has commercial value.) Criminals sometimes steal designs for inventions to make knock-off products that look like the originals. Others copy artists' ideas for movies, books, or songs. The original owners, however, can sue thieves who use their intellectual property, because the U.S. Patent Office registers designs for new products, and the U.S. Copyright Office issues copyrights for books, movies, magazines, music, and other intellectual property. Some things, such as titles, cannot be copyrighted, but specifically arranged words on a page, certain ideas, song lyrics and tunes, trademarks, and mechanical designs are all protected.

With the advances in digital technology and the global reach of the Internet, however, these thefts are harder to track. In addition, many companies manufacture their products overseas. Often IP piracy occurs in the countries where the products are made or printed. Not all countries follow the same copyright and patent policies that the United States does, so these thefts may not always be prosecuted.

Fighting copyright piracy

Clashes between businesses and IP pirates are often dramatic. The pirates often face severe penalties. For example, the owners of Tomato Garden, a

Chinese company convicted in 2009 of making an unauthorized version of Microsoft XP, not only had to give up all their business earnings and go to jail, but the company was also fined three times what it had earned in sales. In 2010 Microsoft also sued the owner of Internet cafés in Dongguan, China, that had illegally used their software. Backed by the Dongguan City Internet Service Association and Dongguan Digital Times, Microsoft China required all cafés in the city to switch to licensed software by 2015. The high cost of paying for authentic versions may force as many as one-third of the cafés to close.

In addition to lawsuits, businesses have experimented with various methods to control IP piracy, including: giving pirates amnesty (freedom from prosecution), collaborating with them, or undercutting their prices. Some companies have tried working jointly with the businesses that are pirating to make sure only legitimate products are produced. Another strategy is to sell authentic products for lower prices so consumers choose them over the pirated copies. Other manufacturers add special features to their genuine products to make them more competitive with, or better than, the lower-priced copies.

Studies have shown that IP piracy occurs most often in countries with low standards of living. People often cannot afford authentic products. Altium, an Australian company, took that into account when it offered amnesty to people who were using pirated versions of its software. Altium offered low prices to upgrade to newer, authentic versions and opened training centers for tech support. By giving people better service and value at a price they can afford, Altium hoped to reduce the need for piracy.

Many governments are also working to combat IP piracy. In 2000 the Office of the U.S. Trade Representative (USTR) began an annual review called Special 301. The review involves examining intellectual property protection in foreign countries. When the annual review first began, it studied about eighty-five countries. By 2010 that number had fallen to about forty-five countries. Many of the countries on the early lists worked hard to control the problem, but others have remained on the list year after year.

In 2003 Congress formed the International Anti-Piracy Caucus, a committee to study the problem of IP theft. The seventy members look for ways to prevent IP piracy, assist the House and Senate with laws and hearings, and brief (inform) congressional delegations traveling to other countries. They also compile a yearly report.

Does IP Piracy Really Hurt Sales?

Although many large companies complain that IP piracy is hurting their sales, others in the industry dispute those claims. Some studies and experiments have shown that wide distribution of pirated materials can often help sales. This has been found to be true in both the music and book industries.

A 2004 study by Felix Oberholzer-Gee, a Harvard Business School professor, and Koleman Strumpf, a professor from the University of North Carolina Chapel Hill, showed little connection between piracy and reduced sales. They concluded in *The Effect of File Sharing on Record Sales: An Empirical Analysis* that "the most heavily downloaded songs showed no decrease in CD sales as a result of increasing downloads. In fact, albums that sold more than 600,000 copies during this period appeared to sell better when downloaded more heavily."

As for how many sales are actually lost through pirating, the Oberholzer-Gee and Strumpf study indicated that "five thousand downloads are needed to displace a single album sale." This contradicts industry estimates, which count each pirated item as a lost sale. The fact is that most IP pirates would never buy all the items they download.

Pirated movies can also do well at the box office. For example, *Avatar* (2009) grossed more than one billion in sales in spite of an estimated nine hundred thousand illegal downloads during its first week in theaters.

The same appears to hold true for books. Although not pirated, Cory Doctorow's best-selling books have been released simultaneously in print and electronic editions. Doctorow advocates liberalizing copyright laws for free sharing of all digital media, so his e-books were published under a Creative Commons License, which allows readers to share the books as long as they do not sell them or create derivative works (other works based on his books).

Another success story is Jeff Kinney's *Diary of a Wimpy Kid*, which he first posted online. Although the Web site averaged seventy thousand readers a day, the book sold well and stayed on the *New York Times* best seller list for more than one year.

As David Rosen, head programmer at Wolfire Games, points out on the *Wolfire Games Blog*, "Anecdotally and from studies by companies like the BSA [Business Software Alliance], it's clear that pirates for the most part have very little income. They are unemployed students, or live in countries with very low per-capita GDP [gross domestic product], where the price of a $60 game is more like $1000 (in terms of purchasing power parity [equality] and income percentage). When Reflexive games performed a series of experiments with anti-piracy measures, they found that they only made one extra sale for every 1000 pirated copies they blocked."

Although questions will always exist as to whether or not IP piracy damages sales, it is clear that some products succeed in spite of, or perhaps even because of, piracy.

International Piracy Watch List

The first year the Anti-Piracy Caucus met, it released the *2003 International Piracy Watch List*. This report included eight countries: Brazil, China,

Customers look at pirated DVDs at a shop in Beijing, China, in January 2010. The Anti-Piracy Caucus included China on its 2010 International Piracy Watch List. WANG SHAO/AFP/GETTY IMAGES.

Pakistan, Russia, Taiwan, Thailand, Malaysia, and Mexico. Each year thereafter they continued to identify countries that they believed were the greatest threats to IP rights. Following the release of these yearly lists, some countries changed their policies and worked to reduce IP piracy. Others remained on the list, and new countries were added.

On May 19, 2010, at a press conference in Washington, D.C., the Anti-Piracy Caucus presented the *2010 International Piracy Watch List.* The chairpersons of the committee, Representatives Adam B. Schiff (D-CA) and Bob Goodlatte (R-VA) and Senators Sheldon Whitehouse (D-RI) and Orrin Hatch (R-UT) cited the problems with IP piracy in five main countries: Russia, Canada, Mexico, China, and Spain.

One of the committee's greatest concerns was the pirating of digital technology. New equipment for games, movies, videos, music, books, software, and other media grew faster between 2000 and 2010 than it had the whole century before. At the same time, the ability to steal these new technologies also increased. According to Senator Whitehouse in a press release on the *U.S. Senator Orrin G. Hatch Official Web Site*, "The United States has been on the losing end of the largest theft of intellectual property in history."

Congressman Goodlatte said in the same press release, "It is tempting to think of crimes involving piracy, or intellectual property theft, as victimless, but this is simply untrue." Artists lost billions of sales because of Web sites offering illegal downloads of copyrighted works. Congressman Schiff added, "To assure the continued creation and distribution of music, movies, software and books, from which we all benefit, we must ensure that out artists, creators and producers are paid for their work, and take much stronger action to ensure countries on the anti-piracy watch list are forced to take piracy seriously."

Things to remember while reading the excerpt from the *2010 International Piracy Watch List*:

- In Russia and Mexico, IP pirates use camcorders in movie theaters to record the movie they are watching, then sell the pirated copies. Although Russians who are caught are ejected from the theater, they can sue and get reimbursed for the cost of their tickets if they claim they were filming for personal use.

- In December 2009 alone, Spain had more than 1.2 million illegal downloads through peer-to-peer (P2P) file sharing. (P2P file sharing software allows computer users to directly access files from one another's hard drives.)

- A study done in 2009 by Dexin Tian and Chin-Chung Chao, published in the *Journal of Information, Law, and Technology*, indicates that "what is considered copyright infringement by the Americans may be treated as fair use by the Chinese." Historically, the Chinese have valued collective ownership and sharing information. Tian and Chao explain, "Even today, many educated consumers in China contend that IPR [intellectual property rights] should only apply to tangible goods and not intangibles like information."

- Some countries resent the U.S. Piracy Watch List and say the list is politically motivated by special interest groups.

- Another criticism of the Piracy Watch List is that American and European consumers often buy pirated goods from other countries, but do not face similar disapproval.

• • •

2010 Country Watch List

Canada

. . . Canada continues to lack adequate laws to allow copyright holders to protect their works from online piracy or to enable a legitimate digital marketplace to develop. This failure has been acknowledged within Canada. Indeed, numerous government reports and Throne Speeches over the past decade and a half have called for comprehensive copyright reform. Successive Canadian governments have failed to follow through on these pledges, however.

As a result, Canada remains an international safe haven for Internet pirates. It is a leading host of commercial operators of illegitimate file sharing sites. For example, at one point in 2009, five of the world's top ten illegitimate **"bittorrent"** sites were registered, located, or operated out of Canada. Moreover, some site operators and users boast openly of their **immunity** under Canadian law. One such site, *isoHunt*—which has been found **liable** in the U.S. for inducing copyright **infringement**—has in fact sued Canadian rights holders in order to establish its protection under Canadian law.

Canada also still has failed to enact urgently needed reforms that would bring it into compliance with the World Intellectual Property Organization (WIPO) Internet Treaties. For example, it still must prohibit both **circumvention** of technological copyright protection measures and the **trafficking** of circumvention devices. It also must enact an effective legal framework governing Internet Service Provider (ISP) liability and responsibility. Until it enacts these and other reforms, Canada is likely to serve as an international **transshipment** hub for circumvention devices, such as "mod chips" and "game copiers," that allow for the use and reproduction of unauthorized copies of popular entertainment software products. . . .

China

. . . China's toleration of massive physical piracy is well-known, having been documented in our previous reports, USTR's annual Special 301 reports, and elsewhere. Nonetheless, the export and transshipment of pirated high-quality CDs and DVDs of U.S. films from and through China continues to grow. Transshipments flow out of China to destinations worldwide, including the U.S. The recent emergence of high-quality, **counterfeit** *Blu-ray* DVDs sold online by Chinese retail and auction websites is one of the latest examples of China's export piracy problem. China has also emerged as the global epicenter **epicenter** for the production and export of circumvention devices.

Bittorrent: A file-sharing method that allows for faster downloads by getting the files from several different sources at one time.

Immunity: Freedom from punishment.

Liable: Legally responsible for.

Infringement: A violation of the law.

Circumvention: Going around.

Trafficking: Transporting illicit or illegal items.

Transshipment: To change from one form of transportation or vessel to another.

Counterfeit: Fake.

Epicenter: Center of focus.

Physical piracy also remains problematic for the U.S. book publishing industry, whether it be illegal printing of academic books and commercial bestsellers, unauthorized commercial-scale photocopying, or production of DVDs containing numerous pirated titles. China also continues to tolerate excessive levels of software license infringement in government and in state-owned and private enterprises. . . .

China's online and mobile markets now have become contaminated with pirated materials via an array of illegal websites, user-generated content sites such as *Tudou.com* and *Youku.com*, and so-called "deep-linking" sites such as the search engine *Baidu* that connect users to infringing websites and content. Close to half of the audiovisual content available on the world's "top sites" is sourced from user-generated content sites in China. Internet piracy also severely affects online academic and professional journals as commercial entities provide unauthorized access to electronic copies of scientific journal articles published by U.S. publishers. Scanned books are also made available for download through websites such as *Taobao*.

The Chinese government has made numerous **bilateral** commitments to address these forms of piracy. We urge it to follow through with meaningful reforms and enforcement. . . .

Mexico

While we are aware of a perceived willingness to address copyright issues on the part of Mexican officials, the sheer dimension of the piracy problems in Mexican markets remains severe. For example, Mexico has the most **prolific** camcording problem in Latin America, hurting the U.S. film industry in Mexico and the broader Latin American market. According to industry analysis using watermarks, there has been a 700% increase in identified camcorded copies sourced from Mexico since 2005. Growing Internet piracy, fueled by a lack of cooperation from ISPs, also continues to go unaddressed. As an example of the scope of the problem, an industry analysis found that the number of illegal music files downloaded in Mexico each year is more than six times the number of songs contained in the CDs sold legally in Mexico. Piracy of hard goods and unauthorized use of software also remain severe problems.

We recognize the efforts of Mexican enforcement agencies, and note with appreciation the high level of cooperation between authorities and rights holder organizations. We also commend the Government of Mexico for passing legislation providing **ex officio** law enforcement authority, a long-standing priority of our Caucus. . . .

Bilateral: Action by two nations.

Prolific: Fast-growing.

Ex officio: By virtue of or because of holding an office.

Russia

The U.S.-Russia IPR Agreement, signed in November 2006, provides a mutually agreed upon roadmap for effective enforcement of intellectual property rights. It is imperative that Russia work **expeditiously** to fulfill its obligations under the Agreement. The Russian government has taken some positive steps, including enforcement actions against retail establishments and warehouses. There has been a decline in enforcement actions over the past two years, however, and much remains to be done. In particular, we are disappointed with the inadequate progress in addressing Internet piracy and the ongoing lack of **deterrent penalties**. To tackle this problem, Russia needs to amend its Civil Code to provide for meaningful cooperation from ISPs, and to establish a specialized Internet IPR Unit within the Ministry of Interior. Russia also should adopt updated and uniform procedures for investigation and prosecution of copyright infringement. . . .

It also is important that Russia implement an optical disc licensing **regime** and pass *ex officio* legislation, both important elements of the U.S.-Russia Agreement. According to industry reports, hard goods piracy remains rampant in many cities. In St. Petersburg, for example, it is not uncommon for legitimate retail chains to carry pirated products. The motion picture industry also reports that an explosion in camcorder piracy in 2009 has made Russia the world's leading source of illicit full-video recordings of films from theaters.

Spain

According to reports from the music industry, Spain's music market has fallen by 70% over the last eight years and 40,000 jobs have been lost in the last five years. Other copyright industries face similar challenges in Spain. Inadequacies in the existing Spanish legal and regulatory structure have given rise to this problem, and it is time for urgent action. In the past year, the Spanish Government has introduced a new piece of legislation to tackle piracy through websites. We welcome and support this development. . . .

Contributing to Spain's high online piracy levels are the government's policies preventing identification of the direct **infringer**, and that decriminalize illegal downloading of content distributed via peer-to-peer file sharing. Spanish Police also refuse to take Internet enforcement actions. The Circular from the Officer of the Prosecutor General supporting these policies should be **rescinded**. Greater accountability and **deterrence** must be established in Spanish law. Until that happens, even voluntary agreements between copyright owners and ISPs to enable the efficient takedown of infringing hosted content will be nearly impossible to achieve. . . .

Expeditiously: Quickly.

Deterrent penalties: Punishments that prevent a crime.

Regime: Process.

Infringer: A person or company who copies copyrighted material without permission.

Rescinded: Repealed.

Deterrence: Preventing crime through fear of punishment.

A street vendor selling pirated CDs in Spain. ALBERTO PAREDES/GETTY IMAGES.

• • •

What happened next ...

One country that reacted strongly to the *2010 International Piracy Watch List* was Canada. Michael Geist, a law professor at the University of Ottawa, accused the United States of "bullying." He said on his web site, "This year's report is particularly embarrassing for the U.S. since it not only lacks in credible data, but ignores the submission from CCIA [Computer & Communications Industry Association] that argued that it is completely inappropriate to place Canada on the list." In an *Ars Technica* article, Howard Knopf, a Canadian copyright lawyer, contended that "Canadian copyright law is much stronger than US copyright law."

Pirate Party

Not everyone agrees that IP piracy is bad. Sharing files with friends who have not paid for the software, movie, music, or e-book is illegal, but many people do it. Popular Web sites, such as Canada's *IsoHunt*, Germany's *RapidShare*, China's *Baidu*, Ukraine's *mp3fiesta*, and Luxembourg's *RMX4U.com* (all listed as threats by the Anti-Piracy Caucus), provide copyrighted products free of charge. Judging by the amount of global traffic they attract, it appears that quite a few people are eager to download pirated goods. Many younger adults who grew up using the Internet believe everyone should have equal access to these types of files.

Some people feel so strongly about this that they have formed a political party. The Pirate Party began in Sweden in 2006 to support *ThePirateBay.org*, a popular Web site that was convicted of copyright infringement for file sharing. The party grew rapidly, and in 2009 sent its first representatives to Parliament (the Swedish legislative body).

Following Sweden's lead, thirty-three other countries now have Pirate Parties. Candidates have run under Pirate Parties International in the Czech Republic, the Netherlands, and the United Kingdom. Pirate Party members in Germany have held municipal seats.

The leader of the Canadian Pirate Party, Jake Daynes, a nineteen-year-old video-game-design student, is typical of many in the new party—

The flag of the Pirate Party. WOLFGANG KUMM/DPA/ LANDOV.

young, Internet savvy, and convinced that digital information should be freely shared. He and others in the party support government transparency along with copyright and patent law reform, including ending patents on pharmaceuticals (medicine) and software. Daynes says in an article by Mike Barber for the *National Post*, "We think that for the dissemination (spreading) of culture—music, books, movies, you name it—that should be fair use."

Canada was not the only critic. Other countries also saw the United States as hypocritical. As Henry Blodget explained in an article in *Slate* magazine, "Now that [America has] stolen IP, polluted the environment, and exploited workers to move up the value chain, we want to ban the practices in other countries. . . . The U.S. didn't get really tough on intellectual-property rights, people note, until we had intellectual property to lose. . . . "

In spite of these negative reactions, many countries around the world met in the summer of 2010 to create a uniform set of rules to reduce IP piracy. These meetings, which began in June 2008, were held in different countries and were attended by Australia, Canada, the European Union, Japan, Korea, Mexico, Morocco, New Zealand, Singapore, Switzerland, and the United States. Coming to a consensus on an Anti-Counterfeiting Trade Agreement (ACTA), however, involves a great deal of compromise. Objections to ACTA include the secrecy surrounding the meetings (although some of the drafts of the agreement were leaked to the press) and the possible threats to freedom and individual rights. But with the costs of piracy to businesses and individuals mounting into the billions each year, these countries believe the threat must be jointly addressed and laws uniformly enforced.

Did you know . . .

- Organized crime is involved in IP piracy in many foreign countries, and criminals are using arms-smuggling and drug-trafficking routes to move illegal DVDs and CDs.
- Countries, such as France and the United Kingdom, who passed laws making Internet service providers (ISPs) legally responsible for their customers' illegal downloads believe it will help curb piracy, but critics point out that spoofers (hackers who illegally take over someone else's computer without their knowledge) will still profit while the person whose computer is hijacked will lose Internet service.
- In 2009 U.S. businesses lost an estimated $25 billion in sales due to global piracy.
- A 2010 study by Tera Consultants showed that Europe could lose 1.2 million jobs in the creative industries by 2015 if piracy is not stopped.
- Peer-to-peer (P2P) file sharing accounts for most Internet piracy.
- When the USTR released its 2010 Special 301 Report, Canada was again placed on the Priority Watch List along with Algeria, Argentina, Chile, China, India, Indonesia, Pakistan, Russia, Thailand, and Venezuela.
- According to a 2010 report by the Government Accountability Office, the three main government studies that give estimates of

how much money is lost due to piracy are not based on facts but are only assumptions. Gathering actual data on these losses is difficult, so estimates are often made instead.

Consider the following . . .

- Some of the countries on the Watch List have actually experienced a significant reduction in IP theft over the past few years. If a country is making strides to reduce piracy, should it be placed on the Watch List?
- Studies have shown that piracy is highest in countries where people's yearly income is low. Is it fair to limit access to intellectual property to people who can afford it? If not, what can be done to equalize access?
- Many people buy music, software, video games, and e-books, then share them with their friends. They feel that as long as they are not selling these items, it is fair use. What is your opinion on this?
- Suppose you are a songwriter and have spent many hours writing a song. Would you rather have many people hear and enjoy your song, even if you do not make money on it, or would you prefer to make money for your labor, even if it means only a limited number of people will hear it?
- How might the Chinese proverb "He who shares is to be rewarded; he who does not, condemned" influence Asian attitudes toward IP theft?

For More Information

BOOKS

Bingham, Jane. *Internet Freedom: Where Is the Limit?* Mankato, MN: Heinemann-Raintree, 2007.

Engdahl, Sylvia, ed. *Issues on Trial: Intellectual Property Rights.* Farmington Hills, MI: Greenhaven, 2009.

Hunnewell, Lee. *Essential Viewpoints: Internet Piracy.* Edina, MN: ABDO Publishing, 2007.

Riley, Gail. *Controversy! Internet Piracy.* New York: Benchmark Books, 2010.

PERIODICALS

"Altium Offers Amnesty to Chinese Pirates." *Printed Circuit Design & Fab* 25, no. 9 (September 2008): 8.

Anderson, Nate. "Canadians Drop Gloves, Punch U.S. in Face over Piracy List," *Ars Technica* (May 2010). Available online at http://arstechnica.com/tech-policy/news/2010/05/canadians-drop-gloves-punch-us-in-face-over-piracy-watchlist.ars (accessed on January 3, 2011).

Barber, Mike. "Pirate Party of Canada Calls for Canadian Copyright Reform," *National Post* (May 1, 2010). Available online at www.nationalpost.com/story.html?id=2975789 (accessed on January 3, 2011).

Blodget, Henry. "How to Solve China's Piracy Problem," *Slate* (April 12, 2005). Available online at www.slate.com/id/2116629 (accessed on January 3, 2011).

Bu, Kitty. "Chinese Surfers See Red over Microsoft Blackouts," *eWeek* (October 22, 2008). Available online at www.eweek.com/c/a/Security/Chinese-Surfers-See-Red-over-Microsoft-Blackouts/ (accessed on January 3, 2011).

Business Software Alliance and IDC. *Sixth Annual BSA-IDC Global Software Piracy Study* (May 2009). Available online at http://images.autodesk.com/adsk/files/globalpiracy2008.pdf (accessed on January 3, 2011).

European Trade Commission. *The Anti-Counterfeiting Trade Agreement Fact Sheet* (November 2008). Available online at http://trade.ec.europa.eu/doclib/docs/2008/october/tradoc_140836.11.08.pdf (accessed on January 3, 2011).

Knight, Will. "Net Music Piracy 'Does Not Harm Record Sales.'" *New Scientist* (March 2004). Available online at www.newscientist.com/article/dn4831-net-music-piracy-does-not-harm-record-sales.html (accessed on January 3, 2011).

Oberholzer, Felix, and Koleman Strumpf. *The Effect of File Sharing on Record Sales: An Empirical Analysis.* (March 2004). Available online at www.unc.edu/~cigar/papers/FileSharing_March2004.pdf (accessed on January 3, 2011).

U.S. Government Accountability Office. *Intellectual Property: Observations on Efforts to Quantify the Economic Effects of Counterfeit and Pirated Goods* (April 2010). Available online at http://www.gao.gov/new.items/d10423.pdf (accessed on January 3, 2011).

WEB SITES

Geist, Michael. "USTR's Bully Report Unfairly Blames Canada Again." *Michael Geist.* www.michaelgeist.ca/content/view/4997/125/ (accessed on January 3, 2011).

Hatch, Orrin. "Hatch, International Anti-Piracy Caucus Unveils '2010 International Piracy Watch List.'" *U.S. Senator Orrin G. Hatch Official Web Site.* http://hatch.senate.gov/public/index.cfm?FuseAction=PressReleases.Print&PressRelease_id=b109414b-1b78-be3e-e0b8-34869d0477c4&suppresslayouts=true (accessed on January 3, 2011).

Rosen, David. "Another View of Game Piracy." *Wolfire Games Blog* (May 6, 2010). http://blog.wolfire.com/2010/05/Another-view-of-game-piracy (accessed on January 3, 2011).

Where to Learn More

Books

Burgess, Douglas R., Jr. *The Pirates' Pact: The Secret Alliances Between History's Most Notorious Buccaneers and Colonial America.* New York: McGraw-Hill, 2009.

Carpenter, John Reeve. *Pirates: Scourge of the Seas.* New York: Sterling, 2006.

Cawthorne, Nigel. *Pirates of the 21st Century: How Modern-day Buccaneers Are Terrorising the World's Oceans.* London: John Blake, 2010.

Clifford, Barry. *Expedition Whydah: The Story of the World's First Excavation of a Pirate Ship.* New York: Cliff Street Books, 1999.

Cordingly, David. *Under the Black Flag: The Romance and the Reality of Life Among the Pirates.* New York: Random House, 2006.

———, ed. *Pirates: Terror on the High Seas from the Caribbean to the South China Sea.* North Dighton, MA: World Publications Group, 2006.

Crowley, Roger. *Empires of the Sea: The Siege of Malta, the Battle of Lepanto, and the Contest for the Center of the World.* New York: Random House, 2008.

Druett, Joan. *She Captains: Heroines and Hellions of the Sea.* New York: Simon and Schuster, 2001.

Forester, C.S. *The Barbary Pirates.* New York: Sterling Point, 2008.

Heller-Roazen, Daniel. *The Enemy of All: Piracy and the Law of Nations.* New York: Zone Books, 2009.

Johnson, Captain Charles. *A General History of the Robberies and Murders of the Most Notorious Pirates.* Guilford, CT: The Lyons Press, 1998, 2002.

Konstam, Angus. *The History of Pirates.* Guilford, CT: The Lyons Press, 2002.

———. *Piracy: The Complete History.* Oxford, England: Osprey, 2008.

Lane, Kris E. *Pillaging the Empire: Piracy in the Americas, 1500–1750.* Armonk, NY: Sharpe, 1998.

Lewis, Jon E., ed. *The Mammoth Book of Pirates: Over 25 True Tales of Devilry and Daring by the Most Infamous Pirates of All Time.* Philadelphia, PA: Running Press, 2006.

Little, Benerson. *The Sea Rover's Practice: Pirate Tactics and Techniques, 1630–1730.* Dulles, VA: Potomac Books, 2007.

Lloyd, Christopher. *English Corsairs on the Barbary Coast.* London: William Collins Sons, 1981.

Matthews, John. *Pirates.* New York: Atheneum, 2006.

Murray, Dian H. *Pirates of the South China Coast, 1790–1810.* California: Stanford University Press, 1987.

Ormerod, Henry A. *Piracy in the Ancient World.* Baltimore: Johns Hopkins University Press, 1996.

Pennell, C.R., ed. *Bandits at Sea.* New York: New York University Press, 2001.

Perry, Dan. *Blackbeard: The Real Pirate of the Caribbean.* New York: Basic Books, 2006.

Rediker, Marcus. *Between the Devil and the Deep Blue Sea: Merchant Seamen, Pirates and the Anglo-American Maritime World, 1700–1750.* Cambridge, UK: Cambridge University Press, 1987.

———. *Villains of All Nations: Atlantic Pirates in the Golden Age.* Boston, MA: Beacon Press, 2004.

Sanders, Richard. *If a Pirate I Must Be . . . The True Story of "Black Bart," King of the Caribbean Pirates.* New York: Skyhorse Publishing, 2009.

Sharp, Anne Wallace. *Daring Pirate Women.* Minneapolis, MN: Lerner, 2002.

Travers, Tim. *Pirates: A History.* Stroud, Gloucestershire, UK: Tempus, 2007.

Wilson, Peter Lamborn. *Pirate Utopias: Moorish Corsairs and European Renegades.* 2nd ed. Rye Brook, NY: Autonomedia, 2003.

Woodard, Colin. *The Republic of Pirates: Being the True and Surprising Story of the Caribbean Pirates and the Man Who Brought Them Down.* New York: Harcourt, 2007.

Wren, Laura Lee. *Pirates and Privateers of the High Seas.* Berkeley Heights, NJ: Enslow, 2003.

Yolen, Jane. *Sea Queens: Women Pirates Around the World.* Watertown, MA: Charlesbridge, 2008.

Zacks, Richard. *The Pirate Coast: Thomas Jefferson, the First Marines, and the Secret Mission of 1805.* New York: Hyperion, 2005.

Periodicals

Antony, Robert. "Piracy in Early Modern China," *IIAS Newsletter,* 36 (March 2005). Also available online at http://www.iias.nl/nl/36/IIAS_NL36_07.pdf (accessed on January 3, 2011).

Baldauf, Scott. "Who Are Somalia's Pirates?" *Christian Science Monitor* (November 20, 2008). Also available online at http://www.csmonitor.com/World/Africa/2008/1120/p25s22-woaf.html (accessed on January 3, 2011).

De Souza, Philip. "Ancient Rome and the Pirates." *History Today* 51, no. 7 (2001).

Gettleman, Jeffrey. "Somalia's Pirates Flourish in a Lawless Nation" *New York Times* (October 31, 2008). Available online at www.nytimes.com/2008/10/31/world/africa/31pirates.html (accessed on January 3, 2011).

Gwin, Peter. "Dangerous Straits." *National Geographic* (October 2007). Also available online at http://ngm.nationalgeographic.com/2007/10/malacca-strait-pirates/pirates-text.html (accessed on January 3, 2011).

Johnson, Keith. "Who's a Pirate? U.S. Court Sees Duel over Definition." *Wall Street Journal* (August 14, 2010). Available online at http://online.wsj.com/article/SB20001424052748703988304575413470900570834.html (accessed on January 3, 2011).

Murray, Dian H. "Pirates of the South China Coast 1790–1810," *Journal of the Economic and Social History of the Orient* 33, no. 2 (1990): 234–6.

Rediker, Marcus. "When Women Pirates Sailed the Seas." *The Wilson Quarterly* 17, no. 4 (Autumn 1993):102–10.

Tabarrok, Alexander. "The Rise, Fall, and Rise Again of Privateers," *Independent Review* 11, no. 4 (Spring 2007):565–77.

Web Sites

Adow, Mohammed. "The Pirate Kings of Puntland." *Al Jazeera.net* (June 17, 2009). http://english.aljazeera.net/news/africa/2009/06/2009614125245860630.html (accessed on January 3, 2011).

Davis, Robert. "British Slaves on the Barbary Coast." *BBC British History in Depth.* http://www.bbc.co.uk/history/british/empire_seapower/white_slaves_01.shtml (accessed on January 3, 2011).

Krystek, Lee. "The Golden Age of Piracy." *The Unmuseum.* www.unmuseum.org/pirate.htm (accessed on January 3, 2011).

"Pirates." *National Maritime Museum.* http://www.nmm.ac.uk/explore/sea-and-ships/facts/ships-and-seafarers/pirates (accessed on January 3, 2011).

"Pirates of the Whydah." *National Geographic.* http://www.nationalgeographic.com/whydah/main.html (accessed on January 3, 2011).

Rothwell, Donald R. "Maritime Piracy and International Law." *Crimes of War Project* (February 24, 2009). http://www.crimesofwar.org/onnews/news-piracy.html (accessed on January 3, 2011).

Index

Bold type indicates major entries. Illustrations are marked by (ill.).